FOR PLEASURE

MINORITARIAN AESTHETICS
General Editors: Uri McMillan, Sandra Ruiz, Shane Vogel

Minoritarian Aesthetics promotes scholarship that develops a minor position toward aesthetics and an aesthetic stance toward minoritarian experience. The aesthetic—the domain of sensation, beauty, value, taste, (dis)pleasure, and the sublime—instructs not only representations and judgments of the social but the relational bonds that form between objects, subjects, and entities across spatial-temporal domains.

Deadpan: The Aesthetics of Black Inexpression
Tina Post

For Pleasure: Race, Experimentalism, and Aesthetics
Rachel Jane Carroll

For Pleasure

Race, Experimentalism, and Aesthetics

Rachel Jane Carroll

NEW YORK UNIVERSITY PRESS
New York

NEW YORK UNIVERSITY PRESS
New York
www.nyupress.org

© 2023 by New York University
All rights reserved

Please contact the Library of Congress for Cataloging-in-Publication data.
ISBN: 9781479826728 (hardback)
ISBN: 9781479826735 (paperback)
ISBN: 9781479826742 (library ebook)
ISBN: 9781479826711 (consumer ebook)

This book is printed on acid-free paper, and its binding materials are chosen for strength and durability. We strive to use environmentally responsible suppliers and materials to the greatest extent possible in publishing our books.

Manufactured in the United States of America

10 9 8 7 6 5 4 3 2 1

Also available as an ebook

For Gully, a pure soul

CONTENTS

Introduction: Attentional Movements   1

1. What Can Beauty Do?   39

2. Yoko Ono's Whimsy   87

3. Pure Color   123

4. Difficult Pleasures   165

   Conclusion: Being Moved   211

   Acknowledgments   219

   Notes   221

   Bibliography   249

   Index   265

   About the Author   279

Introduction

Attentional Movements

Primordial scenes of Earth's formation collide against roaring suburban lawnmowers, bearing down on video artist Ulysses Jenkins, supine in the too-green grass of a California lawn. The tubes of a deconstructed television soar through a black void, like spacecraft floating with cetacean grace. Environmental disasters erupt: volcanoes spewing smoke, an oil tanker on fire, torrential storms, floods, weeping bystanders. An ill man lies under a brightly patterned quilt, surrounded by medicine bottles, as another man leans down to care for him—perhaps an early representation of a person with HIV/AIDS. Chimpanzees hawk motor oil. A white man brandishes a rifle against his thigh, leaning against pickup trucks as the word "Invasion" flashes across the screen. A Black woman fries bacon on a flattop grill as newscasters grimly announce that wages are not keeping up with skyrocketing prices. Ronald Reagan's national security advisor prophesies an era of ideas and the inevitable fall of communism. Reagan promises that the United States will solve the social and economic problems at hand "as we've solved them for the past two hundred years," a declaration that feels more like a threat than a reassurance amid this apocalyptic crush of images.

These are some of the video sequences that make up Jenkins's 1981 experimental video, *Inconsequential Doggereal*. Doggerel is poetry that has an irregular rhythm or rhyme used for comic effect, often vulgar and poorly written. In his concept of "dogge*real*," Jenkins's addition of an *a* suggests that his heteroclite visual and sonic rhythms reveal a reality obscured by the smooth cadences of conventional aesthetics. The "real" in "doggereal" also functions as a homonym for "reel," calling attention to the method and materials of aesthetic production rather than simply the images that make up the "content" of the video.

Living in the interstices of its collage is the protagonist of *Inconsequential Doggereal*, played by Jenkins, who reckons with this chaotic "mass of images."[1] This character appears in a state of existential dread, sipping from a coffee mug with a look of terror and disgust as he gazes at something lurking out of frame, shitting and urinating, sobbing next to his toilet as his mental unraveling is intercut with images of an elegant Black woman smiling like a model for the camera, bordered by lush greenery in a soft-focus dream. The protagonist's crisis is accompanied by scenes of interpersonal conflict between a handful of additional characters. In these performances, unnamed characters argue while roughly passing a football back and forth, their pairings referencing familiar narratives of racial and gendered discord: a white man and a Black man arguing; a Black man and a Black woman arguing; a white woman mooning at her white male partner who doesn't take her seriously; an Asian woman who talks to the camera, critiquing the instrument of her image-making as if it were a lover. These stylized sequences often play out with satiric humor, heightening the absurdism of the video. The football, the plaything of a distinctly American and brutal sport, functions as a symbol of systematized violent competition between differently positioned people in a hierarchical society. Ostensibly an object of pleasure, the thing that allows the game to be played and the talisman that must be ferried across the goal line to win, here the football represents a game dominated by anger, dread, and resentment that never seems to end. These short, performed sequences arise throughout the video with its frenetic editing style, sound and image sloshing over its edges.

Through video collage, Jenkins manages to show disaster at multiple scales, connecting the intimately personal to the planetary—the friction of a personal argument against the fallout from the Cold War and Reaganism, lurching with a high-pitched shriek of laughter. In this way, he restores the context that is missing from the scenes of dispute and existential terror. The racial and gendered animosity depicted is not merely the failure of individuals to "get along" but part of a system that is far too vast and complicated to be narrated in a simple, linear structure. Collage helps viewers understand that there is a larger scale, both temporally and in the network of relations, for interpersonal conflict and psychological horror. By recontextualizing racial and gendered distress within the planetary scale of racial capitalism, *Inconsequential Doggereal* denaturalizes disharmony and restores context to the overpowering feelings on view in the video.[2]

The aesthetic intervention of *Inconsequential Doggereal* is not merely to provide corrective images, interceding in racial and gendered acts of harm or rivalry through representation. Rather, Jenkins's surrealism interferes in the flow of conventional media and art that reinforces the realism of racial capitalism. Surrealism makes available different positions in relation to the mainstream. As such, *Inconsequential Doggereal* is exemplary of the thesis of this book, showing how art can serve to connect the intimate to the systemic, exploring the affective impact of global systems of oppression while showing how the relationality of art can produce alternative social worlds and philosophical orientations. This is the experimental rhythm of a new real.

Like much of Jenkins's work, *Inconsequential Doggereal* channels the existential terror of racial capitalism yet offers a hopeful, if ambiguous, ending. The protagonist leaves his home, a space of isolation where he appeared to be sinking deeper and deeper into despair, carrying a cardboard box full of the symbolic footballs. When we next see him, it is at a distance, in stark contrast from the close-ups and mid-shots that create a sense of gnarly apprehension throughout the video. The view is suddenly open. He is nude, walking through a grassy green park, a football in one hand, as the final movement of Los Angeles composer William Kraft's *Contextures: Riots—Decade '60* (1967) plays in the background.[3] The shot is framed by foliage, as if viewers are peering through the bushes, unseen by the protagonist, watching at a distance. The protagonist winds his way down the sloping lawn draped in morning mist. Without any clear objective, he pauses to kneel and pick a dandelion puff, blowing its fuzz into the gray dawn. In contrast to previous scenes where the protagonist's nudity feels abject, at the end of the video, his nakedness feels more like a rebirth than the stripping down of dignity. The protagonist tucks a dandelion behind his ear as he tosses the football in a preoccupied manner.

Like much experimental art and literature, *Inconsequential Doggereal* is about the risks and pleasures of aesthetic interpretation, using experimental aesthetic techniques to cue the viewer to reflect on their habits of interpretation, the ways that interpretive conventions shape reality, and how shifts in methods of interpretation might intervene in social life. It is thus instructive for understanding the aims of this book as a whole. Experimentalism is attuned to interpretation as a mutable field, considering how formal conventions shape interpretative habits and audience expectations. Experimentalism directs the reader or viewer to consider the project of aesthetic evaluation, prompting audiences to reflect on aesthetic judgment and interpretation as praxes that impact social realities. As I will explain, aesthetic form directs our attention. By experimenting with aesthetic form, artists make different scenes of attention more accessible, a perceptual restructuring that meaningfully affects the social relations of aesthetic judgment. Thinking of form in this way, we can begin to understand the aesthetic itself as a social condition that makes some ideas, relations, and events possible and inhibits others.

As Jenkins's concept of *doggereal* suggests, a substantial mediation of form, a different rhythm perhaps, will allow us to perceive reality in a new way. For Jenkins, this is wrought through the affordances of video editing, which literally allows Jenkins and his audience to see differently. The received sequences of image and sound can be taken apart and redistributed—slowing things down, pausing, repeating, introducing new visual and auditory effects, and recontextualizing. *For Pleasure* attempts to cultivate methods of interpretation from the critical positions made available by formal experimentation, critical positions that recognize the role that aesthetic pleasure plays in racial practices. In this process, aesthetic pleasure becomes visible as a social relation.

At the end of the video, Jenkins's protagonist arrives at a scene of unhurried beauty set against Kraft's disquieting score for the uprisings against white supremacy. In this ending, the video suggests that those uprisings produced a new world, laying the ground for the protagonist's absorption in natural beauty as he wanders vulnerable yet poised and thoughtful, tethered to the political by the football palmed in his hand. The uprisings are not over, even though they are out of sight. As music, they fill the morning of this world, setting the tone for the protagonist's gentle ambulations. The struggle for freedom against white supremacy through collective action creates the conditions for this pursuit of beauty. But perhaps the reverse is also true; the beauty that the protagonist seeks out and reproduces, blowing the dandelion seeds out into the hushed green space to root and flower, also recontextualizes the music of uprising. With the dandelion tucked behind the protagonist's ear, beauty serves to propagate something else beyond the misery and violence of the real that racial capitalism has built.

Throughout *For Pleasure*, I delve into experimental art and literature like *Inconsequential Doggereal* that provide insight into the relationship between aesthetic pleasure and racial practices and formations in the United States. This book offers methods for reading experimental literature and art produced by racially minoritized authors and artists working in and around the United States in the mid-twentieth century. In a study of work by authors and artists, including Isaac Julien, Nella Larsen, Yoko Ono, Jack Whitten, Byron Kim, Glenn Ligon, Zora Neale Hurston, Theresa Hak Kyung Cha, and Cici Wu, among others, *For Pleasure* argues that aesthetic pleasure plays a key role in both racial practices and struggles against racist domination. I define experimentalism as aesthetic forms and techniques that significantly innovate within, or depart from, existing aesthetic conventions, while directing the reader or viewer to consider their immediate project of interpretation. I argue that while experimental forms are not inherently liberatory, they can generate new social arrangements through their imaginative capacity and ability to disarm, delight, and surprise. Pleasure is worthy of our attention.

This book is not a chronology of experimentalism but the search for a method for understanding experimentalism's relevance to a global racial order and its undoing. *For Pleasure* asserts that the aesthetic is a space of social relation where racial meaning is produced, circulated, and transformed. As such, it plays a vital role in racial practices and formations, providing links between the ideological, psychic, cultural, and material. Not only is aesthetic experience commingled with production and circulation of racial meaning, but the Western study of aesthetics has played an integral role in the development of race and racism as global systems, namely through their shared modern origins in the Enlightenment. Aesthetic theory, its discourse on value, naturalization of certain aesthetic judgments, and production of exemplary aesthetic subjects has been indispensable to racial capitalism, rationalizing and legitimizing the feelings-based and ideological hierarchies of value that buttress systems of racial dominance.

However, the modern story of the aesthetic is hardly a tale of absolute oppression. On the contrary, in pursuing a minoritarian aesthetics analytic, we see on full view the human capacity for indomitability and ingenuity. The aesthetic is a place where we can observe people's ability to organize psychically and socially around the expansion of life possibility, despite the naturalized relationship between gratuitous violence and value that composes our world. This capacity is on display in Jenkins's *Inconsequential Doggereal* and in the majority of the other artworks and texts examined in this book. Experimentalism highlights the dynamic between the mainstream of violence and minoritarian countercurrents while offering alternative understandings of aesthetic and social value.

This study of aesthetic pleasure and race is neither censoriously against pleasure nor a denial of art's capacity for harm. Rather, it is an attempt to cultivate interpretative and aesthetic practices that do not depend on racial dominance. Following these premises, the chapters in this book guide readers through three main models of interpretation and analysis that center questions of race and racialization: how to understand aesthetic judgment as a relation of power (chapter 1 on beauty and chapter 2 on whimsy); how experimentalism can be a tool against oppression (chapter 2 and chapter 3 on color abstraction); and how aesthetic pleasure can be a social space where sameness and difference might be navigated ethically (chapter 4 on dreaminess and difficulty).

This book imagines that experimental art and literature can intervene in the habituated practices of interpretation and aesthetic judgment that support social relations built on racial domination. *For Pleasure* thus intercedes in assumptions about who makes experimental work, experimentalism's relationships to freedom and social change, and the pleasures that both experimental aesthetics and social change promise to deliver. My arguments are based on the premise that experimental aesthetics have a significant racial aspect that is not separate from more conservative strains of aesthetic production and theory. Despite this, experimentalism nevertheless provides opportunities for deep aesthetic gratification and the generation of new social worlds. In exploring the entanglements between experimental aesthetics and race, I draw from the work of scholars, such Sylvia Wynter, Denise Ferreira da Silva, Fred Moten, and Robert Bernasconi, who have re-narrated the Enlightenment's contribution to aesthetic theory. These thinkers have pushed us to reevaluate conventional European-derived and Kantian-inflected aesthetic theories, not as synonymous with egalitarian universalism but as productive of the violent racial asymmetry undergirding European colonialism and transatlantic slavery, resulting in the hierarchies of human and nonhuman difference that sustain a global racial order.

Although movements and artists associated with experimentalism have often positioned themselves politically and aesthetically against a mainstream aesthetic sensibility, experimentalism does not in fact escape collusions with systemic racism. Non-white writers and artists have historically been excluded from the category of the experimental through a false binary in which art by racialized artists is automatically associated with social "content" and art that is recognized as formally experimental or difficult is associated with racial whiteness. Among the several deleterious effects of this false bifurcation is that the formal innovations produced by artists of color are ignored and misrecognized, their meanings crudely interpreted through default racialist lenses, while the racial meanings of "experimental" white art are obscured or denied. This is part of the argument made in the poet and essayist Cathy Park Hong's rousing critique of the racial politics of the avant-garde in the world of twentieth- and twenty-first-century poetry. In "Delusions of Whiteness in the Avant-Garde," Hong skewers what we might counterintuitively dub the "tradition" of the avant-garde as a racist enterprise, resulting in a contemporary poetry world governed by a "delusion of whiteness" that is "the luxurious option that anyone can be 'post-identity' and can casually slip in and out of identities like a video game avatar, when there are those who are consistently harassed, surveilled, profiled, or deported for whom they are."[4]

However, a focus on the exclusionary aspects of the avant-garde's racism gets us only so far, as Hong goes on to contend. While this book does center the work of racially minoritized artists and writers, hoping to loosen whiteness's grip on the idea of aesthetic experimentation and debunk the racial binary that segregates (white) "form" from (non-white) "content," it also hopes to show that the concepts of experimentalism and the avant-garde themselves are not racially neutral but rather are participants in manufacturing the hierarchies of aesthetic and social value. I believe we require a reevaluation of what it means to be experimental. To this end, my aim is not so much to narrate the histories of racially minoritized experimentalisms but to restore context to the interpretive frameworks and habits that structure encounters with the experimental.

As Hong suggests in the mic-drop at the end of her essay, the idea of the avant-garde—or experimental, as I put it—might not be worth saving: "Fuck the avant-garde. We must hew our own path."[5] The discourse of the avant-garde or experimental can easily become a self-valorizing tool for encoding and protecting whiteness. This is something that I have wrestled with quite a bit while writing this book—How useful is the experimental as a frame of analysis? Does the invocation of experimentalism simply re-inscribe a hierarchy of value that is at best fruitless, at worst irredeemable? I proceed with experimentalism as the subject of this book with caution. As I will explain, experimentalism names some important dynamics within the history of aesthetics that still need to be drawn out, as well as a set of aesthetic and critical desires that I think continue to be a cause for optimism. Given racial capitalism's hyper-flexibility and ability to co-opt literally anything, no matter how contradictory, as evidence of its entitlement to produce reality, experimentalism's capacity to generate new, interruptive, and defamiliarizing experiences remains crucial to any role aesthetics might play in disturbing the realism of global racial capitalism and its conceit that value must necessarily be produced through violence. However, should the usefulness of experimentalism as an idea dissolve or another framework come to take its place, so be it. My attachments are to the need to imagine different social relations through the aesthetic, not to experimentalism as a heroic tool.

Method

My process is to historicize and contextualize what is aesthetically and conceptually unique about the texts, films, performances, and artworks explored in this book within systems of racial meaning, social relations, and historical power struggle. This is a book that tries to understand how a circuit can be broken and rerouted in an attempt to bring a more just world into being. It asserts that subordination is not a value to uphold, while recognizing that minoritized positions can present vital alternative perspectives on the social. In a state of unfreedom constituted by anti-Blackness, ableism, colonialism, racial capitalism, trans antagonism, and cisheteropatriarchy, to study form and aesthetic pleasure, however one might define *study*, can be a means of being changed by what we do not recognize.[6] From that experience, we might cultivate methods of interpretation that serve projects of justly living in difference.

While this book has overt political commitments to the ending of racial capitalism and to optimism for the role that the aesthetic might play in that process, it is important to emphasize that interventions in the politics of aesthetics are not replacements for other forms of political action. Just as an overreliance on the representational as a predictable tool for political intervention can distract from the need for more direct and material changes, a valorization of the experimental can lead us to stop at the scene of "possibility," "potentiality," or "the new." It is difficult to conceive of a radical politics that does not exercise thrilling creativity while imagining a profoundly different set of relations between humans and nonhumans. Yet in the academic humanities, there is perhaps too much contentment with gallant abstractions and a tendency to rest on the vagaries of what *could be* when it comes to addressing the real social systems in which we live. It should be acknowledged here that while this book tries to bridge that gap between the utopian horizon and the practical materiality of the past and the present through historicization and recontextualization, aesthetic analysis is not a sufficient basis for social change. A radical transformation of society will certainly require both the denaturalization of the given and the propagation of strange ideas for how we might proceed toward a more just world. These are things that the experimental can provide for us. But that is not the entirety of the work that needs doing, and I would not like to claim otherwise.

Culture is the place where people process their lived experiences alongside others, and as such, it tells us not only about the material conditions of people's lives but how people understand those conditions, attach to them, divest from them, or use them as jumping-off points. Art can help us understand the lived textures of oppression, its mechanics, and the conditions that produce it in such a unique way that we can imagine the crumbling of those oppressive systems. Thus far, the study of the aesthetic in the West has traditionally split the difference between the individual and the collective through the idea of universality, narrating aesthetic pleasure as an entirely subjective experience that nevertheless occurs in response to that subject's encounter with universal feelings. This history of the aesthetic is addressed in detail in chapter 1 on beauty, aesthetic judgment, and Black aesthetics, but to briefly gloss here, the aesthetic is often discussed as a space of universality where difference is suspended and positive social transformation can take place. As Kantian aesthetic theorist Thierry de Duve puts it, "The social function of art—if art has a function and if it can be called social—is to testify that humans ought to be living in harmony with each other when everything demonstrates that they can't."[7] Although sentiments of social harmony, equality, and amicability might be well-meaning, they obscure the racialization of the concepts that support these elysian ideals. Whose universality? Who decides what is "common" and what is exceptional, disposable, or kept separate? Whose fantasy of "equality"? This book proposes that we must study aesthetic pleasure through the lens of its racial imbrications, historical and contemporary. We must return to the basic assumptions of the conventional Western aesthetic model and consider their complicity with anti-Blackness, colonialism, slavery, and global racial capitalism. These systems share the same historical and geographic points of emergence with modern Euro-American aesthetic theory; indeed, they have informed each other from the beginning. Aesthetics and experimentalism do not diverge from the history of race; they are a part of it. In exploring what the experimental can tell us about race and aesthetics in the twentieth-century United States, we not only see aesthetic pleasure from a new vantage point but are given opportunities to reimagine its role in building a more just world.

For Pleasure revises our understanding of aesthetic pleasure from the perspective of a critical study of race, with the goal of developing ethical methods of critique that acknowledge the fundamental interrelationality of aesthetic pleasure. By "for pleasure," I mean both prioritizing the analysis of pleasure in the interpretation of a text or artwork and honoring pleasure as a vital aspect of literature, art, and a life that is more than survival. I argue that the aesthetic, as a structure of pleasure in which meaning and power are produced and negotiated, is a location for the creation of ethical social relations.

Key Terms

In the pages that follow, I offer an overview of four key terms that provide foundational ideas for my analysis. They are *aesthetic*, *pleasure*, *experimental*, and *race*. I then offer an explanation of my understanding of minoritarian aesthetics and how this concept informs the work in this book. I hope these sections will set the stage for the book's arguments and serve as a helpful guide for the reader.

Aesthetic

Aesthetic judgment has long been a means of categorizing people within a hierarchy of the human. As Kandice Chuh writes, "The incapacity for proper aesthetic judgment signaled the difference between those who would and would not realize human potential by achieving full self-consciousness."[8] In this model, a proper aesthetic subject knows the difference between good and bad art, or art and not art, and "knowing" that difference manufactures the social differences of race, gender, and other categories of the human. The aesthetic subject feels "correctly" in relation to aesthetic forms, an affective relation that is deployed to differentiate groups of people according to their levels of disposability and vulnerability to violence.

In the study of the aesthetic, European-derived notions of the human that are inseparable from the production of modern race and racism continue to dominate scholarly discussion, a legacy that is covered in chapter 1 on beauty. Yet the prevalence of this iteration of the Human with a capital *H* has hardly gone without critique. The commanding presence of a modern iteration of the Human and his relationship to the aesthetic (I say "his" pointedly) as it emerged with colonialism, racial slavery, and racial capitalism has been explored in reevaluations of history and liberal subjectivity by scholars such as Sylvia Wynter, Lisa Lowe, Kandice Chuh, and Denise Ferreira da Silva, to name only a few.[9] The Human and the aesthetic entwine in an Enlightenment ideal of a liberal subject whose agency, rationality, and access to the universal is based in his ability to make proper aesthetic judgments. As these scholars note, the Human as aesthetic subject is inseparable from the emergence of racial whiteness, or what Dylan Rodríguez calls "White Being," "a narrative, ceremonial practice of human being that pivots on relations of dominance with other beings (human and otherwise) and aspirational mastery over the wildness and unknowabilities of nature and the physical universe."[10] "Proper" aesthetic judgments are exactly the kind of "narrative, ceremonial practice" that enacts those relations of dominance through one's ability to discern. In this understanding, aesthetic pleasure is a property of whiteness in both senses of the word—as an elemental aspect of racial whiteness and as a possession of the subject, something that is masterfully apprehended and held in the space of the subject. Here, I also look to Rodríguez's definition of white supremacy as inherently aspirational, an orientation toward forever further mastery. Rodríguez conceptualizes white supremacy as "a *violence of aspiration* and *logic of social organization* that invents, reproduces, revises, and transforms changing modalities of social domination and systemic, targeted physiological and ecological violence. This domination and violence occurs through the planning, imagination, (re-)planning, and institutionalization of group-based human and cultural hierarchies, spanning the environmental and economic to the epistemic and aesthetic."[11] Aesthetic judgment certainly can and does function in this aspirational mode, upholding those "group-based human and cultural hierarchies." *For Pleasure* investigates the aesthetic practices of racial domination in which aesthetic pleasure is a possession of whiteness, while also exploring how aesthetic pleasure might undo white supremacy. Living within such conditions, an attendance to the ethics of aesthetic pleasure is not an attitude of prohibition but an attempt to cultivate interpretative practices and aesthetic experiences that do not depend on racial domination. I attempt a mode of interpretation that contextualizes aesthetic pleasure within a modern history of racial capitalism and asks us to use this context as a basis for understanding aesthetic relationality.

In this book, *aesthetic* will describe assemblages of sensation, form, and value where social relations are sorted amid power struggle. We come together in aesthetic judgment as a nexus of feeling, meaning, and power to articulate what is valued within the social. The aesthetic participates in the production of racial difference but also in the creation of ways of living in difference that rebuke racism's structures of premature death.[12] Throughout this book, I consider how aesthetic judgments are subjective experiences yet are never made in true isolation given the aesthetic's innate sociality and, indeed, its role in building reality, topics discussed in detail in chapters 2 and 4. Even when aesthetic judgments are not spoken aloud, we feel and process them in relation to others and the world. The object or event prompting aesthetic judgment is sensed and therefore connected to a broader network of material and social relations. Those relations resonate within aesthetic judgment. Moreover, and going beyond the basic materiality of sensation in aesthetic experience, the reflex of aesthetic response is itself a form of address premised on social connection.

Aesthetic theorist Sianne Ngai argues that every aesthetic judgment is "an outward-facing act of address, a perlocutionary speech act, and an improvisatory performance."[13] Thierry de Duve concurs, stating as the first principle of aesthetic judgment, "*Aesthetic judgments imply a universal address.*"[14] The strange sociality of the aesthetic, the paradox of its simultaneous subjectivity and sharedness, has been at the core of Western aesthetic theory for centuries, perhaps most notably in Kant's *Critique of Judgment* and its concepts of subjective universality and the *sensus communis*, a text and concepts discussed in depth in chapter 1. I argue, however, that the ideas of subjective universality and the *sensus communis* are insufficient foundations for considering the ethical questions raised by the interrelationality of aesthetic experience. In particular, I focus on the ethical questions related to race and Kant's central participation in the formation of its modern iterations, finding that despite the ostensible collective spirit of subjective universality and the *sensus communis*, these two concepts have meaningfully contributed to the hierarchical racial sorting of human difference.

The premise of my theorizing here is that aesthetic experience and critique are opportunities to metacognitively attend to our relations to others as our shared realities are built through the aesthetic. As feeling and sensation are heightened, guided by form and in relation to a set of ideas and social possibilities, we are pointed toward each other in mutual regard. At this moment, we may rise to the challenge of self-observation and analysis of a social dynamic wherein ethical considerations are immanent. This book models a mode of interpretation that begins with the uneven sociality of aesthetic judgment, its potential for harm as well as its utopian promise, for example in the way that the demand to recognize beauty can be wielded by both oppressive and freedom-seeking groups (chapter 1), how absurdist humor can prompt the reevaluation of the given norms that shape reality (chapter 2), how the history of color adumbrates questions of artistic freedom (chapter 3), and how aesthetic experiences can prompt us to recognize our intense interrelationality with others within the social relation of aesthetic judgment (chapter 4).

Pleasure

There is no aesthetic without pleasure. Sensations of pleasure or unpleasure as they are attached to experiences of form are what distinguishes the aesthetic from other modes of subjective experience, such as cognition. However, even those other non-aesthetic modes can be aestheticized—for example, the pleasure of a beautiful thought. As you will see throughout this book, the experience of aesthetic pleasure is rarely, if ever, affectively one-dimensional. It is more often accompanied by a mélange of other feelings, even seemingly contradictory ones like anger, grief, boredom, or irritation. Aesthetic pleasure is inseparable from other kinds of affective experiences; we have feelings about aesthetic pleasure, or pleasure can be attached to other feelings and desires. We might feel guilty about finding something beautiful, or we might find a certain beauty in something that makes us feel extremely sad. We might have an idea about the aesthetic pleasure we are experiencing that makes us feel annoyance, shame, or joy. You can see how it quickly becomes difficult to tease out aesthetic pleasure from other modes of subjective experience, and even why it can be less than useful to do so. It certainly can be helpful to identify a chain of relations (the pleasurable aesthetic response prompts an idea that prompts a feeling) and to sort out the different components of aesthetic experience. But isolating modes of experience (aesthetic, cognitive, affective) from each other in aesthetic analysis and critique can also obscure the importance of these connections and their mutually influential impact on the psyche and the world. While pleasure might seem an obvious kind of subjective experience, in practice it can be anything but.

This complicated interfacing of feeling and form is an important part of what makes aesthetic pleasure a social experience, even as it is entirely subjective. As Sara Ahmed writes in *The Cultural Politics of Emotion*, such feelings, or emotions in her language, are what connect us to others: "Emotions are not 'in' either the individual or the social, but produce the very surfaces and boundaries that allow the individual and the social to be delineated as if they are objects. The objects of emotion create the very surfaces and boundaries that allow all kinds of objects to be delineated."[15] As such, objects of emotion, aesthetic objects, and aesthetic pleasure help to circulate ideas and feelings, creating arrangements of the surfaces and boundaries that connect and separate us in the social.

Despite the centrality of pleasure to the aesthetic, pleasure is not typically the first thing we tend to think of when the topic of race and aesthetics arises. Anecdotally, the study of race is associated with "negative" affective responses, such as trauma, grief, and anger. Aesthetic experiences characterized by such intense negative feeling are distinguished by the palpable absence of pleasure—joylessness, fear, disgust. As the previous paragraphs would suggest, however, understanding aesthetic experience is more complex than sorting experiences into "positive" and "negative" buckets. We encounter the subject of pleasure when broaching vexed topics such as fetish, stereotype, and definitions of beauty and taste. Here, pleasure is certainly at play, although the delights enjoyed by some do harm to others. Much of the scholarship that addresses the relation between race and aesthetics is necessarily critical of pleasure, pointing to the ways that the enjoyment of certain representations, styles, genres, and texts contributes to the dehumanization and suffering of racialized groups. Because of the central role that aesthetics play in the production of racial difference, this work has been exceedingly important. However, to critique aesthetics or question the ethics of certain kinds of aesthetic pleasure is not to forswear aesthetic pleasure altogether or mark the enjoyment of aesthetic pleasure as irrelevant to the study of race and racism.

Unfortunately, attention to the ways that the aesthetic can circulate ideas, enact social positions, and reinforce power dynamics has not always been warmly received in the relatively conservative field of aesthetic theory. When questions about the ethics and politics of aesthetic pleasure are raised, those critiques of aesthetic pleasure, often called "political" or "ideological" criticism, can be misrepresented as wholesale renunciations of aesthetic pleasure. "Political" criticism in this context can name a vast range of critical styles and objectives, including Marxism, feminism, and anti-racist critique. The "political" critic is represented as constitutively against pleasure, regarding beauty with skepticism and contempt. In these caricatures, the paranoid political critic salivates over the aesthetic as a tempting but poisonous delicacy, delights that cloud the moral mind with an intoxicating haze. Meanwhile, the champions of the aesthetic argue that aesthetic pleasure is anything but oppressive; in fact, aesthetic pleasure in its highest form is freedom itself. The aesthetic primes us for utterly unique and transformative human experiences where we might become unshackled from the limitations of the political and the social while living more harmoniously with others.

Michel Chaouli's *Thinking with Kant's Critique of Judgment* offers such a depiction of disdain for beauty, claiming that the key terms from Kant's *Critique* and aesthetic theory more broadly have become unfashionable and distrusted in both art and scholarship:

> Are we not guilty of naïveté, or worse, of deluding ourselves into believing that these concepts continue to have a grip on our experience? Have artists, critics, and theorists not exposed them as falsehoods, handsome masks that disguise the true face of social violence? Pleasure, we are reminded from every side, communicates a merely decorous liking that serves as an index of how the modern subject has learned to arrange itself with the brutal conditions it inhabits. To really shake things up, you need stronger stuff, so writers reach for enjoyment and *juissance* [sic] and affect; they reach for the supposedly untamed sublime. Taste, for its part, has been revealed as a technique for creating and maintaining social difference, and so "having taste" in fact comes to signify above all an embrace of social and commercial norms. *Beauty* our third term, has suffered the greatest loss of prestige. It now finds few advocates among thoughtful writers and artists. The most ambitious among these—those intent on making and thinking in new ways—have not only found no use for it but have directed their efforts at disparaging it. The last thing a serious artist wants is to be caught in the company of an entity that is now unashamedly at home only in places like beauty contests and beauty parlors.[16]

In the narrative of political criticism and art pursued by Chaouli, while the political critic ostracizes beauty from proper academic research, relegating it to lowly commercial (and feminine) spaces such as pageants and salons, those scholars secretly relish and are motivated by the milder gratifications of aesthetic pleasure in their pursuit of knowledge. This is the premise of Timothy Aubrey's *Guilty Aesthetic Pleasures*, which works to bridge some ground between the diametrically opposed scholarly groups of "the formalists who once determined the direction of English studies and the politically oriented scholars who succeeded them."¹⁷ In Aubrey's narrative, like Chaouli's, at some point at the end of the twentieth century, pleasure was banished from the academy, and like Chaouli, Aubrey imagines this as a succession of regimes, the aesthetic being replaced with the political or ideological:

> Aesthetic pleasure can never be innocent. To seek it out is to commit the sin of trying to evade politics—sin that paradoxically sustains existing political arrangements. Moreover, if aesthetic pleasure is irresponsible, then aesthetic judgment is downright pernicious: under the guise of disinterestedness, it inevitably supports the interests of the privileged, the powerful, and the socially dominant over those of the underserved, the weak, and the marginalized. This, at least, was the view that served to justify efforts to banish aesthetic criticism from academic literature departments in the final decades of the twentieth century, in favor of ideological critique.¹⁸

Chaouli's and Aubrey's books, published in 2017 and 2018, respectively, claim to mark a long reign of the political, identitarian, or ideological critic that is due for reassessment. Arguably, it is Elaine Scarry's *On Beauty and Being Just*, originally delivered as part of the Tanner Lectures on Human Values at Yale University in 1998, that offers the most iconic iteration of this argument and has had the most lasting impact on the discussion of beauty and its dismissal from the academy. In this oft-cited treatise on beauty, Scarry articulates the argument, now familiar to us, that beauty has been banished from the academy and artworld by a new regime motivated by moral and political righteousness. This regime has judged beauty to be an agent of oppression, although it remains secretly desired and hoarded. Scarry makes the case that beauty is "innocent" of these charges and proceeds to disembowel the "incoherent" political arguments against beauty.¹⁹ Without citing any specific scholars, Scarry outlines what she sees as the contradictory double argument against beauty pursued by the political critic:

> The first [argument] urges that beauty, by preoccupying our attention, distracts attention from wrong social arrangements. It makes us inattentive, and therefore eventually indifferent, to the project of bringing

about arrangements that are just. The second argument holds that when we stare at something beautiful, make it an object of sustained regard, our act is destructive to the object. This argument is most often prompted when the gaze is directed toward a human face or form, but the case presumably applies equally when the beautiful thing is a mourning dove, or a trellis spilling over with sweet pea, or a book whose pages are being folded back for the first time. The complaint has given rise to a generalized discrediting of the act of "looking," which is charged with "reifying" the very object that appears to be the subject of admiration.[20]

Without reference to specific texts or critics, it is somewhat difficult to respond to Scarry's description of the political argument against beauty. However, I object to Scarry's claim that it might be presumed that the gaze is as destructive to a human being as it is to a vine of sweet pea or a book (things that do not need to be objectified because they are already objects), unless the plant and book are sentient creatures living in the legacy of genocide, enslavement, and gender-based oppression that provides the historical context of such critiques of looking.

I find bizarre and even disingenuous the idea that political critiques of pleasure regard all kinds of pleasure as equally destructive, or that political critics believe that beauty inevitably succors us into indifference. I do not buy the argument that there is an embargo against pleasure. Rather, as I hope to show throughout this book through my citation of other scholars and example texts, there are specific critiques that identify distinct ways of looking and representation as they have been shaped by histories of cisheteropatriarchy, capitalism, sexual violence, colonialism, slavery, anti-Blackness, and white supremacy. Obviously, the quality and interest of such scholarship varies, but, nevertheless, this scholarship teaches us that it not only matters whether one is looking at a flower or a human face; but it matters who is doing the looking, who or what is being gazed upon, how they are being look at, and in what context. If aesthetic pleasure is a social relation—and I argue that it is—that relation is constituted by dynamics of power and difference and is thus accountable to ethical consideration. Accountability is not prohibition.

The erasure of particularity creates an over-stuffed strawman: the political critic who abjures pleasure. However, if one spends time with the scholarship that could be called "political" or "ideological"—such as is much of the research to which this book is indebted—I believe that one finds not a censorious dismissal of beauty and pleasure but a yearning for it and a belief in its importance. In this sense, I am sympathetic to Aubrey's argument that aesthetic pleasure never really left humanities scholarship; it just started to look different. The narrative of an adversarial relationship between the political and the aesthetic unhelpfully contributes to misapprehensions about the nature of "political" arguments as against pleasure and to the assumption that "aesthetic" critics are without a political stake.

The idea that "political" aesthetic critique is only forbidding, or that it has no stake in pleasure, is a misinterpretation that foreshortens the depth of a rich body of scholarship examining the relationship between race and a range of aesthetic issues. The stringent separation of the political from pleasure represents politics itself as joyless and without humor, its entire strategic and tactical array centered, in the interest of a reducing harm, on making people less free to enjoy themselves. Although the political critic is represented as inveterately against pleasure (while secretly craving it), the aesthetic critic rarely claims to be against the utopian goals of freedom, which politics is ostensibly supposed to bring about. In fact, aesthetic critics are wont to argue that aesthetic pleasure itself, especially beauty, brings about the goals sought by the political critic: freedom, truth, and justice. This is a familiar tension within the academy—that justice-oriented scholars threaten the true freedom of unfettered expression and exploration, that any freedom secured through prohibition and denial is ultimately shortsighted and limiting of human potential. But these arguments do not take into account the history of the aesthetic in the West and its associations with hierarchies of the human—a topic discussed in detail in chapter 1 on beauty and chapter 3 on the freedom to make—considering how the abstraction of the universal aesthetic subject has been strategically aligned with whiteness. While the examples presented in scholarship such as Scarry's tend to be simple and benign—mourning doves, sweet peas, and palm trees—actual aesthetic experiences are complex, raising important questions about whose freedom is secured through different kinds of pleasure.

Both academic and popular conversations on aesthetic pleasure tend to hinge on an unnuanced binary of prohibition and freedom: does one have it, or does one not? This frames pleasure as individual property, an object that the subject holds onto against the onslaughts of moral censure, identitarians, and killjoys.[21] In this framework, pleasure must be defended, and attempts to address pleasure's harms are met as threats to individual freedom and disruptions to societal harmony. The spoiling of aesthetic pleasure is framed as a failure of readers and audiences to move beyond injury in order to see what is universally good or useful in a work of art—which may be merely that it exists.

I would like to suggest that representing aesthetic pleasure simply as an object one *has* (an individual possession that must be guarded), a tool or instrument that someone uses (for better or worse), or an on-off switch is insufficient for describing how aesthetic pleasure works and its role in culture and society and reproduces models of aesthetic subjectivity that leave a global racial order, one that emerged in the modern era of European colonialism and racial slavery, to perpetuate itself undisturbed. I propose instead that we regard aesthetic pleasure as a social structure in which feeling, form, concepts, and value come together in procedures of power and knowledge. When we make an aesthetic judgment, feeling aesthetic pleasure, we are never truly alone. Aesthetic experience takes place in the context of historical and social relations, amid the material (even as a psychic response) unfolding with conscious or unconscious attention to the ways that our aesthetic responses are produced as a mode of address. In and of itself, aesthetic pleasure is not good or bad, moral or immoral, useful or useless. But as in any social relation or practice of being with others, aesthetic pleasure provokes ethical questions. We are not being asked here to determine a "right" kind of aesthetic pleasure, to sort "good" kinds of pleasure from "bad." Rather, the question is, How does pleasure index our social arrangements with others or even put us into social relation with other humans and non-humans?

I enter the conversation on race and aesthetic pleasure to address what I take to be a misapprehension of the problem at hand. To critique pleasure is not the same thing as calling for an injunction against it. The context in which we experience pleasure, the way it connects us to others, and its role in the production of reality, collectively, has a meaningful impact on the world and the beings in it. This impact can be positive, negative, or, most likely, a mix of the two. Thus, the question ought to be, How do we cultivate aesthetic pleasure as a social relation that contributes to a more just world?

Experimental

What is considered experimental is highly variable, but when people talk about the experimental, they are typically saying something about form and its relationship to convention, popularity, and accessibility. The experimental tends to be defined against these things—unconventional, unpopular, ugly, and difficult. Another way that people are apt to use the term *experimental* is to make an argument for the value of a work of art—a work of literature, film, painting, or performance—by claiming that it is somehow new.[22] Its value lies in the pleasures and promises of novelty and the potential for bringing about a transformation—of the self, an idea, a society, or art. It can be delightful to encounter the unexpected, to experience the intense gratification of a previously unthought idea, and the experimental often rubs elbows with the jocosity of the absurd. Even when the newness of a work of literature or art carries with it intense negative experiences such as disillusionment, disenchantment, grief, or horror, there is often an attendant attribution of value that comes with a sense of clarity or the feeling of realization, an ability to see that has been made possible by a previously unencountered presentation of form. The awareness of value is integral to aesthetic pleasure.

For Pleasure traverses media to think about form, aesthetic pleasure, and race. I consider novels, paintings, poems, performances, conceptual art, and films. I have chosen the term *experimental* to give myself enough latitude to bring works in different media into conversation with each other around a shared aesthetic effect. However, its use might be a little idiosyncratic here. I occasionally use it interchangeably with *avant-garde*, although I try to avoid this term for its militaristic and progressivist connotations. *Experimentalism* is most often employed as a term to talk about literature and film. Within these categories, there are debatable, but navigable, distinctions between a mainstream that tends toward narrative, realism, and representation and an underground, or minor flows of creative expression that embrace formal difficulty, innovation, and diversions from representational and conventional forms. The visual arts function a bit differently in relation to *experimental*, where the term is less often in use as a category or genre. Since the rise of abstraction, conceptual art, and performance art in the mid-twentieth century, experimental visual artists have become the mainstream, more or less, as these previously avant-garde forms were absorbed into the very art markets that they were often rebelling against.

I retain *experimental* as a useful term for signaling a certain history of critical attention to innovations in form, as well as a certain desire (on the part of maker, audience, and/or critic) for transformation to take place. The downside of such faith in form is that it can result in an overestimation of its power to act on the world in a predictable and advantageous way. It is naïve to expect forms in and of themselves to only or always do a particular thing. We cannot control the life of a form and what it does. This faith extends to the value of newness itself, that simply by being new, a form, a method, or a material might create an opening for more freedom. But the history of experimentalism clearly demonstrates that newness does not equal liberation; the embroilment of Ezra Pound's call to "make it new" with his embrace of fascism, racism, and anti-Semitism is one of the most well-known examples of the ways that avant-garde, experimental, and new aesthetic forms can just as easily be harnessed to oppressive political visions (something I explore in more detail in chapter 3). And yet I believe that art and literature can and do catalyze social transformation. A desire for new forms is integral to radical and utopian social projects that yearn for a profoundly different world. We often look to art to help us manifest ideas that cannot yet be thought, to give a sensible, shareable shape to aqueous feelings, to create processes that cannot yet been practiced, and to have experiences that cannot yet be imagined.

In this book, I conceptualize form as an aesthetic method of directing attention. The repetition of a sound in a poem, the composition of a painting, the recontextualization of an object in a piece of conceptual art all might guide audiences toward a set of ideas, feelings, contexts, relationships, or bodily sensations. Experimentalism uses aesthetic forms and methods in unexpected ways, shifting our attention away from the habitual and the given, making different perspectives, ideas, feelings, and realities available. Experiments in aesthetic form are prized in this book as methods of redirecting attention, diversions that make certain social forms visible.

The experimental prompts us to consider the moment of aesthetic judgment itself and the practice of interpretation, considering, How is this different from what I expected, or what I have experienced before? and Why is that important? The attentional movements brought about by experimental forms can help us recognize how social violence is created, circulated, and reproduced through aesthetic forms. But the true promise of the experimental perhaps lies in its contributions to the flourishing of new ideas through the unexpected rearrangement of our perceptions of the world. In my most optimistic moments within this book, I find hope in the experimental and its potential to make available social relations not based in domination. Not all the texts or artists in this book might be thought of as obviously experimental, but I use the term to signal a critical method of centering aesthetic risk-taking and the desire to produce new ways of understanding the world rather than as a means of identifying a discrete set of qualities or techniques.

Thinking about form as the aesthetic phenomenon that directs attention also helps us dismantle the figure of the aesthetic subject that has monopolized how we imagine aesthetic judgment in the West since the Enlightenment. Recent scholarship on attention provides alternatives to the idea of a self-contained subject or agent who drives or directs attention. In the study of consciousness, this is sometimes referred to as an interior agent or "controller" who causes mental actions. Drawing from Buddhist texts of the Theravāda tradition written in the Pāli language, philosopher of the mind Jonardon Ganeri argues that contrary to the notion of the self as an agent that precedes mental actions such as aesthetic judgment, it is attention that precedes, and is indeed necessary for, any sense of self.[23] According to Ganeri, attention describes a field of awareness inseparable from any mental activity, so that there is no "detached agent" who "acts in the centre of a space of action" or "detached witness" who "watches from the centre of a space of experience."[24] That is, "attention is not a space of awareness distinct from and occupied by exercises of experience and agency, but the ongoing structure of experience and action."[25] Similarly, the anthropologist Tim Ingold defines attention as "the *stretch* of human life," emphasizing, as with Ganeri, that attention is not so much the purposeful action of an internal agent as it is the quality of one's relation to the world.[26] As Ingold puts it, "I have come to understand that paying attention is not about shining a spotlight on this or that object in the world, but about going along with things, opening up to them and doing their bidding. Intention is premised upon attentionality, not attention on intentionality."[27]

The artist and writer Jenny Odell's observations on attention complement these ideas about attention's capacity to wedge open the world and so fracture the intactness of the liberal self. In her book *How to Do Nothing*, Odell recounts her experience of seeing a live performance of pieces from John Cage's *Song Books* at San Francisco's Davies Symphony Hall. Odell was familiar with Cage as an icon of the mid-century avant-garde and with his belief that "everything is music," but this was her first time seeing a live Cage performance. In Odell's telling, this is no ordinary night at the symphony:

> Instead of the customary rows of musicians dressed in all black, the people onstage were dressed in plain clothes, moving about various props and devices like a typewriter, a set of cards, or a blender. Three vocalists made strange and haunting sounds while someone shuffled cards into a microphone and another walked into the audience to give someone a present—all, in some way, part of the score. As I imagine is the case at many Cage performances, the audience seemed to be shifting in their seats, trying very hard not to laugh, which would be inappropriate in a symphony hall. But the breaking point came when Michael Tilson Thomas, the conductor of the San Francisco Symphony, used the blender to make a smoothie. He took a sip and appeared satisfied. After that, all bets were off, with laughter tumbling down from the seats toward the stage and integrating itself into the piece.[28]

However, the most impressive transformation for Odell is not the metamorphosis of the symphony from stuffy temple of the arts to juice bar but what happens to her after she leaves the hall: "I walked out of the symphony hall down Grove Street to catch the MUNI, and heard every sound with a new clarity—the cars, the footsteps, the wind, the electric buses. Actually, it wasn't so much that I heard these clearly as that I heard them *at all*. How was it, I wondered, that I could have lived in a city for four years already—even having walked down this street after a symphony performance so many times—and never have actually heard anything?"[29]

For Odell, the answer is attention. Her experience at the Cage performance altered her attentional field so that "for months after this, I was a different person," a person who hears the street sounds that previously had not existed for her, among other new habits of noticing.[30] Odell argues that this demonstrates how attention affects the self. Not only does the act of "leav[ing] behind the coordinates of what we habitually notice" enable different relations to the idea of the self and being in the world, but it also encourages us to notice attention itself: "Thrown back on ourselves by a 'wall' and not a window, we can begin to see ourselves seeing."[31] The task, then, in encountering experimental forms—like the performance of Cage's work—is to remain open to the guidance of form and where it might lead, how it might throw us back on ourselves, however counterintuitive. As sensing, interpreting, attending beings, we are not completely in control of our aesthetic experiences, but nor are we completely at their disposal. The interpretative praxis that I advocate for here embraces an ethic of humility and openness and requires us to set aside the notion of a self who directs our aesthetic experiences, allowing ourselves to be moved differently, while staying alert to our position and impact in the world. The satisfaction of predictable experiences gives way to the pleasures of surprise.

When we consider the potential of experimental forms for meaningfully redirecting attention, the valorization of the experimental as a bringer of the new is understandable. In a world that is unbearably hostile to so many, the desire for the new can be a life-saving optimism. The new must come to be if there is to be survival and then more than survival. How else might such reality-shifting change take place except through a radical alteration in how we perceive the world and what is possible and valuable within it? This contention that experimental aesthetic forms can move us to make the attentional shifts necessary for a just world is at the center of each chapter in this book. Throughout, I contemplate how racially minoritized authors and artists have turned to experimental forms and methods to imagine social relations that are not based in racial domination yet live within an aesthetic history shaped by racial capitalism. The experimentalism I study here seeks to redefine aesthetic experience as a space of pleasure and freedom by starting from the premise that a violent global racial order shapes the aesthetic but does not fully define its limits. *Experimental* is a flawed way to describe such beautiful things. But the imperfections of *experimental* as a term also tell us something important about the racial history of aesthetic forms and pleasure. It functions in this book as a marker, rather than a description or definition, of a set of hopes on the one hand and a contradictory and problematic history on the other.

Most notably for this project, while the work of non-white artists and authors has often served as inspiration for white experimentalists, the actual work of artists and authors of color has historically been excluded from critical discourse, high-profile venues, and central spaces for publication and circulation. Scholars have already intervened to correct this omission, thoroughly critiquing the interpretative framework that reads "ethnic" literatures as content-driven explorations of "identity" lacking formal elements of significant literary value. As the scholar of Asian American poetry Dorothy Wang writes, "While 'hard-core' or 'real' literary and poetry critics talk about questions of etymology, prosody, and form, minority poets and poetry are too often left out of the conversation about the literary (or simply left out)."[32] Should an author of color pursue questions of race or other forms of identity, this "operates as a disqualification to participation in avant-gardism," as scholar of experimentalism Natalia Cecire puts it.[33]

The *literary*, the *experimental*, the *aesthetic*—these are all shorthand terms that describe the positive valuation of form, particularly when an author's or artist's use of form is identified as ingenious or new for the time period. In the last two decades especially, scholars like Wang, GerShun Avilez, Anthony Reed, Evie Shockley, Timothy Yu, Nathanial Mackey, and Joseph Jonghyun Jeon, among others, have been working to debunk this binary of race/identity/content on the one side and the unraced/universal/form on the other. While the work done by each individual scholar in this group is unique, all have shown that while the discourse of experimentalism and the avant-garde is raced, this interpretative framework does not reflect the actual creative production of artists and authors of color, who have demonstrated a formal abundance. By deploying the term *experimental*, I am asking us to consider the racial politics of experimentalism, the avant-garde, and the aesthetic, revising these terms from the perspective of minoritarian aesthetic histories.

The concept of *experimental* also helps me explain the periodization of this book. *Experimental* is not only a way of describing critical and aesthetic desires for form, but also, as Cecire has written, a "historical formation."[34] Cecire argues that the historical formation of the experimental contains a double periodization, in which "experimentalism is rooted in the early twentieth century *as reinterpreted by the late twentieth century*, produced by the overlaying of what was present in the early twentieth century with what certain writer-critics of the later twentieth century were ready to see."[35] While such reinterpretations contain serious pitfalls, *For Pleasure* focuses on what can be socially and politically promising in thinking about experimentalism as a mode of interpretation rather than a set of identifiable forms or techniques. In other words, rather than identifying a collection of forms, artists, or genealogies as "experimental," this book uses experimental as a critical lens. *For Pleasure* moves across a broad period of time, focused strongly on the twentieth century with the earliest text produced in 1926 and the latest in 2020. The temporality of the book attempts to contextualize aesthetic forms both within their historical moment of production and also within newer meanings that become available from the moment of our present. Thus, the chapters model a way of reading across period that historically situates forms, artists, and texts while also placing them in conversation with each other across time and category. The chapters work together to historicize and theorize aesthetic forms, methods, and judgments that demonstrate the relationships between aesthetic pleasure and the production and circulation of racial meaning throughout the twentieth century and into the twenty-first. Experimental is a shorthand for a contradictory repertoire of aesthetic histories and feelings around race and form. It is being asked to hold a lot here—to mark an interpretative tradition of racial production and exclusion, a hopeful, utopian attitude toward newness, and to name and make visible minoritarian traditions of aesthetic boldness.

Race

One of my anonymous readers suggested that what I am actually discussing in this book is racialization, not race, and they are correct. I use the term *race* as an umbrella term, signaling the discussion of racial practices, formations, and racism and the ways that racial meaning circulates through the aesthetic. Because the category of experimentalism has been predominantly defined as inseparable from whiteness, this book centers the work of racially minoritized experimentalists. In doing so, I hope to broaden our understanding of who makes experimental literature and art and to offer a revision of the term *experimental* drawn from the work that has lived at the edges of this idea. In building my archive, I draw heavily from my training in Black studies and Asian American studies, and as a result, the majority of the texts explored here are created by Black and Asian artists and examine the contexts of those artworks in relation to histories of Blackness and Asianness within the United States, though not exclusively. This archive allows me to examine key historical and cultural pressure points within the twentieth-century United States necessary to understanding the ways that experimentalism and its aesthetic pleasures have participated in US racial formation. The four body chapters in *For Pleasure* consider four cases where non-white experimentalists have made critical interventions at the intersection of aesthetics and racial practices: the central role of Black modernism and a Black experimentalism in cultivating alternative aesthetic theories against white supremacy (chapter 1); conceptualism's antagonistic response to the increasingly significant role of global war and immigration policy and enforcement as technologies of race-making in the mid-twentieth-century and the centrality of Asians and Asian Americans within this history (chapter 2); the avant-garde's use of anti-Blackness as grounds for aesthetic freedom (chapter 3); and experimentalism's revolutionary potential as it is connected to anticolonial and feminist movements in response to global decolonization, emergent neoliberalism, and Cold War forms of imperialism and warfare that launched a new era of Asian diaspora and migration to the United States and elsewhere (chapter 4).

The focus on Black and Asian American authors and artists also reflects a significant historical relationship between those groups within the history of racial formation and anti-racist movements in the twentieth-century United States. The shifts in availability and desirability of different forms of racialized labor after the official end of slavery and the rise of immigration from Asia led to a complex interrelationality between Blackness and Asianness in the context of American white supremacy. The mutually informing racial formations and practices that emerged as a result have had numerous effects on politics in the latter half of the nineteenth century through the twentieth century. As Lisa Lowe has written, the concept of "free labor" as it emerged in the seventeenth and eighteenth centuries enabled a new mode of racialization and expropriation through the forced and coerced migrations of slavery and colonial labor. Later, with the Page Act (1875), the Immigration Act of 1917, the Johnson-Reed Act (1924), and the invention of "illegal aliens" in the nineteenth and twentieth centuries, immigration policy became a technology of race-making, with Chinese exclusion becoming the prototype for later forms of criminalization, racialization, detention and caging, and deportation embedded in immigration policy, which has had a devastating effect on non-white migrants to the United States ever since. The mythic "good" Asian immigrant subject was weaponized against Black people. Practices of gratuitous violence and exploitation became normalized through narratives of racial essentialism and social determinism that were fundamentally anti-Black. American wars and military imperialism (and against the backdrop of Japanese imperialism) in the Philippines, the Korean peninsula, Vietnam, Cambodia, and Laos resulted in devastating violence, destabilization, and diasporic migration, while the desegregation of the military during the American war in Korea and the institution of the draft during the war in Vietnam demonstrably impacted Black social identity and politics in relation to Asia and the Pacific.

However, Black and Asian relationality was not fully determined by the global racial capitalism and colonialisms that shaped them. There also developed political solidarities, shared practices of political resistance, and collaborative experimentations with different forms of cultural production, appreciation, appropriation, and borrowing. In the eras of the civil rights movement and Black Power, Black political organizing and theorizing became the premiere model for fighting against white supremacy and colonialism internal to the United States. In the era of decolonization in Africa and Southeast Asia especially, many Black and Asian leftist political formations in the United States recognized white supremacy and capitalism as their shared enemies, regarding each other as partners with a shared stake in its demise and as part of the global fight against capitalism and colonialism.

This of course is only a partial view of the shifting racial politics in the mid-twentieth-century United States. A more complete picture would encompass the ongoing project of settler colonialism and Indigenous dispossession, genocide, and resistance, the devastation and continued legacy of Spanish conquest, Manifest Destiny, the complex racial politics of the political, social, and economic restructuring resulting from the Mexican-American War and the Treaty of Guadalupe Hidalgo, the racialization of Latin American labor via US hemispheric politics and anti-communist militarism, the birth of neoliberal authoritarianism as with the bloody Pinochet regime, and so many more world historical factors that have played into the interrelationality between Indigenous, Black, Latinx, Chicanx, and Asian racial formations within and beyond the United States. The interrelationality of racial practices and positions as they impacted Black and Asian formations unfolds in this dense and morphing context as a set of histories and ideas critical to understanding aesthetics and experimentalism in the mid-twentieth century.

In reading Black and Asian traditions together, I take a relational rather than comparative approach, in keeping with Alexander Weheliye's use of those terms. As Weheliye writes in *Habeas Viscus*, "Relationality provides a productive model for critical inquiry and political action within the context of black and critical ethnic studies, because it reveals the global and systemic dimensions of racialized, sexualized, and gendered subjugation, while not losing sight of the many ways political violence has given rise to ongoing practices of freedom within various traditions of the oppressed."[36] In contrast, traditional comparison, which treats social groups as discrete, can reify existing categories while placing oppressed groups in competition with one another to the detriment of all but white supremacy. Each chapter situates the texts and artists historically within the relevant aesthetic and historical context, but I also try to weave connections across chapters, showing how these alternative narratives and interpretations complement each other in building new understandings of the experimental as a minoritarian aesthetics and its possibilities for social change. In this sense, the book also reflects Lisa Marie Cacho's revised definition of the comparative analytic. As she writes:

> A comparative analytic centers relational, contingent, and conditional processes of devaluation, which makes it particularly useful for examining the ways in which interconnected processes of valuation, valorization, and devaluation (i.e., race, gender, sexuality, class, nation, legality, etc.) work interdependently to reify value and relations of inequality as normative, natural, and obvious. Although it is informed by the differential

devaluation of racialized groups, this approach does not necessarily entail an explicit comparison of two or more racial groups because relations of value are not always explicit.[37]

Cacho's emphasis on value and racialization as a mode of normativized devaluation is particularly pertinent to thinking about aesthetics. Aesthetics is a domain of value. It is a social relation wherein sensation and cognition meet on the scene of culture and history to resolve questions of value. Thus, Cacho's definition of the comparative analytic complements Weheliye's concept of the relational, as both demand that scholars situate their objects of analysis within political systems in which no social category can be properly understood as separate from any other but always conditioning and impacting contingent relations of power.

I have no intention of representing anything close to an exhaustive or chronological history of race and experimentalism. Instead, I hope to demonstrate a method of interpretation that takes as its starting context the ways that the aesthetic and the racial have been intertwined. Thus, in this book, each chapter functions as a case study examining a significant phenomenon or concept within the history of race and experimentalism in the twentieth-century United States. In my approach, I do not mean that this is the only way to interpret or engage with the texts studied here or that the "point" of every text, art object, or aesthetic experience is race. However, I hope that the offered readings will model how experimentalism has been shaped by the aesthetic as a racializing structure of feeling and also how experimentalism can intervene in and recircuit that structure, providing different kinds of aesthetic experiences and alternative social arrangements.

A key premise here is that aesthetic theory and the idea of what it means to experience aesthetic pleasure has been fundamentally entangled with whiteness since the Enlightenment, especially in the wake of the influence of Kant's *Critique of Judgment*. This idea is explored in depth in chapter 1, which lays much of the groundwork for how this book understands the relationship between aesthetic judgment and racialization. As Cedric Robinson writes in his influential work *Black Marxism*, race and racism were not the products of European colonialism but endemic to the society that could imagine and pursue such systemic violence:

What concerns us is that we understand that racialism and its permutations persisted, rooted not in a particular era but in the civilization itself. And though our era might seem a particularly fitting one for depositing the origins of racism, that judgment merely reflects how resistant the idea is to examination and how powerful and natural its specifications have become. Our confusions, however, are not unique. As an enduring principle of European social order, the effects of racialism were bound to appear in the social expression of every strata of every European society no matter the structures upon which they were formed. None was immune.[38]

This book spends time with the racialism of aesthetic experience and aesthetic theory that has been naturalized and resists our examination.

While I do make the effort to correct racialized interpretive modes that have historically governed our understanding of the experimental, I do not make the argument that any one racial group is essentially associated with a particular form or that a social or historical context inevitably produces certain kinds of forms. On the contrary, while I encourage readers to stay attuned to social and historical context as part of the method presented here, I argue that we need to interrupt our expectations for what that relation between form and context might be. I attempt to read the work under study in this book against the grain of racialized habits of interpretation, staying open to the social and political possibilities of aesthetic response that can jam those meaning-making patterns. While it is a core argument in the book that writers and artists use experimental forms to intervene in structures of race and racism, I do not argue that any one form is inevitably linked to a racial tradition or context. I want to cultivate a reading practice in which we can be surprised and, through surprise, be changed.

Minoritarian Aesthetics

My thinking on the definition of minoritarian aesthetics is informed by queer theorist José Esteban Muñoz's use of the term *minoritarian*. In Muñoz's work, *minoritarian* describes a relationship to dominance (not necessarily based in numbers) within a social body that can be quite brutal. As he evocatively writes in an essay theorizing both the burdens and the possibilities of live performance for Latinx subjects, "Minoritarian subjects do not always dance because they are happy; sometimes they dance because their feet are being shot at."[39] Despite the bleakness of this image, *minoritarian* also carries with it a sense of hopefulness, that when the majoritarian paradigms are so crushing, minoritarian ways can be a living example of a different and realizable world. Joshua Chambers-Letson brings added clarification of the term and its use in Muñoz's work and the performance studies scholarship that has followed. He explains that the minoritarian is not intended to "subsume, flatten, or obliterate the differences between the different types of subjects who might choose to gather under that name. Rather, it describes a place of (often uncomfortable) gathering, a cover, umbrella, expanse, or refuge under and in which subjects marked by racial, sexual, gender, class, and national minority might choose to come together in tactical struggle, both because of what we share (often domination in some form by the major or dominant culture) and because of what makes us different."[40] Thus, *minoritarian* signals an improvisational and tactical relationship to power, as well as a desire to create social forms that are not structured by domination.

Readers might take note of a romantic valence to these definitions. Indeed, in the utopianism expressed in Muñoz's work and its legacy in queer studies and beyond, there is unavoidably a kind of romance, an expression of desire for something that seems so good that it is extremely difficult to imagine not wanting it. However, with the romance of minoritarianism comes a legitimate concern about the valorization of subordination in and of itself. It is not my intention to argue that minoritization is necessarily a positive thing, although this book does value the knowledge that minoritized experience can offer. What is signaled by minoritarian in this book is not ideal social or aesthetic forms but relations to social dominance, capital, and state power (rather than a set of identities); and practices in pursuit of survival, pleasure, and the abolition of unfreedom. The paths taken to these latter goals are often far from perfect, and I certainly do not believe that suffering and trauma are the necessary means to achieve them. As philosopher Olúfẹ́mi O. Táíwò observes, "Contra the old expression, pain, whether born of oppression or not, is a poor teacher. Suffering is partial, short-sighted, and self-absorbed. We shouldn't have a politics that expects different. Oppression is not a prep school."[41] And also, trauma "is a concrete, experiential manifestation of the vulnerability that connects me to most of the people on this earth. It comes between me and other people not as a wall, but as a bridge."[42] Suffering is not the pedagogical imperative for building a just world, but it is the felt experience of the interconnectedness of global oppressions. In using minoritarian aesthetics as an analytic, I have no desire to glorify the suffering that follows minoritization as a tool of systemic oppression or to suggest that such pain is the teacher one needs if one is to learn how to build a better world. Rather, a minoritarian aesthetics framework helps us understand aesthetics as a modern social relation, to acknowledge ongoing freedom struggles, and to learn from the tactical ingenuity of those who improvise brilliantly toward a more just and beautiful world. A minoritarian aesthetics helps us understand aesthetic forms as historical and active in practices of racialization in the United States. It links aesthetic forms to social forms through the world-making structure of aesthetic judgment. It surmises that as forms change, these changes have social impacts. It explores how minoritized individuals and groups take the given forms that function destructively toward their life possibilities and reconstruct them into forms that create more possibility. Finally, minoritarian aesthetics refuses the policing of pleasure as a structure of racial subordination and embraces the cultivation of aesthetic pleasure as a means of intervening in structures of racial dominance.

Chapter Summaries

Each chapter in this book represents a case study exhibiting a method of interpretation that centers questions of how the aesthetic participates in racial formation and how it might interrupt the racial order. Each chapter discusses one element of aesthetic pleasure: chapter 1 on beauty, chapter 2 on whimsy, chapter 3 on the freedom to make, and chapter 4 on collectivity. This is not an exhaustive list of the kinds of pleasures associated with the aesthetic. While there are many other kinds of pleasure that might be taken up, I selected these four for their connection to the experimental.

Beauty is somewhat unavoidable as a topic of aesthetic pleasure, undoubtedly the aesthetic experience that has garnered the most attention in criticism since Kant's *Critique of Judgment*, and the aesthetic and beauty are often discussed interchangeably. Popularly speaking, beauty is frequently understood to be the "point" of art, or the premier type of pleasure that one receives from art. Alongside beauty's dominance in the discussion of aesthetic pleasure is experimentalism's supposedly antagonistic relationship to the beautiful. However, in chapter 1, I hope to show that experimental forms and techniques have much to teach us about the beautiful, its aesthetic history, and its social promise. I show that experimentalism, specifically as it emerges from a Black aesthetic tradition, provides a much-needed revision of Western beauty regimes. The first chapter of this book demonstrates the necessity of re-theorizing beauty and aesthetic judgment from the ground of Black aesthetics, explaining how aesthetic theory has propelled anti-Blackness as a global system and how Black aesthetic traditions have offered other models for understanding beauty and aesthetic judgment beyond the Kantian standard. The chapter shows how Black aesthetics must be a starting point for any conversation on the liberatory potential of the aesthetic.

While there are many moments within the history of Black experimentalism that might elucidate the beautiful and its role in social life, chapter 1 focuses on the Harlem Renaissance and its legacy as a historical punctum. Examining classic works including W. E. B. Du Bois's "Criteria of Negro Art" (1926), Nella Larsen's *Passing* (1929), and Isaac Julien's *Looking for Langston* (1989), I demonstrate how we might analyze aesthetic judgment as a relation of power, wherein beauty judgments are integral to the modern racial understanding of the human. In my readings, I argue that these exemplary texts are not only beautiful in and of themselves but stage beauty judgments as their subject. The chapter traces a question that is inseparable from the history of Black politics: What can beauty do—if it does anything at all?

In chapter 2, I return to Kant's *Critique of Judgment* and its aesthetic taxonomies to theorize the aesthetic category of whimsy through readings of Yoko Ono's conceptualism in the 1960s and 1970s. The chapter contextualizes Ono's experimentalism within anti-war movements, American military imperialism in Southeast Asia, and mid-century American immigration policy. I consider how the US bureaucratic management of movement is also the production and management of racial difference by examining themes of racial administration into Ono's poetry. Drawing from Kant's less than celebratory conceptualization of whimsy, I argue that Ono uses the humor of the irrational and the impossible to turn the administration of human beings into a source of aesthetic pleasure, irritating the violent project of administrating race and gender. Ono's playful conceptualism enables us to see the administrative as an aesthetic experience, one that impacts our lives quite deeply. Through whimsy, racism's "rational" violence becomes obvious, and the possibility of refusing its coercions through aesthetic pleasure becomes available.

While the first two chapters focus on aesthetic judgment as a structure of power through which racial meaning is produced and circulates through culture, in chapter 3 I focus on two of the ancillary pleasures most strongly associated with experimentalism: the freedom to create and the freedom to interpret without restraint. Simply stated: It feels good to feel free. The aesthetic is often a place where people go to find this elusive feeling, both as creators and appreciators. In the third chapter, I explore the history of color-based abstraction and monochrome painting—particularly the history of chromatic black monochrome painting—to unpack the racial politics of aesthetic freedom as it has been imagined by a Euro-American avant-garde tradition. The chapter considers the relationship of painterly chromatic black abstraction to the production of racial Blackness, focusing on how Black artists have engaged monochrome and abstract color painting through both aesthetic expression and critique. In readings of works by Jack Whitten, Zora Neale Hurston, Ellen Gallagher, and Glenn Ligon, I argue that color abstraction is not outside the global racial order. On the contrary, abstraction is a site of production and circulation for racialized forms and ideas. Equally important to this alternative history of chromatic black abstraction is the chapter's exploration of how Black artists have recovered chromatic blackness as a nonrepresentational mode with transformative possibilities for thought and expression.

In the fourth and final chapter, focusing on the work and legacy of visual artist, filmmaker, and author Theresa Hak Kyung Cha, I examine the risks and pleasures of being together in aesthetic experience. The experimental often invites an erosion of the self-contained aesthetic subject, presenting experiences that purposefully blur the boundaries between artist, audience, and art object. Not only does Cha's art and writing, informed by conceptualism and performance, beautifully exemplify this experimental ethos, but Cha's legacy as a woman-of-color artist who embraced experimentalism has also become a beacon around which a diverse, multigenerational group of artists and audiences now gathers. Through the belated canonization of her book *Dictee*, Cha has become a literary and artistic icon who is regularly recruited to refute the binary racial frameworks outlined earlier in this introduction and throughout this book. Chapter 4 explores how Cha's ethics of aesthetic relation is key to her current popularity. I argue that her work invites participation in the aesthetic *through*, rather than despite, formal difficulty and that it is her commitment to difficulty that counterintuitively drives her popularity. The dedication of other artists, writers, and readers to Cha's work is clear evidence that Cha's "difficulty" is not separate from her ability to generate inter-relationality through critical and aesthetic feeling. While experimental aesthetic forms may estrange conventional interpretation or habits of attention, Cha shows us that they can also draw us in through the invention of new and desperately needed ways of understanding and being in the world.

1

What Can Beauty Do?

Can beauty provide an antidote to dishonor, and love a way to "exhume buried cries" and reanimate the dead?
—Saidiya Hartman, "Venus in Two Acts"

In an early sequence of Isaac Julien's film *Looking for Langston* (1989), Julien confronts the viewer with a discomforting beauty shot. The camera pans slowly, stopping in tight close-up on Julien's face, posed in a casket, head cradled in a halo of effulgent white flowers. Julien's calm, radiantly lit face resting in its coronal cushion registers as a classic beauty shot. A soft glow gently sculpts Julien's face in a style reminiscent of the work of glamor photographers from Hollywood's golden age, for example George Hurrell, who shot stars like Marlene Dietrich and Joan Crawford.[1] However, Julien is neither Dietrich nor Crawford. In 1989, Julien is a queer Black man living within the climate of diffuse threat under the Thatcher and Reagan administrations. His visage disrupts heteronormative and gendered expectations of the cinematic and photographic beauty shot while also signaling a queer history of erotic photography and the funereal photography of James Van Der Zee.[2] The shot performs an acute awareness of the political risks taken by the film. The title screen of *Looking for Langston* calls the film a "meditation," and as the camera lingers on Julien's tenderly filmed, beautiful face, we are prompted to meditate on the moment of aesthetic judgment itself. What happens if we call this funereal image beautiful? What is the meaning of this stylization of death in a moment of eugenic threat to queer Black life?[3] This chapter will attempt, somewhat elliptically, to address these questions through a study of how twentieth-century Black aesthetics has theorized and reimagined beauty and aesthetic judgments.

From this anchoring image, we can read an incendiary friction in *Looking for Langston* between its investment in beauty and its historical exigencies. As Anne Anlin Cheng has written, the affective and political force of beauty can produce ambivalence for racialized subjects.[4] The lines between fetish and liberation can be blurred, a softening of edges on display in the phosphorescence of Julien's film.[5] Beauty "whether it is about witnessing it or having it" thus "enacts a simultaneous process of identification and estrangement that remains central to—yet always displaces—racial difference."[6] The racial, gender, and sexual histories of colonization, identification, and fetish entangled in every gaze discredits Kantian notions of disinterested judgement.

However, while the beautiful in queer Black visual culture may be fraught, beauty also bears an undeniable transformative promise. We are not easily released from our sense of beauty's obviousness or goodness. People tend to imagine that beauty has the capacity to make people freer, or as Elaine Scarry argues, to make the perceiver act more justly in the world.[7] Beautiful, "positive" visualizations of racial difference are regularly recruited in racial projects designed to promote social recognition, dignity, and political power for oppressed groups. And yet racial and colonial oppression, as Cheng argues and *Looking for Langston* suggests, have never been separate from these "positive" representations and feelings. Desire, empathy, admiration, love, and beauty are not anathema to structures of domination but constitutive to them. Moreover, as positive representations become scenes of social and political group formation, they also risk hardening into reified identities, another kind of bell jar to squirm out from under. What practices of making or interpretation would protect Black beauty from the puerile—or self-ennobling—delectation of viewers? What prevents beautiful representations from becoming idealized images of a compulsory way of being, a correction that becomes *the* correct thing? As *Looking for Langston* turns to the beautiful at a moment of political crisis and mass death, it does so searchingly, *looking* for an answer to these questions. In my reading, I argue that the film offers hope for the recovery of aesthetic, visual, and erotic pleasure from fetishism, domination, and exploitation.

In this chapter, I am thinking toward the answers to these questions via the entanglements of beauty, sociality, and politics in the Harlem Renaissance and Black experimentalism. While experimentalism has a reputation for abjuring the beautiful and its incumbent delights that jelly the mind into docile complicity, the Black experimentalists I study here are curious about beauty as a demand for freedom. I hope to show that the Black experimentalists of the historical Harlem Renaissance and its descendants do not abandon beauty as they push aesthetic boundaries but seem to invest in it more deeply, keenly attuned to beauty as a structure of feeling and power. As I will discuss, beauty is intimately entwined with the production of the aesthetic subject as a key figure in modern conceptions of race (as first discussed in the introduction). Thus, the two traditions of Black experimentalism and Black radicalism come together in a profound reevaluation of beauty and social life.

After studying alongside the consummate aesthetes whose work is the foundation of this chapter—Isaac Julien, W. E. B. Du Bois, Nella Larsen—what I have to offer is this: beauty is a relational imaginary long subjected to the frayed suasion of Enlightenment universal reason and aesthetic judgment, which enact forms of racial categorization and domination. However, this tyranny is thin and brittle at its pressure points, its accession incomplete. Beauty judgments are structures of feeling that are also structures of collective demand-making. As such, they can rebuke whiteness's privatization of the universal, producing different forms of universality that deny whiteness's colonizing vision of what it means to be human. By the end of this chapter, I will be coming back to the beginning, returning to Julien in his sensuously lit meditation. But first I sit with two Harlem Renaissance thinkers and artists who frame the hopes and stakes of beauty with exemplary perspicuity—W. E. B. Du Bois and Nella Larsen. This chapter reads two classic Black modernist works—Du Bois's "Criteria of Negro Art" and Larsen's *Passing*—as theories of the beautiful, working through the problem of how to recover the pleasure of the beautiful against Enlightenment regimes of race, aesthetics, and subjectivity. At the end of the chapter, I come back to Isaac Julien's *Looking for Langston*. In my reading, I argue that *Looking for Langston* extends the Harlem Renaissance's experiments with beauty as social and political theory and practice. I demonstrate how we might read aesthetic judgment as a relation of power wherein beauty judgments are integral to the modern racial understanding of the human.

In a reading of Du Bois's classic "Criteria of Negro Art," we hear the echo of Kant's *Critique of Judgment*. I read Du Bois's "Criteria" as a Black political intervention in the Enlightenment aesthetic theory that has shaped the relationship between race, anti-Blackness, and the human, reclaiming the beautiful as the horizon of Black liberation. While Du

Bois lays down a visionary opening salvo, Larsen peers into the unseemly meetings of aesthetic judgment as a social relation, poking a wildness of imagination that ultimately threatens the supposed orderliness of beauty. While the Kantian theory of beauty that has come to dominate Western aesthetics holds that true aesthetic judgment balances the free play of imagination with the limits of universal reason, Larsen's *Passing* explores what happens when beauty is not defined by constraint.

In conversation, Du Bois and Larsen articulate beauty's promise and its dangers in the context of the Harlem Renaissance's experimental spirit. At the end of the chapter, I return to *Looking to Langston*, reading Julien's film as an extension of the aesthetic and political experimentalist traditions set up by artists and thinkers such as Du Bois and Larsen. As I will argue, Julien's *Looking for Langston* stages beauty judgments in a way that troubles the racial regimes maintained through the Kantian mode of aesthetic judgment. Following the philosophical and aesthetic traditions of the Harlem Renaissance, the film explores the possibilities of aesthetic judgment as a collective activity that redefines universality from the position of Black aesthetics and politics. The circular movement of this chapter feels appropriate as I trace a question that recursively arrives and is answered again and again in the history of Black experimental aesthetics, inseparable from the history of Black politics: What can beauty do—if it does anything at all?

Notes on the Experimental

Key to this chapter's arguments is the idea that this exploration of beauty and politics is usefully approached through the lens of experimentalism. *Looking for Langston* cites a queer Black experimentalist drive that helps us see what was distinct about the art of the Harlem Renaissance. Isaac Julien is a prominent figure in the contemporary art world as a filmmaker and installation artist who works across moving image and photography, explores the contingent affordances of multiple channel film, and toys with the relationship between narrative and visual abstraction in deeply researched art films. His groundbreaking early work from the 1980s, including *This Is Not an AIDS Advertisement* (1987), *Looking for Langston* (1989), and *The Attendant* (1993), was central to a new generation of politically mobilized filmmakers who were schooled in poststructuralism, postcolonial theory, cultural studies (Stuart Hall makes cameos in both *Looking for Langston* and *The Attendant*), and what Darius Bost has called the Black gay cultural renaissance.[8] This generation of filmmakers, which included directors such as Gregg Araki, Shu Lea Chang, Cheryl Dunye, Todd Haynes, and Derek Jarman, imagined a new avant-garde cinema based in the perspectives of minoritized filmmakers that could intervene in systems of racial, gender, sexual, and economic oppression. Building his practice in collaboration with Black filmmaking groups such as the Sankofa Film and Video Collective and the Black Audio Film Collective, Julien is credited as being one of the initiators of the New Queer Cinema movement, this loose cohort of independent filmmakers working in the 1980s and 1990s who embraced punk, D.I.Y., and experimental aesthetics in taboo-breaking explorations of queer life that centered sex during the AIDS crisis. Julien's *Looking for Langston* swiftly became a celebrated icon of queer cinema after winning the Teddy Award for Best Short Film at the Berlin International Film Festival in 1989.

With these credentials, naming Julien an "experimental" artist is not a terribly provocative move, although some readers might understandably push back against applying this term to Du Bois and Larsen, two artists and thinkers whose work is much more formally conservative than Julien's. However, as I explain in the introduction, my use of the term *experimental* is expansive, less an identification of a specific set of artistic methods and forms or a strict periodization than a critical method of centering aesthetic risk-taking and the desire to produce new ways of understanding the world. They call our attention to the tensions between mainstream representation and counterforms of aesthetic pleasure, pointing us toward the project of interpretation itself.

Both Du Bois and Larsen center beauty as a social practice of making the world and changing it. Their separate examinations of beauty strive to create new knowledge of, and ways of being in, the world. As literary and philosophical modernists, both participate in new formal and perspectival projects of the period that could be thought of as experimental in their reshaping of genre and discipline. In Larsen's case, her deftly handled foray into the slippery perspectives of the psychological novel (*Passing*, 1929, and *Quicksand*, 1928) reflects a formal experiment in portraying perception and psychological complexity through narrative. Du Bois reevaluates Enlightenment aesthetics by theorizing them from a Black aesthetics perspective.

Finally, the term *experimental* not only refers to questions of form but also names a project of historicization both in my selection of texts and in Julien's depiction of the Harlem Renaissance as an earlier movement of Black aesthetic and social experimentation. As Natalia Cecire has written, the term *experimental* in literary studies performs a double periodization that "rests on a recovery structure."[9] In this double historicization, "Experimentalism is rooted in the early twentieth century as reinterpreted by the late twentieth century, produced by the overlaying of what was present in the early twentieth century with what certain writer-critics of the later twentieth century were ready to see."[10] While Cecire is specifically talking about literature, the concept of experimentalism's double periodization is extremely helpful in understanding the relationship between *Looking for Langston* and its meticulously researched Harlem Renaissance archive.[11]

Looking for Langston draws out the risk-taking of Black artists in the Harlem Renaissance through his incorporation of archival materials and recovered historical knowledge into a film that eschews narrative and normative filmmaking conventions. Julien cites these earlier artists as aesthetic ancestors and influences on his own experimental practice, pulling them into the history of experimentalism. In Cecire's study, she writes that the experimental literature in the late twentieth century "is a recovery canon constructed concertedly from the 1970s through the turn of the millennium, which sought out the features of modernism best suited to serve as antecedents to post-Vietnam concerns."[12] This recovery process means quite differently when we consider how Black artists have been traditionally excluded from mainstream artistic traditions, let alone the traditions of the experimental or avant-garde (a fact to which Cecire also attends). Langston Hughes and W. E. B. Du Bois are perhaps the only figures mentioned in the film who have had a consistent canonical presence in American literature and history. Other artists slipped through the sieve of public memory for much of the twentieth and twenty-first centuries. Unlike white experimental forbearers such as Gertrude Stein and Ezra Pound who have found a foothold within American literary consciousness as both avant-garde and canonical, the work of many Black modernist artists has not been consistently recognized or preserved by mainstream institutions.

Looking for Langston is a project of critical desire as well as queer desire emerging at a moment in African American literary criticism when the recovery and revaluation of Black art and literature was an urgent political and scholarly project. I am thinking here of the research emerging in the 1970s, 1980s, and 1990s by scholars including Houston A. Baker, Jr., Barbara Christian, Henry Louis Gates, Nellie Y. McKay, Arnold Rampersad, Claudia Tate, Cheryl Wall, and Mary Helen Washington, among many others. *Looking for Langston* is perhaps less interested than these redoubtable critics in securing the legacy of Harlem Renaissance artists in the amber of historical truth and more interested in the generativity of transhistorical aesthetic kinship. Yet the idea of some sort of recovery, however flexible in its definition, through archival and historical research is common to both the art film and the scholarly research from which it draws. The film shows that *experimental* can also name the interpretive desire to find possibility in a work of art, perhaps exceeding or even contrary to the intentions of the artist, through the practice of study. Within the waste heaps, apartment buildings burned to the basement, and dusty, unvisited files, one can find not only beautiful works of art but a beautiful desire to make a different kind of world.

Through its citationality, *Looking for Langston* puts forth a legacy of queer Black experimentalism that centers the problem of beauty. In *Looking for Langston* and the earlier Harlem Renaissance texts by Du Bois and Larsen, a Black experimentalist tradition is uniquely positioned to theorize beauty's impact on the social. In fact, there are few aesthetic traditions that have thought as extensively, or as seriously, about the relationship between beautiful art and social change. This may be due to the centrality of anti-Blackness in the Kantian aesthetic theory that has come to dominate Western thinking on the beautiful. Perhaps even more significantly, beauty holds a place of prominence within what Cedric J. Robinson dubbed the Black radical tradition, entwined with socialism and abolitionism.[13]

This chapter focuses on only a few fine threads in a tapestry too sumptuous to schematize. However, my hope is that by staging this conference between Du Bois, Larsen, and Julien, we will see something vital about how beauty is felt and conceptualized in American social and political imaginaries. In the section that follows, I outline the traditional Kantian understanding of aesthetic judgment, as well as critiques from Black studies and philosophy that explain how Kantian aesthetic judgment has come to structure not only aesthetic theories of the beautiful but the racial regime of modern subjectivity. As I will explain below, the ability to make "proper" aesthetic judgments is an endowment of whiteness that structures our modern understanding of the human. The project that follows is an attempt to recover beauty from the privatization by whiteness through Black experimental forays into its redefinition.

Beauty Has a Kant Problem

Beauty judgments are judgments based in feeling. This makes aesthetic judgment a particularly tricky and suspiciously subjective phenomenon to study. As Sianne Ngai writes, the "compulsory sharing of pleasure that refers the subject to a relation among his subjective capacities, which in turn refers him to a relation between the world in general and his ability to know it" can "seem to open a can of worms—that of the undeniable relativism of feeling-based evaluations."[14] In the *Critique of Judgment*, Immanuel Kant famously argues that when a person judges something to be beautiful, "he requires the same liking from others; he then judges not just for himself but for everyone, and speaks of beauty as if it were a property of things."[15] One way to interpret this is to say that when we judge something beautiful, we are also demanding others to feel the same way—to have the same pleasure. This demand to feel in the same way is ubiquitous, a universal demand for all others to agree upon the beauty of the object.

Let's take a moment to examine the demanding orientation of aesthetic judgment in *The Critique of Judgment* more deeply:

> For he must not call it *beautiful* if [he means] only [that] *he* likes it. Many things may be charming and agreeable to him; no one cares about that. But if he proclaims something to be beautiful, then he requires the same liking from others; he then judges not just for himself but for everyone, and speaks of beauty as if it were a property of things. That is why he says: The *thing* is beautiful, and does not count on other people to agree

with his judgment of liking on the ground that he has repeatedly [213] found them agreeing with him; rather, he *demands* that they agree. He reproaches them if they judge differently, and denies that they have taste, which he nevertheless demands of them, as something they ought to have. In view of this [*sofern*] we cannot say that everyone has his own particular taste. That would amount to saying that there is no such thing as taste at all, no aesthetic judgment that could rightfully lay claim to everyone's assent.[16]

In this passage, Kant argues that when a person calls something beautiful, they treat this declaration as an objective statement—making their *demand* on others to recognize a universal feeling. Although a beauty judgment, what Kant calls a "judgment of taste," is a subjective judgment based in feeling (rather than universally observable or logical truths) the judgment *feels* objective. This is the result of a perceived sense of "purposiveness without a purpose," a sense of formal *rightness* that is not due to the object's utility or the perceiver's personal interest in the object.[17] Thus, the viewer feels as if the object itself has an innate, objective quality of beauty that she demands be recognized by others. This is what distinguishes beauty (or what Kant calls "taste") from other "agreeable" aesthetic judgments, to which everyone is entitled to their own opinion. This "common sense," or *sensus communis*, drawn upon by the judgment of taste is what Kant terms subjective universality, "an idea necessary for everyone."[18] It is this sense that any *reasonable* person would agree that the object is beautiful that distinguishes judgments of taste from other kinds of aesthetic judgment.[19]

The power of the beauty judgment is that it is validated by the universality of common sense. To differ from the *sensus communis*, or to be barred from it, is thus to become a person incapable of proper aesthetic judgment. The problem of who is and who is not a part of subjective universality—not only who is capable of a proper judgment of taste but who is recognizable as one who might be called on to agree—is the Kant problem that haunts beauty from the eighteenth-century forward. As I will discuss below in my overview of critiques of Kant coming from Black studies and the critical study of race, it is no coincidence that this theory of beauty that comes to dominate aesthetic theory develops alongside modern conceptions of race.

Allow this language of "demand" to hover; don't let it settle just yet. Allow its velocity to increase, slingshotting us from the domain of the philosophical into the social and even the political. The demand is a lever of political and of social transformation. It is how groups address the world in which they would like to live, or the world as they think it should be, and pull us toward it. Kant tells us that the judging aesthetic subject "requires the same liking from others." He needs it, and he "demands" it of them . . . *to feel in the same way*. The aesthetic judgment is a structure of feeling that enables a kind of collectivity, creating a scene of being together through shared aesthetic pleasure that manufactures and confirms the aesthetic subject capable of making such a judgment. But taking a left from the idealism of Kant's intentions, in this collectivity the line between coercion and consensus is smudged; reined in by the law of reason, the freedom of imagination is haltered. For Kant, artistic beauty, the "beautiful presentation of a thing," should not be too wild, "for in lawless freedom, all its riches [in ideas] produce nothing but nonsense, and it is judgment that adapts the imagination to understanding."[20] The prerequisite for fine art is taste: "Taste, like the power of judgment in general, consists in disciplining (or training) genius. It severely clips its wings, and makes it civilized, or polished. . . . It introduces clarity and order into a wealth of thought and hence makes the ideas durable, fit for approval that is both lasting and universal, and [hence] fit for being followed by others and fit for an ever advancing culture."[21] It is taste's lawfulness that allows the social to take place through forms that enable the universal communication, distinguishing advanced cultures from primitive ones:

> Only in *society* is the beautiful of empirical interest. And if we grant that the urge to society is natural to man but that his fitness and propensity for it, i.e. *sociability*, is a requirement of man as a creature with a vocation for society and hence is a property pertaining to his *humanity*, then we must also inevitably regard taste as an ability to judge whatever allows us to communicate even our *feeling* to everyone else, and hence regard taste as a means of furthering something that everyone's natural inclination demands.[22]

Those who do not meet the demand to feel in the same way become exterior to aesthetic subjectivity and society, simultaneously defining the boundary of the aesthetic subject. Without taste, defined as "the ability to judge something that makes our feeling in a given presentation universally communicable without mediation by a concept," the possibility of society, the communication of everything, "even our *feeling*" breaks down.[23]

The *Robinson Crusoe* style hypothetical that follows this requirement of universal communicability is an interesting example of how Kant positions Europeans at the apex of a civilizational progression—a confident move for someone who never left his hometown:

> Someone abandoned on some desolate island would not, just for himself, adorn either his hut or himself; nor would he look for flowers, let alone grow them, to adorn himself with them. Only in society does it occur to him to be, not merely a human being, but one who is also refined in his own way (this is the beginning of civilization). For we judge someone refined if he has the inclination and the skill to communicate his pleasure to others, and if he is not satisfied with an object unless he can feel his liking for it in community with others. Moreover, a concern for universal communication is something that everyone expects and demands from everyone else, on the basis, as it were, of an original contract dictated by [our] very humanity. Initially, it is true, only charms thus become important in society and become connected with great interest, e.g., the dyes people use to paint themselves (roucou among the Caribs and cinnabar among the Iroquois), or the flowers, seashells, beautifully colored feathers, but eventually also beautiful forms (as in canoes, clothes, etc.) that involve no gratification whatsoever, i.e., no liking of enjoyment. But in the end, when civilization has reached its peak, it makes this communication almost the principle activity of refined inclination, and sensations are valued only to the extent that they are universally communicable. At that point, even if the pleasure that each person has in such an object is inconsiderable and of no significant interest of its own, still its value is increased almost infinitely by the idea of its universal communicability.[24]

Here, although the Indigenous peoples mentioned are assumedly his contemporaries, Kant specifically excludes them from the universal communicability of taste, discussing them as racialized historical subjects rather than aesthetic subjects. Those outside of proper aesthetic judgments, that is, racialized subjects, are outside society, becoming what Denise Ferreira da Silva calls "affectable" subjects.[25] Aesthetic judgment regulates human and nonhuman difference and sameness, articulating a hierarchical distribution of social possibility; it is a practice of racialization. The ethics of engaging beauty's social and political valences become imperative to consider when we realize that Kant's aesthetic theory was meaningfully entwined with his theories of racial taxonomy.

Scholars who engage with Kant's pivotal role in the development of modern racism have shown that his aesthetic theory is inseparable from his participation in the scientific racism of the Enlightenment. As Paul C. Taylor observes, the Western philosophical tradition has regularly excluded Black expressive culture from its examination of beauty.[26] Critics such as Monique Roelofs have persuasively argued that Kant's white supremacy is inextricable from projects of race-based slavery and colonialism, despite Kant's silence on the topic of slavery and his criticism of colonialism.[27] Kant wrote extensively on race, and it is now generally acknowledged that Kant's scientific racism was influential to the establishment of modern racial thought. However, there continues to be debate on how Kant's racism impacts his aesthetic theory, if at all.

Kant's *Observations on the Feeling of the Beautiful and Sublime* is particularly notorious for its fourth section, a travelogue-esque classification of "national characters in so far as they rest upon the different feeling of the sublime and the beautiful," which organizes eighteenth-century racial and cultural groups according to their supposed intellectual, moral, and aesthetic capacities.[28] It is here that we find some of Kant's most blatant commentary on the teleology of racial difference. For an infamous example:

> The Negroes of Africa have by nature no feeling that rises above the ridiculous. Mr. Hume challenges anyone to adduce a single example where a Negro has demonstrated talents, and asserts that among the hundreds of thousands of blacks who have been transported elsewhere from their countries, although very many of them have been set free, nevertheless not a single one has ever been found who has accomplished something great in art or science or shown any other praiseworthy quality, while among the whites there are always those who rise up from the lowest

rabble and through extraordinary gifts earn respect in the world. So essential is the difference between these two human kinds, and it seems to be just as great with regard to the capacities of mind as it is with respect to color.[29]

Reading this passage with the later *Critique*, we can see Kant asserting that Black Africans produce only "nonsense" incapable of the "judgment that adapts the imagination to understanding." Some may argue that the rancid bigotry of these earlier statements are not relevant to Kant's later work on aesthetics. However, scholars such as Robert Bernasconi, Denise Ferreira da Silva, and Fred Moten demonstrate that Kant's racism is not restricted to such glaringly odious comments but are endemic to his philosophy, perceptible in his privileging of teleology, regulation, and purposiveness in the third *Critique*. There is no hygienic barrier between Kant's racial theory, a theory preoccupied with color and the visual signifiers of race, in other words, its aesthetics, and his aesthetic theory. Kant's taxonomical thinking on the aesthetic is a racial logic.

Kant argues that the differences in "capacities of mind" are as great as the differences in skin color (black and white), tying the two together as kinds of racial criteria. By this act, he suggests that there are essential and hierarchical differences between racial types. Robert Bernasconi points out that Kant's arguments on color as a racial criterion rely on purposiveness (purposefulness without purpose), a fundamental element of Kant's aesthetic theory outlined above. As Bernasconi writes, "The blackness of Blacks provided Kant with one of his most powerful illustrations of purposiveness within the biological sphere."[30] Bernasconi connects Kant's teleological theory of race directly to the later *Critique of Judgment*, wherein purposiveness plays a pivotal role in Kant's theory of the beautiful. Bernasconi writes, "If one applies what Kant says about regulative concepts in the *Critique of Judgment* to his discussions of race, then Kant is saying that in the present state of our knowledge the idea of race imposes itself."[31] Simply put, "As Kant understood it, racial differences called for a purposive account."[32] As Sarah Jane Cervenak explains, in Kant's theories of race, "race is an inherited peculiarity that emerges as a purposive differentiation in order to ensure the preservation of the species. Moreover, Kant believes that there is an original diversity within the initial seeds of man that manifests itself when the purpose of species differentiation is required."³³ Some may object here that while Kant's racism is abhorrent, it does not necessarily negate the value of his aesthetic theory. However, arguments of degree debating the extent of the racism in Kant's oeuvre or to what extent Kant's racism does or does not taint the moral clarity of his larger body of work do not interest me. While precision in understanding the specificity of Kant's racial thought is assuredly valuable, negotiations over measures of foulness and acceptability are beside the point. As Bernasconi shows, Kant's white supremacy cannot be quarantined from his theories of aesthetic judgment; the two must be considered in relation to each other in a holistic treatment of Kant's influence of Western culture and philosophy.

Kant's racial teleology is tied to the importance of regulation and purposiveness in his aesthetic theory, a racial logic entwined with a desire to map an orderly schema onto the wildness of aesthetic pleasure—the free play of imagination that must be reined in by reason and the judgment of taste. As Fred Moten writes:

> The regulative discourse on the aesthetic that animates Kant's critical philosophy is inseparable from the question of race as a mode of conceptualizing and regulating human diversity, grounding and justifying inequality and exploitation, as well as marking the limits of human knowledge through the codification of quasi-transcendental philosophical method, which is Kant's acknowledged aim in the critical philosophy.³⁴

This tension between the "nonsense" of lawless imagination and the regulative function of understanding is key to a theory of civilization based in the idea of universal communicability. What feelings can and *must* be shared, and who can share them? Which elements of culture are intelligible as good "taste," and which are discarded as ridiculous? This is the mechanism by which Blackness and the racial Other become both exterior to aesthetic subjectivity and society. Paradoxically, in making Blackness the very thing that is outside the beautiful, Blackness becomes the ground on which aesthetic judgment is theorized. Again, Moten illuminates:

> But Kant certainly did not think that black(ness) was beautiful. In his early observations on the beautiful and the sublime, blackness, in what

he understood to be its irreducible nonbeauty, is detached from the very possibility of truth and rationality, a detachment that is given immediately in the supposed ugliness of the black visage. Strange, then, that in his elaboration of the critical philosophy, race, as embodied in the racial difference that blackness exemplifies, is itself the exemplary form of teleological principle which not only grounds the distinction between simple description and natural history but also, in doing so, helps to make possible that completion of the critical philosophy that is manifest in the very idea of the purposive, in its linking of beauty and morality. Perhaps the beauty of blackness lies in that it has been and continues to be the condition of possibility of the critique of judgment. If so, this beauty justifies an inquiry into the morality symbolized by a raised fist.[35]

The image-gesture of the raised fist, so often associated with Black political movements, for Moten becomes a motif in an alternative aesthetic theory based in Black radicalism.[36] For Moten, "blackness as a radical, abolitionist, critical-historical project" becomes the "ground for a recalibration of the aesthetic."[37] Blackness as that which is Other than aesthetic subjectivity may be the very ground on which beauty and aesthetic judgment are redefined, a pivot from a critique of Kant to a recovery of the beautiful.

Kant does not own beauty. This is despite Kantianism's attempts to turn beauty into the property of whiteness via the exclusivity of subjective universality and the regulatory conveniences of purposiveness that privatize the aesthetic. A Black radical tradition shows us the absurdity of this proprietary relation. The Black radical tradition is an abolitionist force inextricable from the aesthetic, a collective against property and against the ownership of the universal. The imaginative power of Black radicalism to both preserve what has already been made and to constantly imagine new forms of being and belonging presents the work of liberation as an aesthetic undertaking and a political one. Black radicalism shows us that beauty cannot be owned and, perhaps, in this way, undermines the fundamental knowing relation of subject and possession. Central to this aesthetic, social, and political project is the pleasure specific to the beautiful. It is a pleasure sparking both sensorial and cerebral delights. It is also the pleasure of being and feeling with others, even when one is alone. Beauty's collective pleasures rise out from emergent social forms and go on to create others, simultaneous movements of unpropertied freedom. If the Black radical tradition is a force for "anti-instrumental freedom," then I propose the need for a theory of aesthetic judgment that seeks not just to assimilate Blackness into existing aesthetic regimes but to reconsider beauty as a methodology for political demand-making and delight as a political strategy against anti-Blackness.[38]

In raising the raised first, Moten brings to the surface the inextricability of the aesthetic and the radical within the history of Black freedom struggles. The aesthetic is essential to imaginative political praxis and the ability to question the given, the very terms on which a society is based. Art is not a factory for politics. Rather, as I will argue, the praxis of aesthetic judgment, to make and delight in art, is itself a way of inventing an alternative to a society organized by domination as one is living within it. As Saidiya Hartman argues, "Beauty is not a luxury; rather, it is a way of creating possibility in the space of enclosure, a radical art of subsistence, an embrace of our terribleness, a transfiguration of the given."[39] This beauty cannot be said to be instrumental, despite being transfiguring. It is for itself. An art for its own sake. A riotous experimentalism. This is why I perceive a link between the experimental and the practice of beauty in Black aesthetics and politics. The desire for new forms is integral to radical social projects working toward a world that is not structured by domination. Aesthetic judgment as a collective project that marks—or blurs—the boundaries of self and other through the sharing of feeling and ideas attached to particular aesthetic forms and materials—shapes, textures, sounds, images. By *form*, I am not speaking of an abstract ideal or generalized aesthetic technique but rather using the term as a shorthand for the identifiable components of a work of art—the composition of a shot, the perspective of a novel, the rhythm of a poem's line, a shape in a painting, the procedures of a conceptual work, the texture of a material, and so on. Form is the direction of attention; it guides us toward a way of understanding.[40] Formal redirection moves us to forge different social relations via the aesthetic, wherein there are different possibilities for judgment, which have the capacity to radically redefine value. This is what brings the experimental and the beautiful together in the meeting of Black aesthetic and Black radical traditions.

Guided by the understanding of Kantian aesthetic judgment outlined in this section and the possibility of reading differently, this chapter explores the pleasures and unpleasures of the beautiful by studying Black experimentalism's approach to the "recalibration" of the aesthetic. Like Julien working within the anti-Black and anti-queer political ferment of the 1980s, the artists and activists of the Harlem Renaissance were similarly faced with difficult questions about the role of aesthetics in a period of deadly political crisis. In the United States in the early twentieth century, the world was a sulphureous landscape of racial terrorism.[41] Yet alongside the breathless urgency of this historical moment, beauty and the arts emerged as central to the strategies of Black liberation. In the next sections, I will discuss two key texts of the Harlem Renaissance—W. E. B. Du Bois's "Criteria of Negro Art" and Nella Larsen's *Passing*—that consider the relationship between beauty, social life, and politics within a Black aesthetic tradition.

Feeling Into

Influenced by Kantian understandings of aesthetic judgment, common wisdom links beauty to the recognition of shared humanity. To recognize the beauty of another is to recognize their value and to feel that it is somehow connected to one's own, a version of universal communicability and the *sensus communis*. The ability to recognize beauty affirms one's own humanness. By the same logic, beauty might redeem those who have been othered, bringing them into society and making them knowable through what is common to all. Here we depart from close interpretations of Kant's writings and move to contemplate the diffusion of his aesthetic theory into Western culture. The idea of empathetic identification propels this common sense idea that beauty humanizes. Beauty compels us to "feel into" someone else, to "walk in their shoes," shifting our understanding of the Other from object (unrelatable, unidentifiable in every sense, radically different) to subject (a person, relatable, similar). Fascinatingly, the concept of empathy, which is popularly held responsible for the psychic and political transformations catalyzed by beauty, was developed first in the nineteenth century as a way of explaining powerful *aesthetic*, not interpersonal, responses. Empathy was originally a concept that described aesthetic judgments.

Translated from the German *Einfühlung*, which means literally "feeling into," empathy wasn't taken up by psychologists until the early twentieth century. The German Romantic concept of *Einfühlung* was a way to explain feelings of identification with an aesthetic object, premised on a sense of transcendent shared feeling. It was the German philosopher Theodor Lipps in the early twentieth century who first began to think of *Einfühlung* as a form of psychic projection on an object rather than the subject's identification with a higher spirituality or feeling. For Lipps, *Einfühlung* explained how the "leafless tree . . . stands *naked* against the wind, the person *weighed down* with sorrow."[42] As Lauren Wispé parses it, *Einfühlung* was used "to explain how a person grasped the meaning of aesthetic objects and the consciousness of other persons" by describing how "observers project themselves into the objects of perception."[43]

In literature and culture, the degree to which empathetic identification may mobilize political transformation has been linked to a politics of representation, wherein realist representational forms transform objectified Others into humanized subjects. That is, the logic of (positive) realist representation as a form of social change depends on an understanding of empathetic projection quite similar to Lipps's theory of *Einfühlung*, a feeling into the Other via psychic projection, transforming marginalized people from objects to subjects in the process.[44] I question whether this work of *feeling into* another (or an Other) really is imaginative enough to disrupt "the mainstream and its violent relationality."[45]

In Black studies, it is Saidiya Hartman's work that has most generatively explored the substitutive logic of empathy, especially in her early landmark *Scenes of Subjection*. I hope the reader will excuse an extended examination of one of Hartman's prime examples in *Scenes of Subjection* of how fantasies of shared humanity can, perhaps counter to intentions, strengthen rather than erode systems of racial domination. Hartman offers as evidence a letter written by white abolitionist and Presbyterian minister John Rankin in which he attempts to persuade his brother of the cruelties of slavery by narrating an identificatory fantasy in which Rankin himself is enslaved:

> My flighty imagination added much to the tumult of passion by persuading me, for the moment, that I myself was a slave, and with my wife and children placed under the reign of terror. I began *in reality* to feel for

myself, my wife, and my children—the thoughts of being whipped at the pleasure of a morose and capricious master, aroused the strongest feelings of resentment; but when I fancied the cruel lash was approaching my wife and children, and my imagination depicted in lively colors, their tears, their shrieks, and bloody stripes, every indignant principle of my bloody nature was excited to the highest degree.[46]

In this letter, Rankin's empathetic identification with enslaved Black people is disturbing, not only because of the violent imagery of the portrayal (which, Hartman suggests, may itself be a source of aesthetic pleasure) but also because this empathetic identification requires the erasure of actually enslaved Black people, substituting white subjects in their place. Hartman points out that counterintuitively, it is Rankin's empathy in this passage that spoils identification's social promise: "Yet empathy in important respects confounds Rankin's efforts to identify with the enslaved because in making the slave's suffering his own, Rankin begins to feel for himself rather than for those whom this exercise in imagination presumably is designed to reach."[47] Hartman's reading of this aesthetic fantasy of empathetic identification allows us to consider how Rankin's whiteness works as a humanizing or universalizing tool, making Black suffering both visible and invisible. In Hartman's words: "Empathy fails to expand the space of the other but merely places the self in its stead."[48]

Working from Hartman's interrogation of empathetic aesthetic identification, we can push this inquiry a bit further by considering how aesthetic judgments—and, in particular, beauty judgments—supposedly turn objects into subjects within spaces of shared pleasure.[49] As we recall from Kant, the criteria for judging an aesthetic object "beautiful" is that it produces a "universal feeling" in the person doing the judging—a sense that all others must agree that the object is beautiful or else be written out of the unspoken "we" of the *sensus communis*. There is a latent Kantianism within the political strategies that assert beauty's capacity to induce empathy. Such strategies for social change depend on identification—the assertion of a "we," a common sense—to make their claims to moral and political transformation. Empathy and aesthetic judgment are both imagined as tools to broaden who may be included in the "we" and to restructure our relationships to others through the opening of that shared identification. However, the "we" is not a neutral space to begin with; to be made human, to be held in common, is not necessarily to become free.

The history of Black aesthetic theory and praxis demonstrates that beauty does not have an intrinsic politics. Beauty can be both coercive and liberating, utilized by left or right, by oppressed and oppressor. Beauty has been integral to the practice of regulating the human, the creation of whiteness, and its coupling with value. Thus, the social and political stakes of beauty were especially fraught for Black thinkers and artists at the turn of the twentieth century, particularly for the New Negro movement's intellectually dazzling doyen, W. E. B. Du Bois. From the elegant use of color and geometric shape in his presentation of sociological data at the 1900 Paris World's Fair, to the centrality of the spirituals in his arguments in *The Souls of Black Folk*, to the elaborate sets, costumes, and spectacle of the 1913 pageant *The Star of Ethiopia*, his commissioning of Meta Vaux Warrick Fuller's *Ethiopia* sculpture for the 1921 America's Making Exhibition, the prominence of literature and art in the *Crisis* (the extremely influential official magazine of the NAACP founded by Du Bois), and so on, the aesthetic was inseparable from W. E. B. Du Bois's output at the beginning of the century, prolific experiments in what Robin D. G. Kelley might call freedom dreaming.[50] When Du Bois developed his theories of the beautiful in early twentieth-century works such as *The Souls of Black Folk* (1903), *Darkwater* (1920), "The Criteria of Negro Art" (1926), and his novel *Dark Princess* (1928), he drew from a deep knowledge of Romanticism, aesthetic theory, and social science methodologies, bringing together the scientific, philosophical, and aesthetic. At Harvard, Du Bois encountered Kant and Hegel in his studies with George Santayana, the philosopher credited with writing the first major American work on aesthetics.[51] Du Bois later attended the University of Berlin, where, as Kwame Anthony Appiah has written, Du Bois studied historicist methodologies that were "attuned . . . to the contingent and provisional nature of our cultural and social inheritances" believing that "ethical systems weren't baked into some transcendent feature of humanity; they emerged, and unfolded, through social activity, through the shifting internal structures of society."[52] I note Du Bois's experiences in these institutions and his familiarity with German aesthetic philosophy not to credentialize a philosopher who needs no credentializing but to set the scene wherein Du Bois reimagines aesthetic theory. Du Bois did not turn to the question of beauty lightly. His time was precious and the stakes were high. As a social scientist, his interest in beauty was not limited to its effects on individual perception but keyed into questions about the beautiful's role in shaping the material realities of Black lives through the intricacies of social relations.[53]

Much has already been said about the ways that Black artists variously employed aesthetic tactics to transform—or transcend—racial oppression in this period.[54] Questions regarding the role of the arts in antiracist politics animated salons, living rooms, conferences, and classrooms and filled the pages of literary and political publications such as the *Crisis* and *Opportunity*.[55] Thus, Du Bois's Black modernist aesthetic theory is not secondary to the strategic discourses of Black freedom struggle in the early twentieth century; it is fundamental to them. As Nahum Dimitri Chandler writes, "In a word, the most general and profound problem of all Du Bois's work in this early moment and perhaps beyond can be understood as the problem of how to construct and sustain in a practical order new ideals for living, as individuals certainly, but most fundamentally, as forms of collectivity (of a people, a nation, a 'race,' a 'culture,' a 'civilization'). We might also say, the forms of civitas in general."[56] In "Criteria of Negro Art," the transformation of collective being cannot be separated from the aesthetic or, indeed, from beauty. It is a keystone document for early twentieth-century debates on the relationship between art and Black freedom.

As Russ Castronovo writes in his parsing of Du Bois's "Criteria," Du Bois considers beauty "not as a matter of perception but an arena for crafting hegemony," arguing that "Propaganda, above all, represents an aesthetic concern about the form politics should take."[57] Castronovo is not the first to suggest that a dichotomous approach obscures a more complex understanding of art and use, yet the old trap of instrumentalism versus art for art's sake continues to dog Du Bois's provocation: "I do not give a damn for any art that is not used for propaganda."[58] In the "Criteria of Negro Art," Du Bois certainly considers art to be a strategic tool within the struggle for Black liberation. But beauty is no ordinary instrument; it is inseparable from a free world, presented as the end goal of Black radical struggle. Du Bois restages the classic Kantian association of beauty and morality on the ground of a Black radical tradition, so reversing, as we have seen, the conventional conditions of the beautiful that depend on excluding Blackness from the beautiful:

> Thus it is the bounden duty of black America to begin this great work of the creation of Beauty, of the preservation of Beauty, of the realization of Beauty, and we must use in this work all the methods that men have used before. And what have been the tools of the artist in times gone by? First of all, he has used the Truth—not for the sake of truth, not as a scientist seeking truth, but as one upon whom Truth eternally thrusts itself as the highest handmaid of imagination, as the one great vehicle of universal understanding.[59]

Yes, Du Bois's tenor recalls the conservatism of German Romanticism, its exclusionary universalism, its convenient yoking of Truth to Beauty in a philosophical snare. But Du Bois is not simply regurgitating Enlightenment thought in the "Criteria." He is taking back what was already stolen by aesthetic theory. Du Bois refuses to acknowledge whiteness's propriety relation to truth, beauty, and universality by naming the production of Beauty as the work of Black liberation. He points out the internal contradictions and paradoxes of white supremacy when he argues that nothing can be beautiful that is unfree. The fight for freedom itself is beautiful. What is already free must be preserved, shared, carried over as part of the larger freedom-making work of being together in the world. New beauty makes the world more free. Du Bois's task is to frame aesthetic theory as a theory of freedom and belonging taking place within race-making and the racist organization of the world.

Originally given as a speech at the NAACP's annual conference in 1926 and later published in the *Crisis*, in this essay Du Bois positions beauty as the horizon of Black liberation. Du Bois asks his audience to participate in an imaginative exercise: suppose you had citizenship in the fullest sense. Suppose you were free from racial oppression and, moreover, that you had wealth. Then what? In doing so, he reorients the focus of the project of Black freedom from the desire to have "freedom from" oppression toward a desire for the "freedom to" create and take pleasure in life. Du Bois asks:

If you tonight should become full-fledged Americans; if your color faded, or the color line here in Chicago was miraculously forgotten; suppose, too, you became at the same time rich and powerful;—what is it that you would want? What would you immediately seek? Would you buy the most powerful of motor cars and outrace Cook County? Would you buy the most elaborate estate on the North Shore? Would you be a Rotarian or a Lion or a What-not of the very last degree? Would you wear the most striking clothes, give the richest dinners, and buy the longest press notices?[60]

Du Bois wagers not: "Even as you visualize such ideals you know in your hearts that these are not the things you really want . . . there has come to us not only a certain distaste for the tawdry and flamboyant *but a vision of what the world could be if it were really a beautiful world* . . . a world where men know, where men create, where they realize themselves and where they enjoy life. It is that sort of world we want to create for ourselves and for all America."[61] Here, in sketching beauty as the horizon of freedom (that is, a "freedom to"—freedom to know, to create, to realize without imposed limitation), Du Bois describes Black freedom as a scene of aesthetic pleasure: "really a beautiful world." This is an aesthetic pleasure that mobilizes and is indivisible from a scene of collective valuation. The scene of freedom manifests through the "us" called into being by imagining a "beautiful world." The beauty judgment becomes a scene of aesthetic collectivity through freedom-making, enabling Du Bois to imagine freedom as a collective and aesthetic field and to *demand* that freedom as a shared value.

As a signal text of Black modernism and a call to action, through Du Bois's "Criteria" we can begin to theorize beauty judgments as spaces of rendezvous between individual and collective, spaces of generation facilitated by a sense of shared value. Beauty is a way of articulating a sense of belonging as well as the world that this belonging makes possible. It is this active sense of making in the moment and the creation of the new, rather than validation via a referral back to teleology and the fixity of the purposive form, that distinguishes Du Bois's call for freedom from Kantian subjective universality. Of course, not all definitions of freedom mean freedom for all, and not all possibilities contribute to ethical social relations. The kinds of belonging that take place in the moment of a beauty judgment are not identical or equivalent but are embedded in the sociopolitical quagmires of history.

The Promise of Disorder

Du Bois's "Criteria of Negro Art" articulates a freedom-seeking optimism for beauty as a transformative space of collective aesthetic pleasure and alternative valuation. Through beauty, the given might not be affirmed but radically altered. Recalling Hartman, it may be "a transfiguration of the given."[62] However, the actual practice of how such alterations might take place among the imperfect and contradictory undulations of human interaction, desire, and fear is unclear in Du Bois's inspirational call. What happens when beauty cannot be held by the firm hand of the law of understanding? What if beauty's generation of something new does not feel easy, intuitive, or "safe," the feeling that Irene Redfield of Nella Larsen's *Passing* repeatedly seeks out?

In exploring how an altered practice of beauty might play out, I turn to Nella Larsen's classic novel of race and aesthetic desire, *Passing*. *Passing*'s fraught themes of racial identification, humid with queer longing, have been thoroughly scrutinized by critics. I am most interested in returning to *Passing* because it is a novel of high *style*, both in its form and in its preoccupations with raced and feminine beauty, elegant decoration, and sartorial élan. We might easily add an additional item to the list of the novel's major themes: a fixation with beauty. As a Black experimentalist study of the beautiful, *Passing* does not offer a clear or triumphant manifesto for beauty but traces the fine fibers of tension that stretch, contract, and snap within the fraught space of aesthetic judgment as it intersects with racial practices and sexuality. For the characters of Larsen's novel, Beauty is thrilling and terrifying, promising and untrustworthy.

Passing idles in smart, chic descriptions of tastefully furnished rooms, luxurious clothes, beautiful domestic objects, and portraits of the character Clare Kendry that revel in her composed beauty. Like Larsen's previous novel, *Quicksand* (1928), beauty and taste are intertwined with the main characters' desires for the freedom from constraint and the freedom to create. In both novels, white-passing Black women navigate the threats and impasses of racism and sexual exploitation while seeking beauty as a refuge from an ever-present miasma of violence. In both novels, the ekphrastic tableaux is a frequent device used to heighten the sense of stillness offered by beauty—a time and space of reflection and exhalation that hovers slightly outside of a quotidian fanged with sexual and racial violence. As Cherene Sherrard-Johnson explains, these tableaux are not free from racial referents but utterly entwined with what she calls the "iconography of the mulatta" and modernist Orientalism.[63] Indeed, Helga Crane, the protagonist of *Quicksand*, is often framed as an artist figure whose creativity is consistently thwarted, ultimately with a tragic end. While beauty and creativity are held up as a potential means for freedom (which is never quite actualized), when beauty is not of their own making, it can also be turned against the protagonists of *Quicksand* and *Passing*, as in *Quicksand* where throughout the novel men target and commodify Helga Crane via their perceptions of her "exotic" and "primitive" racialized beauty.

Beauty, aesthetic pleasure, and the delight of style come to mark a crossroads of freedom and unfreedom in a world where beauty has been privatized by whiteness. Larsen's work is invaluable for its intense attention to aesthetic judgment. In the space of aesthetic judgment, social relations are hashed out in messy, ethically murky gestures and conflicting desires. The freedom to create worlds unstructured by racial dominance is almost imagined, warming the periphery, but never quite realized.

The plot of *Passing* is propelled by Clare Kendry Bellew, a Black woman from Chicago who has "crossed over the color line" to marry a virulently racist white man (Jack Bellew) who is ostensibly unaware of Clare's Blackness. Irene Redfield is Clare's childhood friend who reconnects with her by chance while both are racially passing at a whites-only hotel restaurant. What Clare and Irene are to each other after this chance meeting is not obvious—friends? lovers? rivals? frenemies? What is obvious is their attraction to each other. They are sucked into a mutual orbit, circling each other, constantly threatening to crash into each other for the rest of the novel. There are many stunning analyses of Clare and Irene's complex, ambivalent relationship, which ends with Irene (probably) pushing Clare out a window. What I find significant about this relationship is that in a novel devoted to the knotty, affective processes of racial identification, female friendship, queer eros, and collective belonging, Larsen makes *aesthetic judgment* a central problematic of the novel—an aesthetic judgment that never feels resolved, as up in the air as the ending with its nauseating drop.

In keeping with Larsen's signature use of ekphrasis and tableau, Clare is an art object within the art object of the novel, repeatedly described in terms that conjure luxury commodities—ivory skin, gold hair, ink-black eyes—repeatedly staged or posed in moments of frozen photographic novel-time where the elements of her beauty are named in a style somewhere between lover's blazon and appraiser's catalogue. *Passing* is narrated in an exceptionally close third-person perspective, meaning Clare is visible to the reader only through Irene's judging gaze—it is Irene's evaluative eye that imprints Clare's iconography on the reader's brain.[64] The reader perceives Clare through the filter of Irene's aesthetic judgment. I propose that the attraction between Clare and Irene is the attraction of a difficult aesthetic judgment. This is a judgment that disables, makes Irene paranoid and unknown to herself, an aesthetic judgment that threatens to reorder the world, a judgment that Irene cannot finish and repeatedly returns to even after she destroys the one who keeps her coming back.

Larsen positions the question of aesthetic judgment as inseparable from race and desire, framing questions of racial collectivity and freedom as aesthetic questions. Clare's proximity to whiteness is both a re-inscription of beauty's racial regimes and a threat to it, just as racial passing both reinforces and undermines racial categories and hierarchies by playing by their rules yet also revealing their fragility and constructedness. The ethical and political quandaries suggested by Irene's obsession with Clare's beauty show that the aesthetic is not a veneered surface obscuring or representing more complex social and political structures humming away underneath; nor is it a relation that can be repaired through "correct" representations. Rather, *Passing*'s staging of aesthetic judgment and fascination with beauty shows us that interpretation and aesthetic judgment are integral to the functioning of social and political systems, not merely reflective of them.

To be clear, I am not seeking to redeem Clare's objectification in *Passing* nor to celebrate it as resistant or revolutionary. Clare's objectification is a problem that arises out of a long history of Black feminine association with objecthood. As Cheng writes in her investigation of the enmeshment between racialized and feminized persons and things, "The black woman has been 'decorated' by culture and law in very specific and corporeal ways."[65] It is not news to say that the "decoration," objectification, or isolation of the body into (sexually) desirable or malleable component parts is integral to systems oppression and subjection. The thingification of the body is part of a strategy to delimit a person's self-determination and bodily autonomy in the interest of maintaining racial and gendered power structures. However, contemporary scholarship in the aesthetics of racialization has complicated default understandings of the phenomenon of objectification.

As Cheng argues, the movements between objectification and personhood are not always as straightforward as one might assume. Likewise, Uri McMillan has offered a compelling theory of Black women's performance in which "performing objecthood" "proves to be a powerful tool for performing one's body, a 'stylized repetition of acts,' that rescripts how black female bodies are perceived by others."[66] Fred Moten's theories of resistant objecthood, particularly in relation to Black experimental art practices, are also relevant. As he announces in the memorable opening line of *In the Break*, "The history of blackness is testament to the fact that objects can and do resist."[67] Speaking to the practices of objectification that have structured understandings of Blackness, Moten argues that the dysregulating puissance of Black performance challenges conventional notions of object and subject. The counterintuitive interest in the social, political, and aesthetic power of the object in and around Black studies is a way of getting at the question, not of what is an object, but what is a person? What does it look like to establish personhood when our very notion of the human is shaped by racial and gendered scenes of domination that specifically exclude Black people from the category of human? What would a personhood not formed through relationships of domination, that is, against the (aesthetic) object, begin to look like?

This problem of objectification ought to inform any reading of *Passing*, but it is especially important to keep in mind as we consider how the novel performs aesthetic judgment as a social relation. *Passing* does not offer an unambiguous representation of aesthetic judgment's ethical, social, and political impacts. It is because of this ambiguity and the novel's near-obsessive return to the scene of aesthetic judgment that the novel can help us better understand the relationship between aesthetic pleasure and domination. It is instructive not because it contains perfect politics or offers anything like a clear solution but because it sits with the difficult questions without flinching.

The novel's initiating moment is a scene of fixation on a beautiful object that threatens to exceed the judging subject's grasp. *Passing* begins with Irene's receipt of a letter from Clare. While the content of the letter unnerves Irene, it is the material aspects of the letter that are the most saturated with feeling and the object of her aesthetic judgments. In her judgment of the letter, Irene privileges its objectness—its textures, materials, design. Even in her analysis of the letter's literary aesthetics, Irene filters her judgment through the lens of materiality. Irene finds the language of the letter too "lavish," suggesting a kind of gauche flaunting of linguistic and affective excess.[68] Irene judges not so much the "content" of the letter, what it communicates, but its thingness, a suggestive but elusive connection between material and feeling. Larsen writes:

> After [Irene's] other ordinary and clearly directed letters the long envelope of thin Italian paper with its almost illegible scrawl seemed out of place and alien. And there was, too, something mysterious and slightly furtive about it. A thin sly *thing* which bore no return address to betray the sender. Not that she hadn't immediately known who its sender was. Some two years ago she had one very like it in outward appearance. Furtive, but yet in some peculiar, determined way a little flaunting. Purple ink. Foreign paper of extraordinary size.[69]

Clare is mixed up with the materiality of her letter. The letter, like Clare's body, is presented in *Passing* as an aesthetic object, and Irene's predominant relationship to it is through aesthetic judgment. These aesthetic evaluations (ink too purple, paper too big, handwriting too scribbly) are what allow Irene to imagine the object as animate, having feelings and even behaviors, characterizing the letter as "sly" and "furtive."

These descriptors bear the aura of racialized and gendered meaning, a kind of coquetry associated with the mulatta figure. The anthropomorphism of the scene recalls Theodor Lipps's aesthetic theory of empathy that enables the viewer to see a leafless tree as "naked" through the act of projection into the object. However, the slyness and furtiveness of the object are not exactly an invitation to "feel into" or feel with the object, but the opposite. The letter is "alien," and it is keeping something from Irene (furtive), scheming against her even (sly). In this sense, Irene's relationship to the letter is more akin to paranoid reading than empathetic reading.[70] She suspects that the gorgeous formal attributes of the letter conceal something threatening. Clare's letter disrupts Irene's world, passing, so to speak, with the "ordinary and clearly directed" mail only to send Irene's life into disorder, just as Clare's startling beauty repeatedly disrupts the order of Irene's moderate bourgeois world. As the narrator explains at the end of the novel just after Clare falls from a window to her death, Clare Kendry is "that beauty that had torn at Irene's placid life."[71] Irene's relationship to Clare, their friendship, rivalry, and erotic attachments, are negotiated through regimes of taste and a series of intense aesthetic evaluations. *Passing* begins with a scene of aesthetic judgment that organizes the rest of the novel in which the aesthetic exceeds the judging subject's ability to apprehend it and, in so doing, threatens to undo the subject herself.

As with the letter that serves as proxy for Clare, Clare herself is consistently described as threateningly aesthetic: her color, texture, and style too evocative of a surface, seeming to imply a meaning that escapes understanding and the regulation of judgment. While Irene conjectures about Clare's thoughts, feelings, and motivations to the point of obsession, the reader never gains clear insight into Clare's inner life. Clare is portrayed as a shimmering repertoire of aesthetic forms, her materiality insistently present but resistant to interpretation. Characters in the novel tend to read Clare through hoary stereotypes of the mulatta figure. Gold hair, light skin, scarlet lips, and dark eyes reappear again and again to signal the mulatta's visual indeterminacy alongside stereotypes regarding her sexual availability and social trespassing.[72] Representations of the mulatta are highly codified, relying on visual tropes to signal the mulatta's veiled presence within white society and establishing a set of criteria for racial identification and classification, what Sherrard-Johnson has termed an "iconography": "dark, almost black, eyes," a "wide mouth like a scarlet flower against the Ivory of her skin" and "pale gold hair."[73] In Larsen's citation of the mulatta trope, Clare's beauty highlights the ways that aesthetic judgments are inseparable from struggles for power and how habitual interpretations bulwark structured domination.

Throughout the novel, Clare's Blackness, presented as immanently detectable yet undetected, is suggested as the secret source of her beauty. The essentialism of the period's racial pseudoscience is readily available here, that the "biological" force of racial Blackness cannot ever be fully subdued or denied, that "blood" will inevitably assert itself. Moreover, even if we interpret the novel as locating Clare's beauty in her Blackness, its counterintuitive manifestation in white features of pale skin and gold hair problematically reinforces racist and colorist conventions of beauty. Thus, in presenting Clare as the primary aesthetic object of the novel, it also presents the problem of aesthetic judgment as indivisible from a contradictory racial schema that is always unraveling. *Passing* centers its problem of aesthetic judgment as a dilemma of racial meaning. The freedom of the novel's characters—Irene, Brian Redfield (Irene's husband), Jack Bellew (Clare's husband), and Clare herself—seems suddenly to depend on what Clare's beauty means. That meaning is continually unclear; the novel is unable to decouple fully the idea of freedom from the repetitive, orderly beauty of whiteness, however, it also maintains a curiously hopeful, desirous attitude toward the ambiguities that unsettle bourgeois regulations of racial identity and sexuality.

And yet Clare's importance in the novel goes beyond her status as a vexed aesthetic object whose social meaning directs how the main characters of the novel perceive themselves and what is possible for them within the order or disorder of their worlds. Although portrayed as a beautiful "thing," she threatens to have an unknowable psychological depth—to be a person—existing beyond either Irene's or the reader's comprehension, unknowable in the mode of judgment at hand. Clare may be figured primarily as a beautiful object, but she refuses to be possessed by other characters, or by the reader. This upsets the proprietary dynamic of Kantian aesthetic judgment itself. She cannot be regulated by interpretation, either by Irene or the reader. She is a lawless beauty. In this way, she upsets the unstated mastery of aesthetic judgment—that the proper judging aesthetic subject knows beauty definitively, and this knowledge endows her with the power to declare the terms of a normative reality. *Passing* explores what happens when the beautiful aesthetic "object" exceeds the inventory of possible social meanings. Reading *Passing* in this way, we might find potential in the failure of interpretive grasping.

Clare suggests affective and social possibilities beyond what Irene allows herself to imagine: "a quality of feeling that was to [Irene] strange, and even repugnant"—a disorderly feeling that threatens to undo the tasteful arrangement of Irene's "placid life."[74] Clare's beauty suggests the freedom promised by beauty as disorder, in opposition to the Kantian model that imagines beauty as the harmonious containment of imagination by the law of understanding, a process that produces whiteness against the antithesis of Blackness. Meanwhile, the fraught relationship between Clare and Irene suggests the difficulty in realizing the possibilities of disordered beauty.

After so much discussion of what other characters—or readers—want from Clare, we might end with a reflection on Clare's desires. The truest answer is that we cannot know what Clare really wants. But reading between the lines, as it were, the novel suggests that what Clare desires most is freedom, a state refused by the racial order, even when troubled by the ambivalent ambiguities of passing. Such wild freedom is a deeply disconcerting concept for Irene. She clings to the relative safety provided by intact, stable social categories and norms, however punishing. Clare appears to be looking for a way of being that is difficult to imagine. In its not-quite-imaginability, there is the thrill of true freedom glowing on the horizon. And yet this possibility is always somewhat decayed by the suggestion that it is Clare's association with whiteness that allows her proximity to such freedom. Perhaps what Irene calls Clare's "having way" signals whiteness's proprietary relation to the world, even if ultimately these same power arrangements precipitate her death. Then again, perhaps the disdainful inappropriateness attached to Clare's "having way" has more to do with what kinds of subjects are allowed to have—or even want—the freedom that Clare desires, which she is ultimately disallowed.

Clare's beauty is a disturbing fixation for Irene because Clare threatens normed possibilities and futures that bring order to Irene's life. A new world comes into view with Clare and yet remains out of focus for both Irene and the reader whose perspective is filtered through Irene's gaze. In the disorderly world brought into view by Clare's beauty, a mother might become free from the obligations of motherhood, a wife might leave her husband or a husband his wife, responsible middle-class doctors might move to Brazil, lesbian erotics could be realized, the color line might attenuate into weak slack—all events that interrupt the normative romances of marriage, family, and nation. It bears noticing that all these non-normative acts and relations *are already* possible, if extremely difficult, within the novel's world and the reader's. People did pursue such things in the 1920s and do so today, although not without hardship and very real material obstacles. But ultimately, in *Passing* their threat to social order is too great to suffer Clare to live. The hazard of Clare's beauty is not only, as others have written, that it promises to undo and destabilize the rubrics of race or the laws of gender and sexuality, but Clare's beauty also challenges the associations of the beautiful with aesthetic orderliness, social stability, moral clarity, and mastery. Clare suggests that beauty can be a scene of disorder, a sociality of improvisation rather than synchronization. However, the political promise of disorder, both frightening and desirable, remains haunted and suspended by whiteness, its orderliness, and its regulatory nature.

In Heaven

Now I arrive back at the beginning: the lambent visage of Isaac Julien, attended by a cortege of white lilies. In *Looking for Langston*, Julien returns to the aesthetic and political questions raised by Du Bois and Larsen during the Harlem Renaissance as he navigates a history of visual pleasure fraught with racial violence. Julien's filmic interpretation of the Harlem Renaissance helps us understand these two authors as practitioners in a Black tradition of aesthetic theory, suggesting that the questions of beauty and politics in *Looking for Langston* are the continuation of an earlier field of study and creative praxis in Black experimentalist art and theory. In *Looking for Langston*, we see the reoccurring problem of beauty's relationship to racial fetishism and whiteness, which we saw explored in Larsen's portrayal of Clare and in Irene's evaluation of her. As in *Passing*, Julien's film considers how the beautiful may undo the painful constraints of aesthetic racism, not by replacing a collection of images or visualizing techniques with "correct" representations but through representation's disarrangement. In the film's unapologetic embrace of beauty amid political crisis, we can detect a Du Boisian conviction that beauty contains the power for social transformation. *Looking for Langston* does not offer a naïve celebration of beauty but contextualizes it within a violent history of looking. Even the choice of monochrome rather than color allows for a dramatically beautiful film that nevertheless conveys a sense of gravity and mourning. Although *Looking for Langston* dives deeply into the harm that aesthetic pleasure has caused, the film maintains optimism for what beauty might be able to do.

At the beginning of the film, a title card calls *Looking for Langston* "a meditation on Langston Hughes and the Harlem Renaissance." It is a lyrical, nonlinear film composed of both archival and original footage, rapturously shot in collaboration with cinematographer Nina Kellgren and photographer Sunil Gupta. As an experimental film at the vanguard of what B. Ruby Rich called the New Queer Cinema, we can also perceive a connection between beauty and the freedom to create, which is so vital to Du Bois's aesthetic theory. It is no coincidence that Julien sets his film in a fantasy of the Harlem Renaissance. The film is looking not only for a Langston who might anchor a tradition of Black gay artists with the filmmaker at its most contemporary iteration but also for a Langston to ground the incandescent surge of political possibility emanating from this moment in the 1980s.

Yet even as *Looking for Langston* finds important similarities between the aesthetic and political movements of the 1920s and the 1980s, Julien's project is not so much one of traditional documentary but one of historical reverie. As Kara Keeling writes, *Looking for Langston* does not imagine history as linear or identity as consistent; instead, "rather than assume an accessible gay identity that is coherent and recognizable over time, Julien's emphasis on 'looking' produces a queer Harlem Renaissance as a present desire in a moment of danger."[75] The film is deeply attuned to the ways that a nonlinear practice of history and memory via experimental form, a temporality that refutes teleology and narrow progressivism, may generate a radical politics of beauty. It is made perhaps within what Jafari S. Allen has called an "*anthological* habit of mind," wherein "the *anthological tradition* is a collection [that] purposefully makes a multivocal statement of the political and aesthetic commitments of a group of artists and/or scholars engaged in what they—or at least the editor—believe is a collective (that is, not necessarily 'unified' but rather harmonious) project."[76] As Grace Kyungwon Hong argues, drawing from the work of critics on the film such as José Muñoz and Manthia Diawara, *Looking for Langston* "demonstrates the ways in which, from the Harlem Renaissance through the present, Blackness has been the fetishized otherness that makes modernist and avant-garde art possible, and in so doing, implies that Black gay life cannot be represented by the avant-garde."[77] In its experimental approach to visuality, identity, time, and the politics of beauty, "*Looking for Langston* thus advances a way of claiming [Langston] Hughes, [James] Baldwin, [Richard Bruce] Nugent, and the unnamed and inaccessible queer subcultures that may have surrounded them, and in so doing, asserts the legitimacy of fiction and imagination as a form of claiming."[78] As film scholar Manthia Diawara argues in his meticulous formal analysis of the film's avant-garde techniques, "The Black imaginary, far from being a fixed place that is guaranteed in nature, is a transforming and transformative space to be filled by freedom-seeking people."[79] Fiction, dream, fantasy, or a little piece of heaven, the name of the gay nightclub where much of the film was shot—scholars writing on *Looking for Langston* repeatedly return to the film's experimental poesis of play, repose, laughter, and desire as the source of its political power.[80]

While *Looking for Langston* is surely invested in the affective, political, and aesthetic power of a Black queer diasporic past, it is also responding to the political exigencies of its present, namely the state-sponsored racism and homophobia of the Reagan and Thatcher regimes and the related devastation of the AIDS pandemic. In the 1980s, political leadership in the United States and the United Kingdom rode a wave of New Right aggression, their platforms built on a commitment to demolishing the modest political gains achieved by social movements in the mid-twentieth century. Kobena Mercer and Paul Gilroy both note that the film and their friendships with Julien were produced during times of riot and crisis. As Mercer writes, at the beginning of *Looking for Langston* we can hear a siren in the background, "signaling a state of emergency in which something buried in the history of Black Atlantic art and culture is being summoned into contemporaneity."[81] Gilroy recalls, "It was rioting that first put me into contact with Isaac. The 'uprisings' of 1981 were an explosive culmination of black communities' bitter struggles against the habitual racism of Britain's police . . . [the uprising of 1981] was also configured by a dawning sense of the chronic, intractable character of the crisis and of the unholy forces unleashed by accelerating deindustrialized urban zones."[82] Communities already vulnerable from long histories of racist and homophobic oppression, exploitation, and wealth extraction, and asymmetrical distribution of resources were further dispossessed by the dissolution of the welfare state, the intensifying brutalities of policing and prison, and the refusal of British and American governments to respond to, or even acknowledge, the institutionalized racism and heterosexism that affected Black and queer people on a daily basis, from their access to health care and housing to their physical safety—even in their own homes.[83]

Artmaking played a crucial role in AIDS activism of the period, although there was not always consensus on what kind of art best served these movements. As Douglas Crimp wrote in 1987, "Art *does* have the power to save lives, and it is this very power that must be recognized, fostered, and supported in every way possible. But if we are to do this, we will have to abandon the idealist conception of art. We don't need a cultural renaissance; we need cultural practices actively participating in the struggle against AIDS. We don't need to transcend the epidemic; we need to end it."[84] Beauty is perhaps the aesthetic judgment most associated with transcendence and the ideal that art can help us overcome particularity and access a universal humanity—and therefore may seem totally oppositional to Crimp's call to end the pandemic. However, as I have been arguing so far, I question whether "transcendence" is precisely what occurs when we encounter beauty. Aesthetic choices amid life-and-death political crises matter profoundly. Faced with racist and homophobic violence perpetrated at the highest levels of government and prestigious cultural echelons, one might understandably worry that beautiful art runs the risk of romanticizing a crisis that is anything but beautiful, indulging in escapist fantasy, or abdicating from a moral duty to resist what Simon Watney referred to as "a dense web of racism, patriotism, and homophobia . . . sticky with blood lust, contempt, hatred, and hysteria."[85] Contrary to these possible objections, I wish to suggest that *Looking for Langston* expands on a rich relationship between beauty, Black aesthetic theory, and politics seen in earlier Black aesthetic iterations, as found in the work of Du Bois and Larsen, that addresses the urgent situation of the film's contemporary moment. In Julien's luxurious film, I read beauty as a faculty of political imagination and argue that beauty judgments function as structures of demand-making. The film mobilizes beauty against fetish and death by staging the moment of aesthetic judgment, dramatizing beauty judgments as sites of affective collectivity, political action, and survival. Julien's portrayal of aesthetic judgment serves as a model for rethinking theories of the beautiful from the ground of Black radicalism.

Here, a summary is in order (in as much as summarizing the film is possible) that will serve to further characterize the film's "freakish" beauty.[86] The film begins with the staging of a funeral. Julien poses as the deceased among a tableau of mourners. His body lies in state, presumably portraying Langston Hughes, although Toni Morrison's eulogy for James Baldwin plays in voiceover here, announcing the film's politics in her references to "rebels" and "dissidents," as well as the film's nonlinear historicism as Morrison's lithic voice rolls across the scene.[87] The eulogy is followed by an archival recording from a memorial broadcast dedicated to Langston Hughes. The camera then pans down, and it appears that the funeral is taking place above a queer night club. Throughout the film, this setting pastiches both Jazz Age glamour and raver glitter—disco balls, voguing, tuxedos, and Bessie Smith seamlessly cohabitate in this fantasy club space. Angels wearing sparkly white BDSM harnesses and tinseled wings observe the party from their perches on a sweeping staircase that appears straight out of the era of film noir, and the scene likewise enjoys this genre's lush lighting with its hard, defined shadows and contrast of bright white light. This is a heavenly cinematic space in which the past, present, and afterlife of decadence mingle like party guests sipping champagne. With one exception (which I will attend to toward the end of this chapter), the characters do not speak, and the film does not depend on a cohesive, overarching plot, although it plays with vignette and narrative-driven sequences.

As this visual and historical collage suggests, Julien imagines beauty as a structure of feeling, a space of collectivity that gains coherence softly, momentarily in the plasma of affect and abstraction rather than through documentary realism. Just in case we were to miss the importance of the beautiful in Julien's decadent, glamorous film, one of the main characters in *Looking for Langston* is actually named Beauty, a reference to Harlem Renaissance artist Richard Bruce Nugent's short story "Smoke, Lilies, and Jade," which is often cited as the first work of African American fiction to feature openly gay characters.[88] Portions of "Smoke,

Lilies, and Jade" are also read in voiceover in the film, reinforcing the connection.

In addition to the references to Nugent and Langston as ancestors of queer Black male beauty, the film also alludes to classical Greek and Roman homoerotic sculpture, Golden Age Hollywood film, and Robert Mapplethorpe's photography. Julien evokes an iconography of conventional beauty through form, treating the viewer to luminous, perfectly balanced tableaux in exquisite monochrome and slow panning shots and actors frozen in poses that suggest still photography, inviting the viewer to linger and delight in the pleasure of looking.[89] While the film counts on the viewer's ability to recognize references to "classical" beauty enshrined in museums, textbooks, and the culture industry, it also plays with the tensions, ambivalences, and revelations made possible by depicting Black queer masculine bodies in relation to this vexed aesthetic history.

By dramatizing the moment of aesthetic judgment, what Cheng calls the "shock of beauty," *Looking for Langston* explores its potential for queer Black politics.[90] *Looking for Langston* is concerned with the ways in which shared feeling circulates through aesthetic forms and how erotic beauty may be recovered from the violence of white supremacy and heteronormativity. In its invocation of Robert Mapplethorpe especially, the film wrestles with fragile distinctions between the gaze of exploitation (what Audre Lorde describes as a look that is really looking away) and a gaze of liberation.[91] *Looking for Langston* seeks to reclaim visual pleasure, and, more specifically, the pleasure of the beautiful, for subjects who have been historically harmed by looking and by beauty as a tool of dominance and violence.

In the film, this conflict is epitomized in the work of Robert Mapplethorpe.[92] Mapplethorpe's photographs of Black men, collected in *The Black Book* (1986), provoked critical attention due to their fetishistic qualities. The photographs present Blackness as molded by the gaze of a white artist, invoking a techno-aesthetic colonial history of photographers and subjects. Mapplethorpe's photographs of Black men elicited an outpouring of incisive critique and annotation from the likes of Kobena Mercer, Glenn Ligon, Essex Hemphill, and Julien himself during the 1980s. However, Mapplethorpe's work also drew criticism—for very different reasons—from the New Right. Mapplethorpe's photographs became a centerpiece in Senator Jesse Helms's arguments against the National Endowment for the Arts, which he argued used funds to "promote, disseminate or produce obscene or indecent materials, including but not limited to depictions of sadomasochism, homoeroticism, the exploitation of children, or individuals engaged in sex acts, or material that denigrates the objects or beliefs of the adherents of a particular religion or nonreligion."[93] In light of both Mapplethorpe's AIDS-related death and the homophobic impetus of New Right censorship movements, critics such as Mercer and José Esteban Muñoz later forged more ambivalent readings of Mapplethorpe's photographs of Black men.

When we dwell in the dreamy panning of the camera across Julien's somnolent face at the beginning of the film, the entanglement of beauty and Blackness rises to our attention, toggling these discourses of liberation, fetish, identification, and disidentification, which cannot be resolved in the scene. Despite claims of beauty's inherent egalitarianism, in practice, beauty's affective intensity and political charge often surge from discord rather than harmony, as responses to Mapplethorpe's photographs exemplify. As I discussed at the beginning of this chapter and in my analysis of *Passing*, beauty's privileged status in Western culture is intimately bound up with racial whiteness. Not only because aesthetic forms and physical attributes that are read as the visual markers of whiteness have come to define the category of the beautiful but also because aesthetic judgment itself, in its manufacture of the proprietary and properly judging aesthetic subject, is part of the production of whiteness.[94] This is certainly not to say that it is impossible for beauty to exist outside of whiteness. But it is to recognize that to call something or someone beautiful is to declare its value, a declaration that creates a social convergence that shapes and is shaped by relations of power. In staging the beauty judgment as he does in *Looking for Langston*, I think that Julien explores the possibility of beauty unpropertied, or beauty that revises our understanding of the relationship between the subject and the universal. By calling up a Black queer collective formed in the cinematic poesis of experimental film, Julien ousts the conventional Kantian aesthetic subject, taking up aesthetic judgment as a collective process of social formation and political demand-making rather than a normative subjective judgment confirmed by the teleology of purposiveness and a universality governed by whiteness.

As in Larsen's *Passing*, *Looking for Langston* stages acts of aesthetic judgment throughout the film. In one motif, a Black man, sometimes the character Beauty, holds a conch shell to his ear as if listening to the ocean. This action is often accompanied by the sound of waves in the soundtrack. The conch shell motif triggers a meditation on beauty judgments and their implications for queer Black politics. Sometimes, in these repetitions, the shell begins to resemble headphones as the man holding the shell sways to the beat of the film's deep house music, water pouring over the lens, the soundtrack belting, "Can you feel it?" When the lyrics ask if "you" can feel "it," the viewer is invited to exist in a moment of aesthetic judgment.[95] The viewer can't tell if this music is diegetic or extra-diegetic, because that difference doesn't even make sense in this film that folds the real and the fictional into each other like the swirl of the conch's spiral. It is unclear who is feeling. The man holding the shell? The viewer? What is the "it" being felt? As the song thumps joyfully across these visual depictions of aesthetic pleasure, the film asks the viewer a question fundamental to the value of aesthetics for social life: Can people share aesthetic feeling, and what does it mean if they do (or don't)?

We should keep in mind that the "sound of the ocean" that we hear when we hold a shell to our ear is really the noise of the shell's resonance with its environment, including our bodies. The shell bounces back the normally unheard sounds of blood and tissue pressing and circulating against the surface of the shell, amplified by its cavity. The sound of the material structure of the shell and its context resounds against the imagination, becoming an instrument that transforms sensation into fantasy and aesthetic feeling. Listening to the "sound of the ocean" in the film is a metaphor for beauty judgments that similarly reflect the subject back onto themselves while creating the effect of objective judgment. We imagine that we're hearing the sound of the ocean as an observable phenomenon, but really it's all in our heads.

If he listens to the shell and then passes it to someone else, will they hear the same sound (or close enough)? In the conch motif, both the performer and the audience seem to be listening to the same music as the boundaries between inside and outside, self and other become porous in this representation of aesthetic judgment. The question remains unanswered—"Can you feel it?"—but the affirmative possibility (or at least the desire for it) hovers over this sequence. With the conch metaphor, Julien grapples with the oceanic materiality of a Black Atlantic past while handling the immateriality of an aesthetic echo with a self-referential origin. This is the invigorating fantasy of communion within a lost or partial history of Black queerness inseparable from aesthetic pleasure. Beauty and pleasure facilitate this Black Atlantic vibration. The sequence stages aesthetic judgment as a club scene; beauty as a socially and politically saturated structure of feeling and a space of collective idealism becomes a way to live amid death and political crisis. Departing from the conventions of Kantian subjective judgment, here aesthetic pleasure and the beautiful are temporary feelings made collectively in a moment that then recedes like the ebb of a beat or a wave.

In thinking through the relationship between shared feeling and aesthetic judgment, I return to the reading of Kant's *Critique of Judgment* discussed at the beginning of this chapter. In doing so, I aim to move into alignment with what I see as the film's "reading" of the ambivalent history of the beautiful, revising classical regimes of beauty in a queer Black aesthetic invocation. As *Looking for Langston* demonstrates, we cannot ethically encounter the discourse of beauty in the West without understanding it as a participant in racial systems. Perhaps the flow of power is sometimes diverted by reading the discourse against itself and through disidentificatory acts that prioritize aesthetic pleasure for those whose pleasure has been previously refused, denied, or stolen. Such counter-readings, Du Boisian readings perhaps, enable a critique of whiteness's propriety relation to beauty.

Here we might draw a connection between the universalizing demand of beauty judgments and the demands of social and political collectives. This might be more obvious in social justice movements that explicitly critique beauty regimes, such as the Harlem Renaissance, Black Arts movement, "Black Is Beautiful," or the new popular politics of representation flourishing in mass culture, especially in social and digital media.[96] The final section of this chapter explores the ways that *Looking for Langston* uses the demand-making structure of the beauty judgment to create a space of queer Black universalism countering whiteness's propriety relationship to beauty.

Although the concept of the universal may feel antithetical to subversive politics, signaling an outdated transcendentalism or humanism (as critiqued by both Crimp and the scholars of liberal humanism mentioned at the outset of this chapter), the conservative tenor of the universal perhaps shifts if we consider the universal to be something that is made and constantly remade rather than preexistent, immutable, or inherited intact. Ernesto Laclau has defined the universal as a "lack," "as an incomplete horizon suturing a dislocated particular identity."[97] In Laclau's theorizing, the particular is the enunciation of identity within the context of the universal, the universal being the political imaginary that would make democracy possible, characterized by its absence rather than by an essence.[98] Rather than thinking of the universal as a prior or singular thing that transcends or eliminates particularity, the universal can be understood as a space of particularity—the partially visualized end of struggle. As Linda Zerilli explains, "This universalism is not One: it is not a preexisting something (essence or form) to which individuals accede, but, rather, the fragile, shifting, and always incomplete achievement of political action; it is not the container of a presence but the placeholder of an absence. . . . Universalism can neither precede nor exceed the political, for it is nothing else but a hegemonic relation of *articulated* differences."[99]

The paradoxical relation between the universal and the particular is what makes collectivity possible. The ultimate consequence of pure difference would be apartheid. Without some concept of an experience that can be shared, disparate groups lose grounds for claim-making. Even worse, a theory of pure difference ignores the fact that "each group is not only different from the others but constitutes in many cases such difference on the basis of the exclusion and subordination of other groups," ignoring the role of power in the production of difference.[100] Conversely, the idea of a stable universal is the source of racism, totalitarianism, subjugation, and indeed the oppressive regulations of Kantian beauty judgments. Perhaps the universal is a useful social and political concept, but it must be understood as being without essence, shifting, momentary. *Looking for Langston* explores beauty's propensity to be utilized by power but also its potential to form universalities that are not deterministic, permanent, or fascistically regulated. I read *Looking for Langston*, like *Passing*, as a Black experimental text that sees beauty as a space of wild imagination unfettered by white, straight universality. However, unlike *Passing*, *Looking for Langston* expresses a protective optimism for this wildness, aesthetic practices that might be joined to create utopian spaces in contradiction to anti-Blackness.

Julien mobilizes what is too particular, too minoritized to have any claim to the universal, by traditional rubrics at least, performing beauty's subversive claim-making. That is, we may read *Looking for Langston* as staging an alternative theory of beauty judgments that rejects whiteness and anti-Blackness as the regulatory frameworks that govern subjective universality. The claim to universality from a minoritized position can help erode the cultural and ideological dominance of an oppressive society, but only if we recognize that universality is a historically and affectively saturated, shifting structure of relation, rather than a fixed essence, and only if we are open to the continual mutation of the universal as an impermanent site, rather than a purposive, transcendental continuity. In this understanding, the universal has content, but it does not stay the same—or does not have to. The universal is not what we *have* in common, as subjects apprehending objects. Rather, maybe the unpropertied universal is about sharing a moment of relinquished subjectivity within the site of particularity, making a claim for difference's value and its capacity to imagine new social relations. In the presence of beauty, we are not confirmed but changed.

In the staging of aesthetic judgment as a scene of shared pleasure in which the subject and object are blurred or even are simply not the relevant concepts, Julien, via the film's argument for the universality of queer Black expression, denaturalizes the universalism of a white heteronormative aesthetic tradition that relies on the idea of a proper judging aesthetic subject. We might ask if *judgment* is even the correct term for an aesthetic experience that does not rely upon individual mastery. However, the importance of the *demand* lingers. The collective feelings arising in the beauty judgment, heard as the demand, are not a practice of *feeling into* in the sense of projection; rather, they summon a temporary space where some things may be shared. Not all of us are invited into all aspects of the film's aesthetic intimacies—and I include myself among those viewers who are at times sitting beside the film rather than within it.[101] Being beside is a kind of connectedness that does not depend on sameness or having the same feeling. It is instead an ethical attention to difference when the relevant values are in alignment—to wait with somebody, to sit alongside them, to hold something for them, to witness for them, to hold a door open or to close it against something. Perhaps a near infinite number of ways of being together and being for without being the same. In this space, subject position (or identity) is not incidental, although they do not determine what is summoned by aesthetic judgment. Within the momentary consensus shaped by the beauty judgment, the older things have not fallen away, and different ways of relating to others become visible as we let ourselves be changed in the company of others.

Beauty's lack of criteria, but not of content, its constitutive demand of agreement and common sense (common feeling) makes it a fitting utopian structure. As José Esteban Muñoz argues, radical politics, perhaps especially queer politics, need spaces of fantasy: "Utopia lets us imagine a space outside of heteronormativity. It permits us to conceptualize new worlds and realities that are not irrevocably constrained by the HIV/AIDS pandemic and institutionalized state homophobia. More important, utopia offers us a critique of the present, of what is, by casting a picture of what *can and perhaps will be*."[102] The beautiful is an integral part of such a political imaginary. In the moment of aesthetic judgment, utopian promises such as those outlined by Muñoz momentarily exist. This is a key premise of *Looking for Langston*, where queer Black freedom is visualized within the protected, temporary (but lasting) spaces of the film. Beauty's insistent presence makes demands that might be judged as improbable or impossible in other contexts but are manifest in the moment of aesthetic judgment. In making this claim, I hope not to erase the specificity of *Looking for Langston*'s Black positionality, dispersing or repurposing what is being demanded by the film. Rather, I wish to suggest that those demands initiate a total restructuring of a tradition of Kantian aesthetic judgment founded in anti-Blackness. This restructuring has a comprehensive effect on how we understand beauty. Thus, the argument here is not that the demands made by *Looking for Langston* might be used or applied in non-Black elsewheres or to participate in the projective empathies critiqued earlier in this chapter but that the film demands that we encounter beauty that is not based in anti-Blackness. Here, we might recall Fred Moten's exploration of "blackness as a radical, abolitionist, critical-historical project" that becomes the "ground for a recalibration of the aesthetic."[103]

We can observe this through the film's portrayal of the character Beauty, who holds the conch shell to his ear among several other unnamed characters, angels and club kids listening to the insistent house beat: *can you feel it?* It is significant that Beauty is not just an object that invites looking (the camera mimics the desiring human eye as it frames Beauty's body) but also a subject who makes promises. With the words of "I'll wait!," the only line in the entire film that is not voiceover narration, Beauty introduces futurity in a film otherwise preoccupied with the present and the past. Beauty waits at the edge of the film and of politics. He waits not just for the character Alex, but as a metaphor for the aesthetic category of beauty, he also waits for the viewer who, on the fringes of the film's world, is not quite there yet.[104] In this scene, Beauty utters the film's promise for queer Black delight.

One important feature to consider within the film's depiction of beauty is that the actor who plays Beauty does not necessarily challenge many dominant beauty ideals. Tall, symmetrical, having little visible body fat, with pronounced musculature and light skin—Beauty's name and symbolic prominence could be seen as reinforcing anti-Black and classed regulations of human difference.[105] Additionally, as in *Passing*, the couple form of Beauty and Alex, like Irene and Clare, comes to assume the conventional structure of aesthetic judgment. Alex frequently encounters Beauty as an art object—as does the viewer—a statue or a photograph come to life, still, posed, nude. On its own, this romance, which is also a story about the thrall of aesthetic encounter (as in *Passing*), can be seen as reproducing the problematic racial and sexual power dynamics of Kantian aesthetic judgment. It is easy for viewers (and critics) to be drawn to this love story because it is the clearest "narrative" of the film with a familiar romantic plot and Nugent's short story recited in voiceover. However, the story of Beauty and Alex does not stand alone. I would argue that this romance, which completes rather early in the runtime of the film, is in fact not the centerpiece of *Looking for Langston*. It is an important component of a film that weaves together many different characters, vignettes, moods, and scenes and a film that formally displaces the convention of a central story around which every other element is oriented. In *Looking for Langston*, we find research-based historical narrative, critiques of white sexual exploitation of Black men, ruminations on the role of pornography in gay male sexuality and culture, scenes of queer nightlife bonding, memorials to ancestors and lost friends, the threat of AIDS stalking the irrepressibility of desire (with poems by Essex Hemphill), and ebullient partying, all unfolding in highly stylized, self-aware, and non-sequential scenes. While it's true that Beauty is portrayed by a conventionally beautiful person, he is far from the only example of beauty in the film. There are so many other characters given their moment of cinematic beauty, including historical figures like James Baldwin, Countee Cullen, Richmond Barthé, Palmer Hayden, and Langston Hughes, who do not fit the typical mold. The bedrock of the film is not a love story culminating in the couple form, a romance of traditional aesthetic relations between aesthetic subject and beautiful object. It is the delight of aesthetic pleasure that plays out through performances by a heterogenous cast flaunting the beauty of human bodily variability. The film perhaps enacts what Jafari S. Allen calls "Black gay time space," a "state of at once exceeding and belonging irreducibly to (one's) time invoked and enabled by the disco ball" where "one can cut into the past and project or imagine a future in which we are still dancing with friends and lovers gone too soon to the ethers of the dance floor and the flickers of the disco ball light."[106] Rather than stopping at Beauty the character and the part he plays in one of the film's several love stories, *Looking for Langston*'s theory of beauty is perhaps best understood in a closing sequence of the film, which stages not the coupling of proper aesthetic subject and aesthetic object but a wild collective imaginary that triumphs over the police.

The joyous partying in the night club is reaching a climax. The dancers move ecstatically to house music, smashing champagne glasses on the floor to the rhythm of the beat. This is intercut with an approaching (mostly white) mob, police in uniform and plain clothes, perhaps joined by some deputized civilians, brandishing truncheons and brutish looks, preparing to raid the club, to hurt and to kill.[107] The mob approaches and the dancers appear completely unaware, revving up their delirious celebration when they could be using this precious time to escape. Tension builds through the increasingly frenetic cuts between dancers and the violence coming for them. Then, at the moment of climax, as the mob enters the club, we are delighted to find that it is empty. The dancers have disappeared in the energy of their own rapturous pleasure. The BDSM angels smirk and laugh mischievously at the mob searching for victims, their anger deflating into flaccid confusion under the rotating starlight of the disco ball.

The fantastic community evades violence through the vigor of its imaginative pleasure. It has made fools of the mob and their fantasies of a murderous restoration of fascistic universalism. The potential of this beautiful group of ravers and aesthetes to manifest political transformation is heightened by the presence of an actual community of artists, activists, and scholars coming together in the meeting ground of the film, including Blackberri, Essex Hemphill, Wayson Jones, Stuart Hall, Jimmy Somerville, and Julien himself. The nightclub, and the film, as spaces reserved exclusively for pleasure, prizing "appearance" over "substance," fleeting feeling over permanence, redefines the landscape of what is possible, the limits of survival and desire. The mob is left waiting for a fantasy that seems witless and improbable. The silent laughter of those watching from the afterlife echoes soundlessly in the non-place. The moment of aesthetic judgment is only a moment, beauty waits, and the viewer is left with the reverberating pleasure of laughter, a laughter that is the aesthetic echo of creativity and survival. In the moment of beauty, which can be held only temporarily, pleasure becomes the feeling of queer Black politics and the structure of political demand-making. Beauty is a victory over the police, that is, the deadly regulation and enforcement of anti-Blackness and sexual normativity.

As the film ends by whisking away the nightclubbers from one heaven to another yet unseen, protected by mirthful angels who linger just to watch the would-be enforcers flounder in their congealing, inutile violence, we might reassess the opening of the film and the image of Julien in the casket—not dead, but sleeping. Not fixed in deadly repose but wildly dreaming in beauty's deregulation. As the camera pans from his face to the scene of the club just beneath his head, the film initiates its sequences of lovingly wrought beauty unfolding in a shared dream: carefully staged tableaux of seashells, silks, roses, and mirrors, glittering wings against the soft black shadows, the collages of archival materials like altars, the open-mouthed smile of a dancer spinning in the disco light refracted by the smoky air. At the end of the film, as the cops stomp and sputter inanely, the camera wanders over to the still-spinning record player. The soundtrack transitions from the call and response collaboration between the poet Essex Hemphill and musician Wayson

Jones, mixed with the house track "Can You Party (Club Mix)" by Royal House, to a recording of Langston Hughes reading his poems accompanied by a jazz band on the 1958 television program *The Subject Is Jazz*. The film ends with a clip of Hughes reading the poem "Night and Morn," closing on the final lines: "I could be blue but / I been blue all night long."[108] "Night and Morn" is a blues poem, almost a lyrical fragment, which gives little narrative detail but through the delicately crafted force of rhythm and repetition conveys rallying optimism, the speaker's spirits rising with the sun after a long night of deep sadness. The lights come up behind Hughes's smiling face as he utters the line, "Sun's a risin'," and it is as if the film, too, is rousing itself from the surreality of a night of grief, music, and beauty, not to return to the "reality" provided by the cold, clear light of day but stepping into the aurora, the point before the day when anything seems possible.

In this opening chapter, I have attempted to establish the stakes of beauty and aesthetic pleasure within a Black experimental tradition and a Black radical tradition as they overlap in the project of redefining beauty and aesthetic judgment. Black experimentalism, an aesthetic tradition and space of political intimacy that exceeds the space and time of Harlem in the 1920s and 1930s, offers a sonorous exploration of the beautiful and its relationship to political imagination, echoing into the twenty-first century. I have argued that Black experimentalists such as Du Bois and Larsen are significant theorists of the beautiful in the United States and Black diasporic contexts. Du Bois and Larsen critique and complicate beauty's Enlightenment legacy and place Black art at the center of the discourse on the beautiful. In *Looking for Langston*, Isaac Julien expands on Black experimentalism's interrogation of the beautiful and the political, suggesting how aesthetic pleasure can be more than a political instrument, how it can be an end in itself, following up on Du Bois's proposed political imaginary while also attending to the risks and pleasures of objectification, as explored in Larsen's *Passing*.

In the chapter that follows, I continue to draw from the *Critique of Judgment*, recovering whimsy from Kant's category of "merely agreeable." Whimsy works as a kind of mischievous foil to the beautiful, unexpectedly altering the criteria for aesthetic judgment and shifting the ground of the *sensus communis*. Through the work of Yoko Ono, especially her conceptualist artist's book *Grapefruit and Film No. 4 (Bot-*

toms), whimsy's irrational delight enables formal and political critiques of the state's management of racialized and gendered subjects. As *Looking for Langston* articulates the political demands of the beautiful for queer Black life, Ono's whimsy demonstrates aesthetic pleasure's analytic capacity, expanding our understanding of the relationship between aesthetic form and social and political imagination.

2

Yoko Ono's Whimsy

But a document can pull a nation out from under you.
—Susan Briante, *Defacing the Monument*

On the first page of Yoko Ono's conceptualist artist's book *Grapefruit: A Book of Instructions and Drawings*, we are invited to provide a little information. The hand-drawn word *synopsis*, underlined with an informal squiggle, precedes the instructions: "Write your own."[1] An arrow points down to an indifferently sketched box that takes up most of the blocky 5 ½ × 5 ½ inch square page. Standing next to the box (for scale, perhaps) is a small humanoid figure, drawn with cartoonish minimalism. A vaguely alien biped: thin, curving legs composed from single lines precariously support a summer-squash-shaped torso, merging into an elongated neck and ending in a round, featureless head gazing toward the box. The torso is decorated with two flicks of the pen to represent primly turned-out arms. A small cross in the bottom third of the torso denotes a bellybutton. Beneath the synopsis box, Ono provides a simple identification form: "Name," "Weight," "Sex," and "Colour."

Before ever encountering the book's "content," Ono invites the reader to provide its synopsis. But what is the reader being asked to describe and summarize? The book? The cutesy humanoid figure? Or the reader herself? In the drawing, the synopsis of a book is confused with the identity of a person. It pulls together multiple forms of reduction (the synopsis, the identification form, the cartoon) and appeals to the reader's desire to neatly categorize. However, like all great minimalists, Ono does not allow the simplicity of form to limit interpretative possibility. Rather, her arrangement of minimal forms generates interpretative profusion and complexity.

In its absurdism, this invitation to categorize can be read as a refusal of classification as a method of understanding, an opening salvo for the anti-administrative whimsy that runs throughout *Grapefruit*. The prompts ask the reader to provide familiar, basic components of modern identification—name, weight, sex, color (suggesting race). We expect such questions in countless bureaucratic encounters—at school, the doctor's, the DMV—but it makes little sense for this information to be collected at the beginning of a work of art, a space of imagination that would seem to be the least likely place for the routine reporting of personal data.

Ono's references to the administrative markers that sort, explain, and control people allow us to see the administrative as an aesthetic experience, one that impacts people's lives quite profoundly. While the tone of this opening with its sociological prompts and clear instructions mimics the impersonality of the administrative form, the informality of Ono's charming doodle gives the form a strangeness and personality that undermines the pursuit of detached information gathering and data production. I read *Grapefruit* and Ono's larger body of conceptualist work from the 1960s and 1970s as a rejection of the administrative aesthetic that naturalizes human categorization within racial capitalism and cisheteropatriarchy. Deploying an aesthetic category I call *whimsy*, Ono uses the humor of the unexpected, the irrational, and the impossible to irritate the administration of human beings and its violent management of race, gender, and other social positions, turning to aesthetic pleasure as a source of unlearning and imagination.

In this chapter, I return to Kant's *Critique of Judgment*, shifting from the demanding exultations of the beautiful toward the more niche aesthetic category of whimsy. Kant's inclusion of whimsy among his quite serious bestiary of aesthetic experiences in the *Critique* may be surprising to some. Kant defines the whimsical as "the talent enabling us to put ourselves at will into a certain mental disposition, in which everything is judged in a way quite different from the usual one (even vice versa), but yet is judged in conformity with certain principles of reason [present] in such a mental attunement."[2] Whimsy has the capacity to create new criteria for aesthetic judgment that upend existing expectations and yet feel right. While Kant quickly dispenses with the whimsical as merely a minor aesthetic experience ultimately inconsequential to his larger project, there is in Kant's definition and dismissal of whimsy a seed of something significant. Whimsy's capacity for being unexpectedly compelling and for delivering delightful reversals makes it particularly promising for intervention in structures of dominance.

Taking Ono's conceptualism from the 1960s and 1970s as a case study in whimsy helps us understand the administration of racial and gender identity in the United States as an acutely joyless aesthetic process, as well as a material and social one. Ono's whimsy prompts us to consider the state and institutional management of identity as an aesthetic question. Ono's conceptualist work from the 1960s and 1970s, including her artist's book *Grapefruit* and her 1966 experimental film *Film No. 4 (Bottoms)*, allows us to perceive identity as a form maintained through tedious and repetitive aesthetic work—the kind of labor that gives you spiritual carpel tunnel, acid reflux triggered by the indigestible bits of daily living, the chronic pain of subtle stress positions—in other words, a slow and ceaseless making up and breaking down of people. *Grapefruit* helps us understand these things through the unremarkable kinds of writing that lubricate the functioning of racial capitalism and the state, such as administrative forms, credentializing genres like the résumé, and even ostensibly democratic forms like the petition. I will call these genres *paperwork*. This wordplay reflects Yoko Ono's whimsy as it collides with the humorlessness of the administrator.[3] Paperwork is the aesthetics of managerial subjection, which I link to so-called high artistic forms, including the lyric tradition.

To study Yoko Ono's conceptualism, one must take humor seriously. Nosing along this line of inquiry, I am not pursuing a broad theory of humor but investigating a more feminized, more childlike, and queerer niche. Yoko Ono's whimsy intervenes in the deadly serious racialization of groups via imperialist war-making and immigration administration. In turning to whimsy in the face of the humorless bureaucratic forms that normalize the sorting of people along a spectrum of desirability and vulnerability, I am not being glib. Whimsy strategically defaces the aesthetics of neutrality that allows race-making and racial violence to unfold in ways that appear rational and natural. My readings position Ono's conceptual absurdisms, which unwaveringly deploy a discourse of peace and love, as responses to what Chandan Reddy has called "racial cruelty," the strategic violence by which the United States "continues to assert its form as the best possible totality for worldwide social relations."[4] The recourse to whimsy counters the aesthetics of rationality that enable such cruelty. As Reddy argues, both liberals and conservatives assert the fundamental rationality of the United States:

> By the twentieth century, US state violence was operating through and constrained by a drive for a monopoly on rationality, figured most often by attempts to concretize the meaning of rational freedom as a freedom from the threat of arbitrariness. The modern state establishes itself in and through practices and their apparatuses that, in a particular historical instance, generate the conditions for the expression of legitimate violence, seeking to conserve those apparatuses for the state exclusively. The state form, then is made possible through epistemologies, epistemes, and institutions that collectively forge the conditions for the universalization of a specific expression of reason or rationality.[5]

These "arbitrary" threats, distinguished from "legitimate" violence, are consistently articulated through practices of racialization and the binarization of gender. My reading of Ono's work rejects the apparent orderliness of state violence by embracing the arbitrary and ignoring the "rationalism" that naturalizes racism and gender conformity. To study Ono's work, to take it seriously, is to explore how irrational, anti-achievement, and unproductive whimsies might erode credulity in the aesthetic forms that produce and manage race and gender as methods of extraction, exploitation, and control. Although much of Ono's work lacks the signifying features that would allow it to register as being "about" race or gender, this is in part the point. The aesthetic practices of racialization and gendering are often deployed as "neutral" categorization, cataloguing of information, and the capturing of data. Presented as objective and routine, paperwork is simply how the world works, even as its procedures become increasingly unwantable. The embrace of whimsy's irrationality places the reader or viewer in the position to perceive and to question the inevitability of structural violence.

Conceptualizing Whimsy

Ono's *Grapefruit*, a hybrid form full of segments, pulp, pith, and pips, is not easily classified, although for the purposes of marketing, its publisher labels the book "poetry." Like the author, it cannot be categorized as a single type or kind. First self-published by Ono in 1964 in a limited run of five hundred copies, *Grapefruit* was later published in 1970 by Simon and Schuster, who published an expanded edition with new material in 2000; this is the edition referred to in this chapter. As suggested by the opening drawing, *Grapefruit* is a funny book—funny-"ha ha" and funny-weird. However, it is also a challenging book. It delights as it befuddles; the pleasure of irrationality is one of its primary idioms. Unlike a riddle, there is no single answer, no rational key that causes incomprehensibility to drop, meaning to fall into place as we are returned to the homeostasis of the given. *Grapefruit* maintains its strangeness.

Grapefruit is most often read as an "artist's book," which is such a capacious category that it can be defined only as a book written by an artist.[6] In its current iteration (*Grapefruit* continues to grow, ripening with each edition), *Grapefruit* contains many different kinds of texts and genres, including drawings, questionnaires, essays, poems, and conceptualist instructions and event scores.[7] The *instruction* is an avant-garde form developed by Ono in the mid-1950s as she was studying music composition and literature at Sarah Lawrence College.[8] These texts are instructions for performances or, as Ono calls them, *events* that can be performed by anyone and appreciated on their own as works of literature, similar to the Fluxus event score.[9] Some instructions can be performed in a more or less literal way, such as "Pea Piece," which instructs the reader to leave peas behind wherever they go. Other instructions are *possible* to complete but highly impractical, such as "Kite Piece I," which tells the reader to borrow the *Mona Lisa* and fly it as a kite. And some instructions are physically impossible to perform but can be performed imaginatively in one's mind, such as "Walk Piece," which advises the reader to stir their brain with a penis then take a walk.

Ono's instructions are an integral part of a larger experimental ecosystem that emerged in New York City in the early to mid-1950s and hit its stride in the mid-1960s. As conceptualism developed, many artists, often having received some conventional training in music, the visual arts, or both, began to create text-based art that required an audience to "complete" the work. Notable examples include John Cage and his invention of the text-based score, the event scores of Fluxus (George Maciunas, La Monte Young, George Brecht, Dick Higgins,

Alison Knowles), the eruption of the happening (Yayoi Kusama, Allan Kaprow), and the development of conceptual art (Sol LeWitt, Adrian Piper, John Baldessari). Ono's work bears similarities to much of this art, and she was an associate of many of the artists listed above, especially Fluxus.[10] For many of the artists in this cohort, the relative accessibility of text allowed for the detachment of artmaking from skill, arts institutions, wealth, and prestige. The conceptualist text rebuffs the idea of an art object that might be bought and sold, absorbing the artist into the existing art world controlled by markets.[11] Ono's instructions and other text-based pieces especially emphasize the role of the audience in performing or completing the work of art. While Ono's instructions emerged from a conceptualist moment of enthusiasm for text, there are important differences between Ono's use of text in her instructions and poems and the use of text in musical composition scores, Fluxus event scores, avant-garde happenings, and conceptualist drawings, text-paintings, and performances.

Most notably, Ono uses literary elements like imagery, symbolism, and narrative to generate readerly meaning. Ono's text-based pieces also tend to contain a stronger emphasis on reader interiority. As Ono explains the difference between her instructions for events and the happenings of the 1960s, "Event, to me, is not an assimilation of all the arts as happenings seems to be, but an extrication from various sensory perceptions. It is not 'a get togetherness' as most happenings are, but dealing with oneself. Also, it has no script as happenings do, although it has something that starts it moving—the closest word for it may be a 'wish' or 'hope.'"[12] Reading is a kind of collective hoping in *Grapefruit*, the participation in another's wish by taking part in *Grapefruit*'s experiments in perception and sensation.

Yoko Ono's whimsy plays a significant role in what makes *Grapefruit* pleasurable, yet it is also what makes it difficult. To read *Grapefruit*, you must go all in. This means letting go of a dominant reality, surrendering to a quixotic practice of seeing the world. Staking publicly such a perspective on the world is embarrassing, in part because of the racialized and gendered epistemologies that define what is true or reasonable. It is embarrassing to invest in something that seems small and whose value is unclear or that simply does not seem real. What, then, would it mean to *really* read this work? To think these thoughts?

Even as whimsy can be a spark for delight, it is also an easy target for ridicule. For example, in a blog post denouncing the whimsical in Fluxus, the well-known art critic John Perreault sneers:

> When whimsy rears its cute little head, Fluxus fails. Whimsy is not humor, whimsy is cute. Whimsy is not an Artopian characteristic, whereas sarcasm is. . . . You know it when you see it. It sickens you and makes even kind persons reach for their fly-swatters [sic], their spitballs, their rubberband [sic] slingshots, and even their b-b guns [sic]. It smells like artificially-flavored and artificially-sweetened bad candy. Examples? Why not start at the top. We adore Saint Yoko, but when she fails in her instruction pieces or her Tweets it is smack down on the whimsy bed-of-nails. I am sickened every time she Tweets 'Love your Mom'. Or 'It is Mother's day in Costa Rico [sic].' Yoko, get over it![13]

In Perreault's bilious characterization, whimsy is disgusting. He holds his nose at its sentimentality, its froth of naïveté. Whimsy is a suitable object for violence, although it is not a true threat. The play weapons of children will dispense it quickly—spitballs, slingshots, BB guns, or even a cruel word. It is interesting that what makes whimsy repulsive is its sweetness and childlike qualities, particularly mother love. It is equally interesting that an aesthetic defined by its inability to be taken seriously draws such bellicosity.

Really reading Ono means questioning assumptions so basic that they feel incontestable. Doing so means taking seriously aspects of society that are conventionally regarded as being without value. What a waste, these sugar-drunk heads softened by soft hearts. It is significant that Perreault's examples of whimsy are so girlish and anti-maternal. And, as we'll see, to be whimsical *is* to embrace the feminine in that whimsy makes it possible to question the rationality of masculine violence. To go with whimsy is not an affectively or socially neutral process, but is attended by the guilt, shame, anxiety, and rancor that comes with spending our time on what is not deemed useful. A preoccupation with productivity and usefulness under racial capitalism, as well as anxiety over the necessity of the "right" choices on how to spend one's diminishing time and energy in critical political moments, leads to a calculus of value in which the clarity of realism and representation often win out.[14] As Rei

Terada writes, "The idea of 'accepting' givens or not—especially on the largest scale, that of the Kantian enabling conditions of space, time, and consciousness—can seem fantastic from the outset. When we persevere in such thoughts anyway, it's with embarrassment about extending them to the areas where they seem to matter least."[15] To question the given is to align yourself with madness and deviance, outcasts partitioned off by institutional walls or the invisible walls that segregate the socially illegible, the dysregulated, drug users, and artists. When questioning the given, if you are not labeled insane, then you may be feminized— the childlike, sentimental idealist, the utopian, lounging in bed to end a war.[16] What feels natural or transparent in aesthetic judgment is very often bound up with systems of domination and power. When we read *Grapefruit*, we should consider how the pejoration of whimsy aligns with racialized and gendered tactics of delegitimization. If a radical transformation of the world is truly what is desired, then we can expect those transformations to require fundamental conceptual shifts that feel strange, unpredictable, and embarrassing.

Ono's talent for whimsical comedy has been seriously underappreciated.[17] Her specific style, as it evolved out of her experiments in creative writing and music composition, attends to the imaginative production of a pleasant weirdness similar to defamiliarization, but not quite.[18] Like Victor Shklovsky's original definition of the term, the poetic quality of Ono's language pushes us to see what is deemed normal as strange while also seeing what is strange as suddenly plausible. Important to whimsy, however, is a distinct sense of pleasure that attends this strangeness—a delight in the weird and witty, and often, yes, the cute or sweet, rather than a sense of unpleasant shock or alienation. This does not mean that Ono's work is without seriousness, darkness, or violence. Rather, part of Ono's radical revision of the world includes centering pleasures that are not taken seriously. These are not the big dramatic pleasures of sublimity, sexual climax (although there is eroticism in Ono's work), or ecstatic beauty. Rather, this is the pleasure of contemplating the smell of the moon, savoring a tuna fish sandwich, or burying the sunrise in your garden.

Ono's conceptualism urges others to radically revise their perception of the world through purposeful, ritualized, and unusual instructions, producing events that often take place as reading. In reading Ono, our attention is drawn to the more banal moments of aesthetic judgment unobtrusively punctuating everyday life like the ticking of a clock.[19] The whimsical is delightful because it treats what is odd or fanciful as utterly normal, an enchantment that interrupts the routine business of living. In this way, whimsy offers special insight into the relationship between aesthetic judgment and norms. Most notably, taking Ono's whimsy seriously allows us insight into relationships between aesthetic judgment and the management of race and gender.

Criticism on what constitutes "the whimsical" as an aesthetic category is meager, leaving a generous amount of space to theorize. However, there is one reliable aesthetic philosopher whose notes on the whimsical offer insight into *Grapefruit*—Immanuel Kant. In the *Critique of Judgment*, the treatise where Kant famously outlines his theories of the beautiful and the sublime, he also spares a moment for the whimsical:

> The *whimsical* manner may also be included with whatever is cheerful and closely akin to the gratification derived from laughter, and which belongs to originality of intellect, but which certainly does not belong to the talent for fine art. For *whimsicality*, in its favorable sense, means the talent enabling us to put ourselves at will into a certain mental disposition in which everything is judged in a way quite different from the usual one (even vice versa), but yet is judged in conformity with certain principles of reason [present] in such a mental attunement. A person who is subject to such changes involuntarily is *moody* [*launisch*]. But someone who can adopt them at will and purposively (so as to enliven his description of something by means of a contrast arousing laughter) is called *whimsical* [*launig*], as is also the way he conveys [his thoughts]. However, this manner belongs more to agreeable than to fine art, because the object of fine art must always show itself as having some dignity; and so an exhibition of it requires a certain seriousness, just as taste does when it judges the object.[20]

What is especially fascinating in this description of the whimsical is the curious relationship between whimsy and its criteria. Kant calls the whimsical "the talent enabling us to put ourselves at will into a certain mental disposition in which everything is judged in a way quite different from the usual one (even vice versa), but yet is judged in conformity with certain principles of reason [present] in such a mental attunement." To take pleasure in whimsy, we must *shift the criteria of aesthetic judgment* while maintaining a *feeling* of logical acceptability. Despite Kant's attempts to contain this upset of criteria, the regulation of judgment is disturbed. Whimsy thus weakens aesthetic judgment's claims to universal reason and the ubiquity of the given simply by showing that aesthetic pleasure can exist without them. As I summarized in the previous chapter, according to Kant, in a beauty judgment, the subjective judgment of taste feels both universal and objective because our sense of the purposiveness of the object is so compelling—all others must feel the same way. But when something is whimsical, the criteria by which we typically judge is unhinged and might even be oppositional to the original criteria for evaluating the aesthetic experience. This is quite remarkable.

Kant's aesthetic theory and his racial theory are entangled through purposiveness, which bestows a rational bearing on racial hierarchies and violent arrangements of extraction, exploitation, and premature death. Acceptance of purposiveness is necessary to racism's functionality. A theory of the beautiful grounded in the Black radical tradition offers the clarity of the demand for undoing purposiveness and the privatization of the beautiful by whiteness. Whimsy offers another entry point from which the social forms of value might be reimagined through aesthetic pleasure in irrationality and originality that is not contained by reason.

One of the problems with whimsy, according to Kant, is that it lacks dignity, unlike the beautiful. But another way of looking at this, and the possible cause of Kant's ultimate dismissal of whimsy, is that the whimsical's perversion of criteria renders absurd the conventionally beautiful and its claims to natural superiority. While beauty judgments can be a way of affirming value through the assertion of serious pleasure, a shifting universal engendered by the solemnity of the demand, whimsy's power lies in its talent for comedy, the destabilization of purposiveness and universality through play. Humor in general has long been recognized for its subversive power, its ability to invert power relations by interrupting with the unexpected, highlighting contradictions, inverting hierarchies, and offering new frames for viewing familiar things. Kant brushes over this talent for transgression with agility by demoting whimsy to the category of "merely agreeable." However, there is something to be said for whimsy's cultivated rejection of seriousness. Both beauty and whimsy are powerful kinds of aesthetic acts. Beauty takes the declarative approach, and whimsy, as Kant suggests (against his own investments), has the potential to upturn the grounds of the aesthetic, if only temporarily.

How does whimsy fit in with other kinds of humor? Whimsy does not bite and snap at the tender parts, as does satire. It is not caught up in the mimicry of parody. It has much in common with the absurd and its embrace of irrationality and subversion. In some forms of absurdist humor, the sudden revelation of life's arbitrariness makes us laugh to keep from crying, now faced with the futility of our actions and the meaninglessness of that which seemed so important moments before. Whimsy similarly embraces the random or out of place, yet it yields to enchantment when encountering the unexpected. Whimsy is tuned in to a sense of wonder, lightness, and play. Although its pleasures might be dismissed as childlike and facile in some quarters, in whimsy we may also find a politics of delight.

Kant's reading of the whimsical assists in conceptualizing how we might take whimsy seriously, although ultimately, as with the discussion of beauty in chapter 1, in ways that meaningfully depart from traditional Kantian aesthetics and Kant's intentions. Perhaps there is a limit to how much weight whimsy can ultimately carry. Or maybe it is like an ant, small but capable of performing acts suited to a significantly larger body, more powerful in the swarm than alone. Whimsy demands unexpected shifts in our understanding of the world, a dramatic change in the criteria for judgment. It relies on our capacity to be surprised and, more importantly, on the suppression of our impulse to correct.

Whimsy is not, of course, an aesthetic category exclusive to Yoko Ono. This chapter focuses on Ono's work from the 1960s and 1970s because these texts uniquely and cohesively address the aesthetics of rationality in the United States at mid-century. Ono's utopianism is quintessentially whimsical in its cheeky defiance of cruelty performed by redefining the standards that naturalize state violence. Simultaneously, her "paperwork" offers us the chance to see how the supposedly neutral forms of racial and gender administration might be recognized and even creatively resisted. Yet there are many other examples of whimsy that might serve as illustration.

This is particularly true in conceptualist art, especially in its heyday in the 1950s through the 1970s, which frequently blends a critique of supposedly neutral procedures and the presentation of information with absurdist humor and whimsical surprises. American conceptualism beyond *Grapefruit* often conveys a rational or neutral tone as it explores unconventional forms of consciousness and sociality that might be initially regarded as "irrational." This contrast between a "neutral" tone or form and unexpected "content" allows for conceptualist artists to draw attention to the forms and mechanisms that disappear into banality. The instruction in particular—a form organized around the apparently rational act of giving direction and setting rules—reappears in conceptualist practice as a whimsical device. For much of conceptualist writing and art, laying down rules prompts opportunities for contradiction, particularly the joyful subversion of social norms and exploration of new experiences. For example, in *Funk Lessons* (1982–84) the conceptual artist and philosopher Adrian Piper uses the instructional form of the lesson to explore the racialization of movement as instructor and students "get down and party together." Not too distant from Ono's conceptualist form of the "instruction," the hierarchical format of the lesson is appropriated for nonconformist ends. Piper's and Ono's conceptualist contemporary John Baldessari has also channeled the lesson's absurdist potential. In his 1972 video *Teaching a Plant the Alphabet*, as the title suggests, Baldessari instructs a potted banana plant on the English alphabet. While Baldessari's lesson does not contain the more overt racial "content" of Piper's *Funk Lessons*, how are we to disentangle the disciplinary methods of English language learning from the classroom as a racialized and racializing space? This is to say, while Baldessari's *Teaching a Plant the Alphabet* is not "about" race, its whimsical reinterpretation of the language lesson spurs questions about discipline and social control inherent to conventional education as a colonial and racial system, particularly regarding language instruction. Similarly, in the 1960s, Benjamin Patterson, a Fluxus member, composer, and classically trained bassist, expressed a strong interest in the overlap between art and education, studying social psychology and game theory alongside his experiments in music and art. Exploring this topic in 1966, Patterson writes, "I require that the central function of the artist be a duality of discoverer and educator: discoverer of the varying possibilities for selecting from environment stimuli specific precepts and organizing these into significant perceptions, and concurrently, as an educator, training a public in the ability to perceive in newly discovered patterns."[21] Patterson blends his interests in pedagogy, experimental psychology, and the avant-garde in such works such as *Seminar II: American Studies* which offers unconventional lessons on American injustice, and the iconic *Pond* (1962), which begins with a lesson on how to perform the score and uses wind-up toy frogs to create a spontaneous musical event.[22]

The history of the American avant-garde, particularly conceptualism, is rich with such examples of whimsical artworks. These artworks, consciously or not, create opportunities to understand the administration of daily life as a series of mundane, completely normalized actions that are inseparable from larger movements of racial capitalism, gender normativity, and sexual policing. From Nam June Paik's TV buddhas, to Asco's anarchic satire, to Félix González Torres's silent go-go dancers wiggling in gold speedos in the museum gallery, whimsy is a frequent companion of conceptualism in its critique of systems of domination. Although whimsy is not limited to conceptualism or the avant-garde, these artistic approaches are instructive examples of how to find a world of delight in irrationality. The whimsical asks us to pay attention to aspects of cultural and social life that are typically subordinated or disregarded because of their association with what is irrational, feminine, non-white, childlike, queer, and imaginary. Importantly, as these other examples from conceptual art show, although whimsy is frequently optimistic, it is not acritical.

The Paper Trail of Identity Work

But how to read *Grapefruit*? How do we get a grip on the relationship between aesthetic pleasure, form, and social formation in this text? Ono offers some guidance in her titling, as well as in her use of line breaks, enjambment, imagery, and the sensible presence of a speaker throughout a section of *Grapefruit* titled "Poetry." In other words, many of Ono's instructions can easily be read as "lyrical." For example, "Cloud Piece," which asks the reader to imagine dripping clouds that the reader might bury in their garden. Such pieces feel poetic in their brevity and lineation but also through their evocative imagery, which is highly sensory and suggestive of metaphor and symbolism. As scholars of Ono's work such as Midori Yoshimoto and Alexandra Munroe explain, the poetic aspects of Ono's instructions draw from her study of both English and Japanese literature, including haiku and Zen koan.[23] Like poetry, these instructions suggest that a literal reading is not the most meaningful reading. Also like poetry, they suggest that the figurative ought to be understood as equal to the literal in importance—or perhaps even more important—in both ascribing value and defining reality.

With this invocation of poetry through form and section titling, we might begin to rethink our assumptions about address circulating within the *idea* of the poem, perhaps especially as American poetry came to be dominated by the mid-century lyric form. While in many ways the lyric became the default form in American poetry, its standardization suggesting a kind of universality or neutrality, as Kamran Javadizadeh has written, the lyric has a racial and gender politics.[24] Perhaps unexpectedly, these politics play out *through* the lyric's performances of private expression and individuated interiority rather than despite them. In this way, Javadizadeh argues that the lyric is "a literary form of white innocence."[25] The impressions of intimacy and unmediated access to the lyric speaker's inner life "resonates with whiteness's implicit claims to universality and unmediated identity, whereby to be white in the United States is to be, apparently, without race and without a role in the erasure of whiteness's racialized others."[26] The lyric subject is not merely a hollow container, waiting to be filled by the poet's individual content. Rather, the lyric's very claims to neutrality and transparency are what produce racial meaning.

Through Ono's generative hybridizations of the lyric and conceptualist instruction, we might explore the deceptive "neutrality" of universalizing forms. In *Grapefruit*, we encounter the poetic reinterpretation of a decidedly unlyrical genre—the administrative form and the attendant drudgery of *paperwork*. Identification forms, questionnaires, multiple-choice tests, surveys, and résumés come to play a central role in Ono's poetry in *Grapefruit*. Both lyric and administrative forms concern themselves with the project of giving definition to a speaking subject. Both forms also have the effect of naturalizing the ways that aesthetic form produces racial subjectivities, whether through lyric or paperwork.

In *The Utopia of Rules*, a book dedicated to the unexpectedly interesting topic of bureaucracy, anthropologist David Graeber notes that the use of the term *paperwork* rises sharply and consistently from the mid-1960s to the mid-2010s, corresponding with "the gradual fusion of public and private power into a single entity, rife with rules and regulations whose ultimate purpose is to extract wealth in the form of profits," leading to what he calls the "total bureaucratization of society."[27] Indeed, the Google Ngram for uses of *paperwork* between 1900 and 2019 shows a near vertical ascent between 1970 (the publication year of *Grapefruit*) and 1979 and then a steady rise continuing over the next few decades, like a dependable employee punching in year after year. Graeber argues that the rise of bureaucracy is significant not only because maddening labyrinths of paperwork and triplicate forms (or online forms, nowadays) regulate more and more aspects of daily life but because bureaucracy has expanded "the range and density of social relations that are ultimately regulated by the threat of violence."[28] Graeber's iconic example is police officers, the state's most visible bureaucrats, who spend precious little time preventing violence, as is popularly represented on television, and a great deal of time administrating state violence. As Graeber explains, "Generations of police sociologists have pointed out that only a very small proportion of what police actually do has anything to do with enforcing criminal law—or with criminal matters of any kind. Most of it has to do with regulations, or, to put it slightly more technically, with the scientific application of physical force, or the threat of physical force, to aid in the resolution of administrative problems." In short, "police are bureaucrats with weapons" who "bring the threat of force to bear on situations that would otherwise have nothing to do with it."[29] Graeber offers as example the regulation prohibiting drivers from hanging items—say, dangling a CD—from their rearview mirror, a common enough practice that might lead to a traffic stop, a sudden escalation of a non-situation to a *situation*, and a potentially devastating interruption in one's life (trauma, arrest, even death).[30] Bureaucracy and its mind-numbing aggregation of compliance procedures, typed forms that must be completed, signed, and filed, and standardized cataloguing of information serves to normalize the threat of real violence that enables the functioning of racial capitalism. Another good example of this is immigration policy and enforcement—a form of militarized policing—which will be taken up in relation to Ono's work later in this chapter.

Paperwork blunts the imagination; a fluorescent glaze is cast over the world. What is simply boring and compulsory comes to be mistaken as rational. Paperwork is a non-literature, utilitarian reading that gives you a headache. This makes it all the more interesting that in *Grapefruit*, paperwork is the unlikely source of inspiration for some of the text's most compelling pieces. For example, in the untitled piece beginning "born: Bird year," which is also the first poem to appear in *Grapefruit*'s "Poetry" section, Ono structures this "poem" in the form of a résumé or CV. "born: Bird year" blends the terse informational tone of the curriculum vitae with the lyrical beauty of a nature poem. The CV is a genre of writing that barely registers as writing and certainly not as literature. Rather, it is part of the apparatus of what Adorno bemoaned as a relentlessly administrative world, a rotating cog in the compositional technologies of identity. The piece first offers a brief accounting of (we assume, in the tradition of the lyric) Ono's life up until the present, recalling essential biographical, educational, and professional credentials and ending with an artist's statement. In this piece, the poem takes the shape of an administrative form—a kind of institutional feedback loop in which the respondent anticipates the institutional hail with the expected responses. Of course, Ono's responses are hardly rote. Her professional biography unfolds formally in a more or less expected way, making use of indentation and punctuation to mimic the look of a résumé, but its substance is strange. Ono reports: as a child and adolescent, she collects skies and seaweeds. In early adulthood, she honed her expertise in snails, clouds, and garbage cans, having "graduated many / schools specializing in these subjects." She notes the birth of her grapefruit. Currently, she is a sought-after expert on these significant topics, and her work has even been officially recognized by one of the preeminent avant-gardists of the period, Allan Kaprow, the inventor of the happening. In her attached artist's statement, she highlights her notable works, including *Cut Piece* and *Stone Piece*, although the description is far more evocative than one might find in a cut-and-dry artist's statement. Ono writes that people cut away the parts of her that they did not like until "there was only the stone remained of me"; however, even after this cruel cutting away, these unnamed people wanted more, they "wanted to know what it's like in the stone."[31] The résumé ends with a P.S.: "If the butterflies in your stomach die, send / yellow death announcements to your friends."[32]

"born: Bird Year" is a critique of the transformation of a life into information. The artist's statement and postscript convey a biting criticism of the life document that coerces people into standardized forms of reductive self-representation. These acts of writing naturalize mechanisms of exploitation and extraction as simply part of the potential employee's identity and linear life history. The image of people who cut away the parts of Ono that they did not like suggests both the immediate context of the CV, which demands a trimmed revelation of the self, tailored to the desires of the prospective employer, but also a larger comment on the compulsion to reveal, which over time cuts away at something precious. The cutting is a clear reference to Ono's well-known work *Cut Piece*, in which Ono arrived at a venue wearing her best clothes, kneeled on stage in front of a pair of scissors, and invited the audience to cut pieces from her clothing while she sat as motionless and unreactive as possible. Scholars have interpreted Ono's *Cut Piece* as both a performance of Buddhist pacifism and a gesture of feminist refusal.[33] However, in "born: Bird Year," an additional laminate of meaning is suggested. Even as Ono courageously explores the possibility of what might emerge in her surrender of the surface, it is not enough. It is not the passivity of surrender that is desired by her audience but Ono's active production of information—the revelation of "what it's like in the stone." This is what she will not give. The desire to possess that information propels the violence against her by the audience—an enforcement of the requirement to reveal. In the melancholic postscript, something beautiful and fragile is at risk, those butterflies that signal excited anticipation, as well as connection to the natural world of seaweed and sky. In the process of producing the legible self, something precious may be destroyed.

It goes without saying that the genre of the administrative form or identification document differs from the lyric in many ways.[34] Not least, the lyric form explores the practice of expression (of ideas or feelings), and (to generalize) we often judge the success or authenticity of lyric expression by its degree of uniqueness. The administrative form, to the contrary, judges the truthfulness or the success of the writing by how closely responses align with what the institution or organization already knows, that is, how closely the answers match existing types of information. Choose one or more. M / F? White, Black, Asian or Pacific Islander, Non-Hispanic Latino? Sedentary, Somewhat Active, Active, Very

Active? However, despite these obvious differences, the administrative form works surprisingly well as the template of a poem, as we can see in "born: Bird Year."[35]

In its lyric responses to the conventions of the CV, "born: Bird Year" also incites discussion of worker identity and legibility. After all, this is the purpose of the genre, to present the picture of a (hopefully) ideal worker, narrating past achievements in an argument for one's value within a labor market. Early in her avant-garde career, Ono often fought for recognition in an avant-garde that, despite its often leftist politics, continued to be dominated by white men. In light of this struggle to be seen as a legitimate artist, the CV can be read as a wry demonstration of her validity as an artist, a performance that speaks to constantly having to present her credentials. In the context of the mid-twentieth-century United States, Ono's lyric CV must also be considered in relation to the overdetermined racial and gendered meanings attached to labor as it was impacted by flows and stoppages of global migration. Ono came from an aristocratic family, and her own immigration experience was more privileged than most. She spent her early childhood in the United States due to her father's banking business there.[36] Later, his leadership role at America's Bank of Tokyo brought the family to Scarsdale, New York, in 1952, leading Ono to attend Sarah Lawrence College and then abscond, newly eloped, with her first husband, pianist and composer Toshi Ichiyanagi, to join the New York avant-garde in 1955.[37] Although in the 1970s, Ono and John Lennon fought a high-profile deportation case prompted by their antiwar activism, Ono was overall less vulnerable to immigration policies and enforcement than most other non-white immigrants in this mid-twentieth-century period.[38] However, although Ono had personal access to resources that gave her some protection, her use of administrative genres, particularly as they prompt for information about race, work history, and health, invites us to read these administrative poems in relation to a larger history of US immigration history and policing, particularly as it relates to Asian women's immigration.

As historian Mae Ngai has shown, immigration law and policy, shaped by relations of labor and capital, are a means of producing new forms of racial difference.[39] Since the Page Act of 1875, the first racially restrictive immigration law that prohibited the immigration of most East

Asian women to the United States, particularly Chinese women, these laws have always revolved upon the racialized and gendered desirability of certain kinds of labor as they intersect (in at times contradictory ways) with racial capitalism and white supremacist, cisheteropatriarchal ideals of national identity. The use of immigration law as a racist tool for shaping population is perhaps most obvious in the establishment of the Johnson-Reed Act of 1924, which ended open immigration from Europe and installed a quota system limiting the number of people who could immigrate from specific countries. Not surprisingly, these quotas were determined in accordance with the desirability of the racialized groups associated with each country. With the Immigration and Naturalization Act of 1965, an explicit racial quota system was disposed of, and a new system of equal quotas was introduced in which each country was given the same admissions cap. While presenting itself as liberalism's egalitarian answer to the crude racism of previous quotas based on race and nation, the equal distribution of "opportunity" naturalized the idea of a quota system, as Ngai writes. The normalization of immigration quotas by stripping them of their explicitly racist features and making them "equal" obscured the ways that racial capitalism and white settler colonialism affects flows of migration while affirming liberal multiculturalism's fantasies of the United States as a level playing field of opportunity—an image that was globally strategic for supporting American nationalism and international power (including wars in Southeast Asia and anti-communist government intervention in the decolonizing world) during the Cold War era. The immigration reforms of the 1950s and 1960s also established preferences for family-based and occupational immigration, offering a "neutral" and "rational" market-driven justification for the preference of some groups over others compatible with an emerging neoliberal multiculturalism, wherein there is no fairer arbitrator than the market.[40] However, not all labor is equally valued, and race and gender were (and continue to be) significant means by which labor could be categorized and moved according to capitalist value.

Within the form of the CV, one articulates their suitability as a worker for a particular career—in this case, artist. The standardization of the self and of a life takes place in this bureaucratic writing that is inherently coercive, forms of self-presentation designed to make a person more pliable to the needs of racial capitalism. Life documents such as the CV naturalize the racialization and gendering of different forms of labor while obscuring the ways that the standardization of identity supports racial capitalism. Yet Ono's self-articulation within this standard form is hardly a full capitulation to forced forms of self-representation. Ono's responses are beautiful in their indifference to usefulness, their dwelling in the cool, fecund imagery of seaweed, snails, clouds, garbage cans, and skies—conjuring a sense of quiet drift, of what is abandoned to its own slow processes of transformation and decay. This turn to the inevitable rhythms of decomposition, the oblique persistence of the mute animal, and the ubiquity of weather contrasts with the fast-paced productivity and display of extractable value expected in such a document. Ono's poetic rendering of the CV embraces this strange beauty, rejecting coerced self-presentation as usable data.

Reading "born: Bird Year" as an obfuscation of the legibility desired by the bureaucracies of transnational racial capitalism also raises the specter of Asian "inscrutability" or the anxiety over dangerously "unreadable" Asian bodies, speech, and culture. Asian American studies has thoroughly explored the "perpetual foreignness" assigned to Asian Americans and the idea that Asians and Asian Americans are menacingly opaque to (white) interpretation, unassimilability threatening the imperforate wholeness of the nation.[41] Leslie Bow, for instance, has written on Ono as a figure perceived through stereotypes of Asian deception and cunning. Bow shows that Ono's vilification as a "foreigner" and "Dragon Lady" who broke up the Beatles is connected to larger narratives of Asian women's sexuality, writing, "Ono's notoriety was thus intrinsically tied to her perceived talent at both sexual and psychological seduction" that was a "political seduction as well—a seduction away from bourgeois modes of perception and from the separation of art from everyday life."[42] The viciousness of attacks against Ono in popular culture reveals a more insidious racial and gender anxiety regarding Asian women's "ability to corrupt men's identification with other men, undermining allegiance to the group or nation" by being difficult to interpret.[43]

While on the one hand, anti-Asian and sexist stereotypes cast Asian and Asian American women as untrustworthy in their inscrutability, on the flipside of what Homi Bhabha has described as the duality of desire and disgust structural to racial fetishism and stereotype, Asian women also have been understood as malleable and passive, that is, as the stereotype of the submissive Asian woman.[44] As Vivian Huang recounts, inscrutability and passivity are dual concepts that link Asian female bodies to the colonial conquest of Asian land and resources:

> The bodies of Asian women are overdetermined by xenophobic and colonial methods of conquest, where the feminized body is aligned with land and natural resources, as part of the fulfillment of manifest destiny. The metaphorical and material practice of penetration (of body, land, and culture) becomes not a discourse about permission to enter (presuming a code of hospitality that precedes the encounter) but rather of manifest entitlement, patriarchal benevolence, and missions to civilize. Meanwhile, women historically have been exempt from receiving hospitality, including access to naturalization or citizenship as with gendered exclusions from the U.S. such as the Page Law of 1975 (which effectively barred the immigration of Chinese and Japanese women, arguing all were prostitutes and therefore morally threatening to the nation).[45]

While racist stereotypes have figured Asian women as incapable of saying "No," Huang points out that the inability to say "Yes," as part of a counter-strategy to undo the harm of such representations, can become a restrictive prohibition. The CV as a poetic form brings to the surface the complex, often contradictory, racial and gender politics of the immigrant's legibility within the long history of US imperialism in Asia and the needs of racial capitalism. This negotiation of coercive self-representation suggests a resistant praxis that is more complex than a simple binary of surrender versus agency. The invocation of paperwork in Ono's literary experiments are acts of wit that suggest connections between artistic "works on paper" and bureaucratic paperwork, making visible the labor that goes into both kinds of work.

In practice, administrative forms and documents inspire tedium or anxiety far more often than they invoke the beautiful. I am not attempting to recuperate these acts of self-representation, which are oppressively dull and even deadly. Rather, I argue that administrative genres actively shape us as racialized, gendered, sexual, and able-bodied or disabled subjects. However, through the whimsical appropriation of the administrative form (altering the criteria of judgment), readers can recognize this administration of identity and begin to imagine new ways of self-expression and self-presentation that might—at least momentarily—undo those managerial systems. As in the beauty judgment, there is an aspect of universality to the administrative form that is produced through normed agreement. This universality is compulsory, coercing the subject into writing themselves into a certain kind of human form. These administrative poems appropriate the power of compulsory self-documentation by shifting the criteria for the responses. The answer becomes an opportunity of imaginative invention rather than a recitation of conventional subjectivities. Let us not forget that the curriculum vitae is literarily the "course of one's life" or one's "life's work." It is an administrative genre that organizes and defines a life both via the "work" that it has accomplished within a capitalist system of value and while highlighting the ways in which "life" is nurtured and cultivated through valued work. In Ono's "born: Bird year," we can see how the notion of identity work as life's work is a literary project.

Choose One of the Following

Toward the end of the "Poetry" section, Ono includes "Questionnaire," a series of forms, true/false, and multiple-choice tests, which could be filled out by the reader if desired. Like "born: Bird Year," this is a poem built using administrative forms. In "Questionnaire," Ono begins with a familiar type of short-answer biographical form that one might encounter in any number of bureaucratic situations. This is the basic information that might be collected by schools, hospitals or doctors' offices, prisons, immigration services, or the DMV. The form asks the respondent for biographical and physical information such as their name, address, sex, height, weight, and occupation, reminiscent of the "Synopsis" form that opens the book. The "Questionnaire" also asks the respondent to provide their "Colour," suggesting race, as well as the respondent's "Disease" and "Physical Peculiarities," categories that resonate with the history of US immigration administration. The questionnaire recalls the kinds of questions one might find on an immigration form, such as an alien registration form or an application for an immigrant visa, as well as the racialized anxiety over immigration as a site of contagion and a threat to the purity and superiority of whiteness (as a criterion of citizenship). This is an anxiety particularly relevant to histories of Asian immigration to the United States and the racist stereotypes embedded in policy, enforcement, and popular culture.[46] US immigration policy cultivates a certain type of (white) life through the regulation, containment, exclusion, and disciplining of non-white transnational bodies. Historically, US immigration policies have been hypervigilant apparatuses of racist anxiety that link "health" to racial whiteness, blurring concepts of racial and hygienic purity.

Following this identification form is a true/false quiz, a testing genre used to confirm and reinforce the existing truths of the world, disenchanting participants of fantasies and falsehoods through a rigid binary of fact and non-fact. As one might expect at this point, Ono's true/false quiz does not abide by normative expectations of what is "obviously" untrue but offers a series of poetic statements that trouble the empirical. For example, "Teeth and bones are solid form of cloud," or "Paper is marble cut so thin it has become soft. (Make marble out of toilet paper.)"[47] In this piece, too, we can see that the social and political are not excluded from a poetic experiment that embraces the absurd. For example, "The structure of the American jury system is taken from the chance music operation by John Cage. (The noted Judge Connolly is said to have said 'all verdicts are beautiful'.)," which prompts the reader to consider the deadly arbitrariness of the ultra-rational American criminal justice system.[48] The statement "Mt. Fuji, whose colour is blue and white from the distance and volcano red when you go near, is a carefully planned modern Japanese project built to attract American tourists," is made more complex in the context of the postwar presence of US state and commercial power in Japan, Japanese student and New Left movements of the 1960s, and the Anpo protests of 1959–60 and 1970 that sought the end of the United States-Japan Security Treaty, which enables the maintenance of US military bases on Japanese soil.[49] Even the statement "The word 'manila envelope' comes from a deeply-rooted racial prejudice," which could be read as a joke about oversensitivity to racial signifiers, actually has a ring of truth about it in that manila envelopes were originally made from abaca, or Manila hemp, a plant native to the Philippines that was cultivated by the Dutch in the Dutch East Indies and the United States in Central America to make fabric and rope. One might observe that the material that enabled an earlier stage of colonial power by providing the cordage necessary for managing a colony across the ocean, later evolved to support the bureaucratic functioning of a range of state and corporate entities, an innocuous beige container for the information needed to administer a military, a corporation, or a country.

In the final section of "Questionnaire," the reader encounters a multiple-choice test that continues the mischievous probing of reality found throughout "Questionnaire." The first question, titled "Yellow Talk," most explicitly addresses questions of racialization and social categorization by using the racial signifier "yellow" and then offering four quotes for the reader to choose from attributed to doctors with East Asian family names:

a) All colours are imaginary except yellow. Yellow is the colour Of sun at its height. Other colours are shades of yellow in Varying degrees which have been given different names, as if Each of them exist independently, purely for idealogical [sic] Purposes.—Dr. Song
b) Yellow is the only imaginary color.—Dr. Suzuki
c) All colours have yellow in it.—Dr. Lee
d) All colours are imaginary.—Dr. Kato

"Yellow Talk" links the aesthetic and the social production of meaning through the weighted signifier "yellow." Throughout the administrative form pieces in *Grapefruit*, including the opening "Synopsis," Ono has used the term *color* at moments when the word "race" could easily be substituted. Yet "colour" leaves ambiguity within this whimsical text—perhaps Ono *does* intend readers to describe their color in a literal, technical way, the way a painter might deliberate on their color choices in a self-portrait (here I am also thinking of Byron Kim's paintings series *Synecdoche*, discussed in the next chapter). Notably, almost all the answer choices in "Yellow Talk" concern the imaginary in some way, except for answer choice c), which reads both as a possible statement on color theory or (pseudoscientific) racial theory. In these choices, racial meaning is positioned as a product of imagination that directly impacts reality. Each answer choice makes a claim to the "truth" while the reader is tasked with proving their mastered knowledge by selecting the fact among fictions. This points the reader back toward the structure of the test itself as a producer of reality and the reader's participation in the assessment as an important part of determining what is rational and true (or untrue). However, given the absurdity of the tests and the answer choices, there is no objectively "correct" answer. The choice can only reveal information about the reader and their place in the world, serving as jumping-off points for further inquiry and reflection, rather than yielding empirical truth. In many ways, the reader is the true "subject" of the test, a reading amplified by the presence of the identification form at the beginning of "Questionnaire." The purpose of these forms and quizzes is not necessarily for the reader to demonstrate their abilities but to produce information about themselves for some unknown purpose, or perhaps no purpose at all, submitted for analysis by an unidentified entity.

"Questionnaire" is a perfect example of how the aesthetic and nonaesthetic can entangle in the act of judgment. The ground of what makes up the world, including social definitions such as the meaning and parameters of race, are opened for readerly play. While formally, the "Questionnaire" blends recognizable genres associated with determined meaning—such as administrative forms and fixed-answer tests—the content of this poem confounds a reader's attempts to select a "correct" answer. The criteria for judgment must shift. Identification forms and tests are tools used for sorting people and collecting information that can be used to extrapolate meaning, rank individuals, identify and standardize differences, and create policy. Although "Questionnaire" is absurd, delightful, and witty—that is, whimsical—the availability of political and social interpretations suggests that *Grapefruit* is not insensitive to the stakes of its hybrid genres. Rather than a dismissal of, or escape from, the insipid tyranny of administration, the turn to aesthetic pleasure enables critique and creates imaginative spaces to dream up alternate realities.

Why Violence?

Ono's paperwork poems explore the relationship between aesthetic judgment and the administration of race and other social formations.

Ono's 1966 film *Film No. 4*, also known as *Bottoms*, and her essay "On Film," which appears in *Grapefruit*, further demonstrate how whimsy intervenes in the disciplinary rationality of the state. *Film No. 4 (Bottoms)* is a sterling example of truth in advertising; this is indeed a film about peoples' bottoms. Ono's essay "On Film" explains her approach to the subject, going beyond the scope of the film itself to offer trenchant perspectives on gender, the body, and state violence. In the film and accompanying essay, whimsy helps us reconsider the associations between rationality and the gendered body. Rather than frame the body in terms of our ability to control it or execute tasks, in short, the body's *effectiveness*, Ono lingers in the pleasures of the body's *disobedience*, its vulnerability, and its errant unpredictability out of sync with gendered efficiency.

In "On Film," Ono writes:

> I wonder why men can get serious at all. They have this delicate long thing hanging outside their bodies, which goes up and down by its own will. . . . the inconsistency of it, like carrying a chance alarm or something. If I were a man I would always be laughing at myself. Humour is probably something the male of the species discovered through their own anatomy. But men are so serious. Why? Why violence?[50]

Before digging into an analysis of this passage, I want to acknowledge the ways that this representation of the penis as inherently male suggests a dated and harmful genital essentialism. We all owe a debt of gratitude to the blossoming of trans* frameworks of analysis, in the work of Susan Stryker, Paisley Currah, C. Riley Snorton, Jian Chen, Marquis Bey, and Che Gossett, to name only a few. This work has significantly altered how we think about the relationship between sex, gender, and the body. However, perhaps it is also possible to read a gender critique into Ono's staged confusion. In such a reading, Ono's portrayal of the penis as vulnerable and fluctuant undermines the idea that violent masculinity is "natural" because it can be found in the biological truth of the body, suggesting, on the contrary, that masculine violence is a willful disavowal of the body as a source of amusement, gentleness, and play, a perspective that contradicts the biological determinism of conventional masculinity. We might also read this passage as being in conversation with the feminist theorizing of the late 1960s and early 1970s, as in the work of Shulamith Firestone in *The Dialectic of Sex* (1970) or Kate Millett's *Sexual Politics* (1970).[51] Both these bestselling feminist texts explore psychoanalysis and its fixation with genitals (particularly the penis) as an agent of patriarchal oppression.[52] In questioning the "reality" of the male body, this passage suggests that gender and sex normativity might be revised through pleasurable experiences, such as laughter.

This reading is complemented by Ono's feminist writings elsewhere, for example her 1972 *New York Times* piece "The Feminization of Society." In this article, Ono argues that since "in the last two thousand years, men have repeatedly shown us failure in their method of running the world," we ought to move toward a total feminization of society. By this she means, "We can change with feminine intelligence and awareness, into a basically organic, noncompetitive society that is based on love rather than reasoning. The result will be balance, peace and contentment. We can evolve rather than revolt, come together rather than claim independence and feel rather than think. These are the characteristics that are considered feminine and that men despise in women. But have men done so well by avoiding the development of these characteristics within themselves?"[53] It feels safe to assume that the answer to this last question is a definite "No." It is possible to read Ono's proposal for "female revolution" as a turn not toward essentialism but toward pleasure as a means of re-gendering the body and society.[54] While these writings continue to rely on the language of the gender binary, they also suggest that gender is changeable and that societal transformation could be incited by pleasure by turning to "love rather than reasoning."

Returning to "On Film," there is certainly a mischievous pleasure in imagining the "delicate" penis as an occasion for mirth rather than a serious symbol of power. However, I am less interested in the symbolic inversion deployed here (the effects of which seem obvious) than the passage's staging of the whimsical. Read alongside "The Feminization of Society," the pleasure of the passage can be interpreted as having a meaningful political valence. The whimsical turn works as a compact hinge, structuring and mobilizing the joint between the gendering of the body and the gendering of structural violence. The gendered body made whimsical—a surprising redefinition of the criteria of judgment—calls into question what we have "agreed" is true about the body, gender politics, and the necessity of warfare. Similarly, the volta in this paragraph—"But men are so serious. Why? Why violence?"—questions the self-evidence of masculine rational violence. Starting by challenging the seriousness of the body gendered male, Ono goes on to question the naturalized relationship between seriousness and violence. Why is militarized state violence assumed to be a rational necessity while we scoff at peace as naïve and impractical? In the context of the American war in Vietnam, which Ono was famously against, this interrogation of gender and violence can be read as part of a larger critique of American militarism as essentially rational. The question "Why violence?" asks the reader to examine their assumptions about the inevitability of violence, particularly as its normalization coincides with a hierarchical gender binary and, as we shall see, colonialism and imperialism.

Imagining the masculine-gendered body as a site of humor and errancy rather than violence, the text reimagines the gendered, sexed body through whimsy. The unpredictability of arousal and the buffooning mechanics of the penis going "up and down by its own will" like a "chance alarm clock" recalls slapstick comedy rather than cool control. This is in line with the "incongruity theory" of humor, which argues that we laugh when we find something out of place. The body, perhaps especially the sexual or vulgar body, is pleasurable and funny because it constantly upsets our expectations; it is always out of place, an absurd iteration of a gendered and sexual ideal, irrational. One might consider Ono's chaotic and pleasurable framing of the body in contrast to the docile body classically theorized in Foucault's *Discipline and Punish* through the figure of the soldier:

> By the late eighteenth century, the soldier has become something that can be made; out of a formless clay, an inapt body, the machine required can be constructed; posture is gradually corrected; a calculated constraint runs slowly through each part of the body, mastering it, making it pliable, ready at all times, turning silently into the automatism of habit.[55]

If, as Foucault goes on to argue, the modern body depends on our ability to coerce, manipulate, and correct our body's fluctuating, inconsistent nature, a sort of material rationality, then this text offers the cockamamie, desiring body as a remedy. Taking pleasure in the body's whimsical unpredictability serves as a counter-politics to disciplinary rigor and rational control.

Directly following her critique that "men are so serious," Ono continues: "Why hatred? Why war? If people want to make war, they should make a colour war, and paint each others city up during the night in pinks and greens. Men have an unusual talent for making a bore out of everything they touch. Art, painting, sculpture, like who wants a cast-iron woman, for instance."[56] As Ono questions the rationality of making war by questioning war's aesthetic value, she raises the stakes of aesthetic judgment—or rather draws our attention to stakes that are already much higher than we might realize. Here, Ono seems to allude to the Vietnam War as a race war (a "colour war"), perhaps referring to anti-colonial critiques of the Vietnam War as a war with imperialist and neocolonial objectives inseparable from white supremacy. Ono uses sly homonymic play—toggling between racial color and pigment (as in the paperwork poems)—suggesting a shift in values away from racial domination toward aesthetic pleasure, marking aesthetic pleasure as opposite to the logic and values that inform American war-making.

War, like a cast-iron woman (a gendered yet unerotic and unchanging body), fails aesthetically in that it fails to conjure delight in the viewer. Again, the text rejects rigid embodiment for a more capricious scene of pleasure. If there *must* be a war for no reason, why not make it beautiful and funny—the image of "soldiers" sneaking into the enemy's city under the cover of night for a bit of extravagant vandalism, perhaps an improvement on the current state of things, bringing vibrant pinks and greens into an urban landscape dominated by browns and grays. Imagine bubblegum-colored skyscrapers and verdant green bridges crisscrossing the urban landscape. This fantasy war is reminiscent of a conceptualist event, happening, or performance-art piece from this period, such as we might find in Yayoi Kusama's work especially.[57] The essay offers aesthetic pleasure as an alternative to violence and, in fact, the truly rational action that corrects the deadly absurdism of war.

More darkly, Ono's "colour war" signals the brutal racial politics that shaped the US government's modus operandi in the war in Vietnam. As Yến Lê Espiritu writes:

American imperialists bolstered their drive into Vietnam with technologies of racialization that depicted United States military intervention as a blessing—one that would bring progress, well-being, and salvation to a people deemed racially, culturally, and even morally inferior. These technologies of racialization formally justified and codified the subordination of the Vietnamese, creating a juridical and cultural space for them as a separate category of beings. This racialization simultaneously helped rationalize and buttress the power of 'civilized' white men, who shouldered the 'white man's burden' of protecting the weak and dispensing justice.[58]

In this paradigm described by Espiritu, American military violence is an unfortunate necessity in instantiating a more just world, what Mimi Thi Nguyen theorizes as the "gift of freedom."[59] American superiority is produced through nationalist ideologies in which the United States claims to strategically utilize violence to bring about a more just and democratic world. Such narratives of a better world through American military violence are inextricable from national projects of white supremacy, as Espiritu points out. As Christian Appy has argued, American military violence in Vietnam was rationalized as a tragic yet unavoidable condition of democracy and freedom. Military violence was portrayed as a common good executed in the interest of building a better world, not only for the United States but also for Christian South Vietnamese people. In reality, this savior narrative was always a fabrication in service of American Cold War politics. Violence suffered by the Vietnamese is figured as unfortunate collateral damage, secondary to the loss or injury of (white) American lives.[60] Perversely, the American war in Vietnam is figured as an American "national trauma," as Sylvia Chong explains, which "imagines the U.S. nation-state as wounded like the soldiers it sent to war, but also calls upon the discourses of forgiveness and redemption to heal the nation of its psychological malaise."[61] Thus, the violence inflicted through war, including bombings, napalm, forced removal, abduction, economic devastation, and mass death, becomes secondary to the more urgent rending of the national (read: masculine, white) psyche and American global power. Chong, like Ono, traces a connection between imperialist violence and heteropatriarchal masculinity in American gender and racial fantasies. In both examples, the neurotic inability to "perform," that is, the errancy of the masculine body, is "treated" through acts of rational violence. When Ono imagines a "colour war" as an antidote to military violence, she marshals irrationality against the violence of white masculinist sanity.

Sign Here, Please.

While "On Film" offers a fascinating inquiry in the gendering of war and rationality, the primary subject of Ono's essay is ostensibly her *Film No. 4 (Bottoms)*.[62] The premise of the film is simple. The camera captures a series of slowly walking nude bottoms in tight close-up. Shot in grainy black-and-white, the framing of the bottoms is the same in every shot, with the natural creases of the body often serving to segment the screen into a quartered, inexact grid.[63] Through the minimalism of *Bottoms*, Ono explains that she wanted to show that "anybody can be a director," fulfilling conceptualist principles that art requires neither craft nor skill.[64] *Bottoms* also serves the purpose of unconventionally documenting "the London scene."[65] Ono expresses the hope that in the future viewers would view the film and "see a sudden swarm of exposed bottoms. . . . And I hope that they would see that the 60's was not only the age of achievements, but of laughter."[66] *Bottoms*, as well as Ono's discussion of it, emphasizes laughter over progress, abstraction over traditional portraiture in a visual ode to the body as a scene of amusement and captivating difference. In the film, Ono conducts an army of soft, nude bottoms marching against the atrocity of war.

The unconventional portraiture in *Bottoms* asks us to think about what differentiates each of these bottoms as an individual. While there are certainly cultural standards for judging the aesthetic or erotic value of bottoms, as well as moral judgments associated with certain kinds of bottoms, (too big or small, muscled or un-muscled, racialization of bottoms, etc.), the bottom is not generally the main bodily feature used to identify others. Ono is in a sense subbing out the face—the traditional object of the filmic close-up and individuation in general—for the bottom, inverting the common criteria we typically use to identify, categorize, and judge other people. In doing so, the film asks us to reconsider the criteria that underpins our aesthetic methods of categorical identification.

As other critics of *Bottoms* have pointed out, while the repetitious series of bottoms can quickly become more tedious than titillating to watch, the bottoms parade also encourages the viewer to become unexpectedly detail-oriented as the eye seeks out ways of differentiating one bottom from another and, surprisingly, finds these bland shots full of variable minutia. In describing his experience of viewing the film, critic Scott MacDonald writes:

> Because Ono's structuring of the visuals is rigorously serial, *No. 4 (Bottoms)* is reminiscent of Muybridge's motion studies.... What we realize from seeing these bottoms, and inevitably comparing them with one another—with our idea of 'bottom'—is both obvious and startling. Not only are people's bottoms remarkably varied in their shape, coloring, and texture, but no two bottoms move in the same way. And most surprisingly (for me), none of the hundreds of buttocks we see is a precisely 'correct' bottom as 'bottom' is defined by the fashion and advertising industries and by conventional film and television. For me, watching *No. 4 (Bottoms)* was a release from self-consciousness; it was as if I realized, for the first time, that my bottom is OK and so is yours—that bottoms are just bottoms, usually a little droopy, often hairy or lined, sometimes blemished ... but endlessly distinctive and entertaining.[67]

MacDonald's body-affirming reading of *Bottoms* points to the lack of an official taxonomy or mainstream nomenclature of the bottom, while also highlighting a near infinite range of interesting differences that become visible without a clear framework for categorization or understanding.

On the political aspirations of *Bottoms*, Ono writes that the film is "like an aimless petition signed by people with their anuses. Next time we wish to make an appeal, we should send this film as the signature list."[68] This unconventional signature, on one level, may be read either as a ribald expression of the right to petition the government or as its opposite, a critique of the efficacy of traditional democratic methods (in that we might as well sign with our bottoms for all the good it will do). However, if we take seriously Ono's criticism of the serious and her turn toward whimsy and delight, then the anal signatures on the petition may be something more than a rude gesture toward conventional politics. Rather, I interpret it as a political fantasy in which the terms of citizenship, political participation, and individuality are revised at the most basic level.

I might point out that "bottom" is a rather cute way to refer to this part of the anatomy, as opposed to more clinical or sexualized terms. *Bottom* is the term one might expect to use with children or when being circumspect. Syllabically, the symmetrical assonance of "bot-tom" emulates the body part's rounded bilateral symmetry, which is a bit precious in its mimicry. Sianne Ngai has written that the aesthetic category of the "cute" is both an "aesthetic of powerlessness" that dramatizes aggression toward helpless things but also reflects a desire for an intimate merger with the other.[69] In Ono's film and her essay on it, we see both aspects of the cute activated. The images of "droopy," passive bottoms that inspire feelings of tender generosity in MacDonald become aggressive in their swarm formation. In keeping with Ngai's definition, the cute is characterized not only by its passivity and tendency toward formlessness but also, unexpectedly, by its capacity for aggression (as in a swarm). Ono's reference to the collective of bottoms as a "swarm" teases anxieties over mass movements of the 1960s. The fear that social justice movements fighting against racism, sexism, homophobia, capitalism, war, and imperialism might "swarm" and overpower the status quo mingles in the playfulness and humor in the image of a swarm of bottoms. In establishing the formal criteria of the cute, Ngai argues that "realist verisimilitude and formal precision tend to work against or even nullify cuteness, which becomes most pronounced in objects with simple round contours and little or no ornamentation or detail. By this logic, the epitome of the cute would be an undifferentiated blob or soft doughy matter."[70] Accordingly, the bottom is potentially the cutest aspect of human anatomy. While any part of the human, including the bottom, may be represented in the sharp drama of high contrast and angularity—Robert Mapplethorpe's photographs would be a quintessential example of this—Ono's *Bottoms* lingers in the body's capacity for softness, blurriness, and stippled differentiation.

In "On Film," Ono connects this "swarm" of bottoms directly to the anti-war movement. She writes that ideally, *Film No. 4* would be the prototype for a film project that would capture a smiling image of every person in the world. Perhaps, Ono muses, people could submit their photographs to the local post office, the postal system being a favored means for the conceptual democratization of art in this era. This film would expand at a nearly constant rate as new people were born; it would become so long that no one would be able to watch it all at once, so it would have to be stored in libraries. Ono imagines the ultimate usurpation of the director as auteur or corporate Hollywood filmmaker. The film depends entirely on the cooperation between people across the globe and their desire to connect with each other through artistic collaboration. Ono conceives of this film as art and artmaking on demand as part of a global sociality. But as elsewhere in *Grapefruit*, this whimsical fantasy of collective filmmaking returns us to its exigent violence: "We can also arrange it with a television network so that whenever you want to see faces of a particular location in the world, all you have to do is to press a button and there it is. This way, if Johnson wants see what sort of people he killed in Vietnam that day, he only has to turn the channel. Before this you were just part of a figure in the newspapers, but after this you become a smiling face."[71] The passage leads the reader through an amusing reverie into an unexpected gut punch, keeping a straight face the whole time.

Ono's "aimless," mirthful, anti-achievement politics joins anal perversity with a wholesome smile politics. The text seems to dismiss the differences between the profanity of the anal signature and the positivity of the smile, instead suggesting that the two are interchangeable sites of human expressiveness. However, I do not read this essay as proposing that the smile will interrupt the cycle of violence, disturbing the consciences of world leaders like Lyndon B. Johnson who tally each dead smile as another item in the mathematics of winning and losing. Far from offering a humanist accounting of the smile as excruciating evidence of war's brutality, this vision of what we might call Smile TV suggests that humanization and individuation are totally compatible with the perpetuation of state-sponsored violence.

The hypothetical faces in Ono's Smile TV are uncanny because we are used to thinking of the war dead in their moments of obliteration—the peak of their suffering. Suffering, as Hartman and Chong show, can be repurposed easily to serve white supremacist and imperialist projects, the pain re-signified in its representational circulation. But the text does not seem interested in representing such pain. A smile can be ecstatic, but more often it is mundane, perhaps noted but not notable. Both the smile and the anus are miniature dramas of delight; although ordinary, they can interrupt and undo the viewer. At times, we cannot look away from their shocking idiosyncrasies, their tender, prosaic eros, or otherwise, we feel compelled to look away from their too-embarrassing vulnerability, breaking from an encounter with genuineness.

The fantasies of the smile film and the *Bottoms* petition do not rely on the rationality of persuasiveness to convince immoral leaders to change their actions (the old chestnut that moral arguments will always fail to convince those without morality seems relevant here); rather, it relies on the aesthetic pleasures available in these bodily sites to shift the reader/viewer's criteria for a rational world. In imagining the smiling faces of every person in the world, Ono is imagining the simultaneous, global potential for relational pleasure. This smile is as open as the nude, blemished, ambulating bottom. The smile doesn't promise anything, it doesn't change anything, perhaps it doesn't mean anything at all. Rather, the smile is a prompt to see what will happen between people. Like most utopians, Ono is vague about what the world she wants might look like, beyond that it is peaceful and loving. As José Esteban Muñoz argues, "Utopia is not prescriptive; it renders potential blueprints of a world not quite here, a horizon of possibility, not a fixed schema. It is productive to think about utopia as flux, a temporal disorganization, as a moment when the here and the now is transcended by a *then* and a *there* that could be and indeed should be."[72] A swarm of smiles and bottoms might be such a horizon.

In this reading, Ono's *Bottoms* and Smile TV are anti-war petitions that would land on the desks of indifferent officials on their way to the waste basket. Not only are most of the signatories assumedly noncitizens, but many of them are already dead. What demands are they in a position to make? This is more paperwork. The bottom and the smile become conceptual forms of writing. But like the anti-achievement celebration of human difference that we find in *Film No. 4 (Bottoms)*—or the paperwork poems to be found in *Grapefruit*—Ono's invocation of the form reworks oppressive procedures of subjection and address. The smile and the anus are asking for something—they have a voice, but LBJ cannot hear it or understand it, and he does not care to. But someone else might hear them. The petitions are not really for the American president or any other government official. They are for the world that would take their place.

Ono's smiles veer dangerously close to liberalism's vaporous hopes and prayers, wishing that the intolerable violence might disappear while at the same time seemingly unable to imagine a society that does not require violence as its fundamental organizing principle. But the crucial difference between liberalism's fragile universalism and the smiles and bottoms is that the latter asks us to radically alter the terms of the world while liberalism asserts that we need only produce more of the same. I ask you, which is more impractical? Although I suppose the answer to this question depends on what you would like to achieve.

Whimsy is a way of thinking about how experimentations in form can produce profound changes in the criteria of aesthetic judgment, altering our sense of the given. Aesthetic experimentation is not separate from the imaginative work required to create new ways of being in the world—or a new world altogether. Whimsy is a challenge to the racial and gendered management of life and the rationality of domination and violence. However, as I will explore in the next chapter, the experimental, the new, and the avant-garde are not liberatory by default. Experimentalism is easily recruited to breathe fresh life into the zombified status quo or to intensify violence and oppression in new, more agile forms. To paraphrase Muñoz, it is clear that the world we want is not here yet.[73] We still have to imagine it—and imagination is Yoko Ono's medium of choice.

3

Pure Color

It was pointed out to me as an art student, years and years ago, that art is like a coin. It has a heads and a tail. On the one side of that coin is sensibility and on the other side of that coin is plasticity. It was years later that I developed a better understanding of the word sensibility. What we are talking about is the ability to feel. If we're artists I have to have a way of structuring that feeling. This is why when people ask me my definition of art—do you know what I tell them?—structured feelings. We have the feelings about something and we have to find a way of giving that feeling a structure. That's where the plasticity comes in. The plasticity is the act of making. So, between sensibility and plasticity, we form and we make something out of who we are.
—Jack Whitten

A superlative inventor, the abstract painter Jack Whitten understood the project of giving form to feeling better than most. Born in Bessemer, Alabama in 1939 and associated with the rise of color painting in the late 1960s and 1970s, Whitten was one of the most innovative painters of his generation, particularly in his experiments with acrylic paint, a relatively new medium that became commercially available in the 1950s, dried much faster than oil paint, and offered exciting new textural and visual effects. Combining "sensibility" and "plasticity" by inventing new ways to make a painting, Whitten's deep exploration of painting-as-process was a decades-long study of giving structure to feeling, both inseparable from color.

Whitten is best known perhaps for his slab paintings, which he created with a special tool that he invented and dubbed "The Developer." The Developer was a very large instrument similar to a rake consisting of a squeegee-like head made of Neoprene rubber attached to a twelve-foot-long handle. It allowed Whitten to drag paint across the surface of enormous canvases laid on the floor, creating a painting in one gesture. This was painting in analogy to photography (signaled in the word play of the tool's name), a method that enabled the creation of an image with a single movement. Later in his career, Whitten created acrylic tesserae, iridescent mosaic-style chips about the size of a thumbnail, by curing acrylic paint in handmade molds or in swirling pools and then chopping them up into shards. He applied the tesserae to canvas in a technique that he referred to as paint-as-collage.

In these experiments, Whitten pushed the physicality of color, finding new forms for it, playing with the ways that the perception of color connects us to the world. Whitten understood that light and color were neither apparitional abstractions nor unwavering essences but interactive material: "We know now that light occurs in extremely small particles. . . . That's what allows us to see—those little fucking photons bouncing around your retina, and blam-o, I can see!"[1] To make a painting was not just to apply and control paint, but to engage with the matter that both enables and exceeds perception, building new ways of seeing from that communion between artist and material.

The palpable pleasure of color—massive swathes of thick streaking color, sparkling constellations of broken color, color as a sigh, a palace, and as a city—is on display in Whitten's work, which demonstrates that the aesthetic pleasure of color-based abstraction lies in the meeting of materiality and boundlessness, the seeming limitlessness of the real. The pleasure of color is one of undefined possibilities for sensation and plasticity, and its transformative nature, the ability to become anything. Color-based abstraction, in other words, revolves around the aesthetic pleasure found in the freedom to make.[2]

In this chapter, I trace a discourse of twentieth-century color abstraction as it intersects with the work of experimental Black artists and the anti-Black racism of the avant-garde. I do this by offering an alternative framework for understanding black monochrome painting as a charged site for ideas about abstraction, race, and the freedom to make, both the making of an artwork and the making of an interpretation of it. I focus on chromatic black monochromes in particular because of their art historical significance. Credited as the first monochrome painting, Kazimir Malevich's *Black Square* (1915) propelled a revolutionary discourse around color-based abstraction in the twentieth century as a "zero point" of painting—a negation that would make true creative freedom possible. The black monochrome has had significant longevity as a punctum, marking art's relationship (or lack thereof) to the social world. Is the black monochrome an antithesis, a transcendence of social meanings (Malevich, Ad Reinhardt)? Or is it the opposite, highlighting painting's imbrication with the social and everyday life (Robert Rauschenberg)? The discourse surrounding the black monochrome is contradictory. Black is a color loaded with symbolic meaning—night, death, evil, spiritual purity—yet it is also the color that color artists in the twentieth century turned to when they hoped to move beyond established meaning. Black's paradoxes unfold, for example, in the artist Louise Nevelson's opaque explanation for her signature use of black in her wooden assemblages:

> But when I fell in love with black, it contained all color. It wasn't a negation of color. It was an acceptance. Because black encompasses all colors. Black is the most aristocratic color of all. The only aristocratic color. For me this is the ultimate. You can be quiet and it contains the whole thing. There is no color that will give you the feeling of totality. Of peace. Of greatness. Of quiet. Of excitement. I have seen things that were transformed into black that took on just greatness. I don't want to use a lesser word. Now if it does that for things I've handled, that means that the *essence* of it is just what you call—alchemy.[3]

Great because it holds everything, including, necessarily, that which is *not* great, the artist's epiphany is to recognize what was mistaken for negation as totality. It would be an understatement to say that the color black holds a particularly significant position in the history of color abstraction.

In this chapter, my arguments are not so much about what the black monochrome does phenomenologically—its "alchemy," as Nevelson says—but how chromatic black's associations with artistic freedom are also entwined with forms of racialization in color discourse. As theorist Jared Sexton writes, "The experience of black—as and in relation to color, as and in relation to all colors—is as much a feat of engineering as it is one of imagination; at once scientific and philosophical, it is a matter of aesthetics and ethics, knowledge and belief, fact and fantasy."[4] The discourse of color abstraction connects the freedom to make with making oneself free, suggesting that one depends on the other. As I will discuss in my analysis of Kazimir Malevich's manifesto on pure color, in the twentieth century abstract color forms became associated with a transcendence of the representational. In this mode of thought, representation is a prison of the mind and spirit; color abstraction is the key that unlocks that cage. Yet when chromatic color abstraction and discourses of racial color become entangled, the monochrome is often a scene of fixity, an irreducible limit, as in Zora Neale Hurston's "I feel most colored when I am thrown against a sharp white background."[5] This chapter not only traces the obscured anti-Blackness in a discourse of abstraction that purports to have no social content. Equally important, if not more so, is the chapter's exploration of how Black artists recovered chromatic blackness as a non-representational mode. In readings of work by Jack Whitten, Zora Neale Hurston, Ellen Gallagher, and Glenn Ligon, I show that modernist discourses of color are inextricable from the juggernaut of racialized abstraction, but also that the interpretive openness of abstraction can be restored by and for Black creative expression and aesthetic pleasure.

The barriers for Black abstractionists working in the twentieth century were not only symbolic or aesthetic. Black artists interested in color abstraction, like Sam Gilliam, Alma Thomas, Peter Bradley, and Jack Whitten, among many others, were subject to critical scrutiny and obstructions that white artists, particularly white male artists, did not encounter. Whitten, for example, struggled from the 1960s through the 1980s to receive recognition for his work. He was not welcomed into the white-dominated mainstream artworld, where gallery representation was necessary and systematically excluded Black artists. His monumental slab paintings, with their color blur, like a photograph taken at the slowest shutter speed, did not register in the dominant representational idioms that were called "Black art." Routes for artistic success were incredibly narrow and often dictated by the racial expectations of gatekeepers. Black artists in this period who worked in highly abstract modes had difficulty gaining traction with gallerists and curators, at times accused of being "inauthentic" and imitating white artists because their art did not obviously reference the discrete set of experiences popularly imagined as Black.[6]

In recent years, a trove of scholarship has emerged exploring the tension between the racism of the avant-garde and the freedom-seeking potential of experimental aesthetic forms. As scholars such as GerShun Avilez, Phillip Brian Harper, Joseph Jonghyun Jeon, Anthony Reed, Evie Shockley, Dorothy Wang, and Timothy Yu have explained, racially minoritized artists have faced persistent exclusion when it comes to making art that challenges formal conventions and representation—whether such art is called experimental, abstract, or avant-garde art—including the systematic refusal of admittance to professional venues and erasure from art histories. Beyond these structural barriers to sharing and receiving compensation for one's work, artists of color often face limiting expectations regarding the form of their work, running up against demands to produce "proper" or "authentic"—that is, often, realist—representations of racialized subjects or else face charges of irrelevance or even the abnegation of social duty. On the other hand, experimentalists of color who gain approval from the academy or avant-garde establishment often have the social or political impact of their work trivialized or erased, held up as an exception that proves the rule, the writer or artist of color whose formally innovative work is not compromised by "identity."

Many of the aforementioned scholars argue that the attention to realist representation has come to dominate criticism on work by authors and artists of color, leading scholars to depend on a prefabricated cluster of racialized readings. As literary critic Phillip Brian Harper has written regarding African American expressive culture, interpretive and political norms "presuppose the social-critical function of African American culture" and "they also generally assume that that function is best served by a type of realist aesthetics that cast racial Blackness in overridingly 'positive' terms. Superficially connoting modes of depiction that are properly race-proud demand that racialized representations perceptibly mirror real-world phenomena, however favorable—or not—any particular portrayal may seem."[7] As art historians Darby English and Kobena Mercer have argued, this "burden of representation" has also produced a set of fixed and predetermined interpretations of the work of Black artists and other artists of color as "about race" without a substantive engagement with how the art object may specifically engage with issues of race or racism—or ideas and questions that are not exclusively "about" race.[8] Literary critic Dorothy Wang enriches these observations by explaining that the categories of experimentalism or the "avant-garde" are frequently read as "universal, overarching, and implicitly 'racially unmarked'" by critics.[9] Formally interesting, aesthetically significant, and, in other words, "literary" writing is pitted against the "cultural" writing of marginalized authors in a trap of mutual exclusion. Commenting on a forum on the state of the "new lyric studies" in a 2008 volume of *PMLA*, the journal of the Modern Language Association, Wang observes:

> what is even more operative here than what is explicitly stated is what is *not* stated, what does not *need* to be stated, or what needs to be stated only by shorthand: "identitarian," "identity politics," "cultural," "social," "political," "anxieties," "prejudices," "exotic," "carelessness," "haphazard" versus "literary," "classic," "classical," "discipline," among other terms. These terms (as does the term "avant-garde") act as placeholders for larger assumptions and beliefs, many of which have largely become normative in shoring up the supposed opposition between the cultural against the literary.[10]

Those artists who are marked by "identity" (largely a shorthand for an author's non-white positionality, but also standing in for other minoritized positions) are excluded from the pleasures of creation and interpretation promised by the freely moving "unmarked" literature characterized by form. They are insufficiently aesthetic and overly social.[11]

Further complicating things, abstraction has been recruited historically as a tool in racist stereotyping. The repetitive use of simplified forms to abstract human features and codify them as racial signifiers has a long and painful history. The most obvious cases include minstrelsy, kitsch, and cartoons. While critics often link abstraction in literary and visual culture to aesthetic and conceptual complexity, in salt and pepper shakers or cartoon minstrel characters like Mickey Mouse and Bugs Bunny, abstraction can also serve the role of generalizing and simplifying both forms and ideas.[12] As Harper argues, abstraction's co-option by racist representational regimes has contributed to demands for realist representations in Black expressive culture where, it is hoped, realism might bring a corrective clarity.[13]

Yet despite all these attempts to contain the complexity and heterogeneity of art by Black artists and other artists of color, Black artists continue to assert the pleasures of aesthetic freedom and radical experimentation through color abstraction. As an example, let us return to the work of Jack Whitten, the scientist of beauty, whose work is exemplary in this way, particularly within the tradition of the black monochrome.

Whitten electrified black monochrome painting. His paintings understand the iridescence of black, its contradictions, its luminous, light-giving capacity, as well as its absorptive quality. In the project of joining sensibility and plasticity through color, Whitten substantively engaged the racial metaphors of chromatic blackness without resorting to easy tropes, which are embedded in the history of modernist color abstraction. His art is not determined by the imbrication of color and race in his black paintings. On the contrary, Whitten's black paintings interact with the social meanings of chromatic black so as to expand possible interpretations, rather than fix them within anti-Blackness.

The relationship between chromatic black and racial Blackness is explored in many of Whitten's paintings, but the best example may be his *Black Monolith* series (1988–2017). In this collection of paintings, Whitten used his acrylic tesserae to memorialize well-known Black figures such as Ralph Ellison, W. E. B. Du Bois, Maya Angelou, Barbara Jordan, and Muhammad Ali in monumental paintings. These paintings are not representational portraits but large-scale color abstractions using his signature tesserae, vibrating compressions of feeling and information. Whitten has compared the tesserae to digital "bytes" of data, a unit that is not one thing but many, sitting at the limits of understanding, finite but inconceivable.[14] The small chips of acrylic paint laboriously affixed to the canvas create a shimmering scene, recalling the undulations of landscape, the luminosity of the cosmos, and the solidity of human mass at multiple scales, from the cellular to the aggregate we call the body. By titling these paintings "monoliths," Whitten conveys the gravity of spiritual architecture and the looming singularity of his subjects. And yet in spite of the unitary, self-contained nature of a monolith, the paintings seem endless in their revelation of complexity. The eye cannot take in all this detail at once, the catching and direction of light that creates a sense of endless variability. The viewer exists with the painting in a dance of focus and refocus, of physical movement around the space of the painting in all directions, relating between the macro of the body-like shapes—human, celestial, terrestrial—and the micro of the tesserae.

These are big paintings. You must interact with them physically, doing the dance of lean forward, step back, wander to the left and right. And yes, the *Black Monoliths* series consistently makes use of chromatic black as an eminent aspect of the palette, inviting the viewer to draw connections to chromatic black and racial Blackness, reflecting on their entanglement and what abstraction may open up for both.

For example, in *Black Monolith VII Du Bois Legacy: For W. E. Burghardt* (2014), Whitten sets a central tesserae-built form against a matte deep-black ground. The central form reads at multiple scales. Its bottom-heavy oblong shape suggests seed, ovum, and cell. Simultaneously, it also recalls the topographical or cartographic, the urban lines of a built environment, looking a bit like the island of Manhattan. Or it could be seen as a meteor in descent, recalling Du Bois's work of political science fiction "The Comet," a story in which a comet kills almost everyone in New York City except for two survivors, a Black man and a white woman, who find each other and must now navigate the racial, gender, and sexual politics of that relation directly after a cataclysm. The shape feels suspended, hovering in time, a moment just before the apocalypse and before the society that would come after. The visual almost-allusions suggested in Whitten's formalism convey the germination of something massive, a transformative, birth-like event, a stele of Du Bois as a generative, even maternal, figure of Black radical thought.[15]

As one spends more time with the painting, attempting to take in the overwhelming detail of the individual tesserae, one is flooded with a cacophonous assemblage of color, pattern, shape, and light: milky swirled violets, bright cobalt blues, jade, neon yellow and orange, a nacreous yellow, bits of gold, topaz, crimson, and mauve, chunks striped with black and white like hard candy. The color forms swirl and march, cohere and cluster, step and flow, building around each other with purpose, an arrangement of feeling like a city or the comings and goings at the quantum level. While at first, the color effect of the painting is dominated by black and darker hues, which, to an uncareful viewer suggests the racial literalism of figurative blackness, a closer engagement with the painting reveals that this overall impact is produced through a remarkably intricate selection of hues, values, and contrast, demonstrating Whitten's distinct intelligence for color. In this painting, color refuses representation and embraces abstraction, finding a new visual language for understanding Du Bois and his legacy in a Black radical tradition. This is an iconography that declines the stillness of representation and predetermined meaning, instead constantly reforming within the play of light.[16] Light, structure, and color enable an interpretative play that produces new meaning that is historical, perceptual, and material. It is a black painting that suggests that we ought to reconsider the individualism of the monochrome when color is fundamentally relational.

Whitten's deep understanding of color was not merely an academic interest but a painterly consciousness forged in the civil rights era and what Whitten referred to as "American apartheid." In interviews, Whitten repeatedly credited his experiences with civil disobedience in Alabama and Louisiana in the 1950s, which included meeting Martin Luther King Jr., as the catalysis for his transformation from pre-med student at Tuskegee University to professional artist.[17] Whitten recalled these experiences as harrowing. As he described them in an interview, "I'm one of the people who lead a march through downtown Baton Rouge. Horrible experience. I will never forget at the steps of the state capital building, praying and people throwing piss out of the offices, bottles and eggs, all kinds of shit . . . then I took a bus from Baton Rouge to New York City."[18] Whitten connected his experimental, process-based practice not only to familiar modernist luminaries like De Kooning but to Black history in the South. He credited the influence of George Washington Carver, who famously taught at Tuskegee University but was also a scientifically minded painter who created his own pigments from peanuts.[19] While Whitten's formalism could easily be mistaken as an attempt to transcend the social through pure color, these paintings are better understood as experiments in color's virtuosity as a material of social relations. As Whitten said in an interview with the Tate Museum, "The political is in the work. I know it's in there because I put it there."[20]

Although for simplicity's sake I will be discussing the "color" black in this chapter, technically, black is more complicated. One can talk about black as light and as pigment. In terms of luminosity, true black is the absence of all visible light and, therefore, not technically a color at all. As a pigment, black is the combination of all colors. To make a chromatic black, painters must effectively combine colors so that each color's wavelength can be canceled out by its complement. Thus, most blacks are not true black but extremely dark hues. There are warm and cool blacks, blacks that are more strongly blue, mauve, or green, and so on. In 1860, the German physicist Gustav Kirchhoff developed the theoretical concept of the "black body," an idealized physical form that absorbs all radiation and is therefore perfectly black. Since the 1990s, technological leaps have enabled scientists to create ever darker blacks, driven by military, industrial, and scientific interest. In 2019, engineers at MIT used carbon nanotube technology to create a black that can absorb 99.995 percent of visible light, the blackest material to date, although the scientists say that undoubtably there are blacker blacks to come.[21]

Both scientific and practical approaches to understanding black are permeated by obliquely acknowledged practices of racialization. The mutual haunting of race and chromatic color has been taken up by artists in countless ways as they wrestle with what color means. While monochrome and minimalist painting have often pursued a direct affective, phenomenological, or spiritual aesthetic experience between the artist or viewer and the artwork, the punctum where race and color meet interrupts quests to separate the aesthetic from the social.

Perhaps one of the most well-known examples of the relationship between color and race in contemporary monochrome painting is Korean American artist Byron Kim's *Synecdoche* series (1991–present). Taking its title from literary terminology—a metaphor in which a part comes to represent the whole—*Synecdoche* is a series of unusual portraits, now numbering over five hundred 10 × 8 inch rectangles that are displayed in a grid on the wall.[22] We do not see a figure in these paintings of Kim's friends, family, neighbors, fellow artists, or strangers met on the steps of the Brooklyn Public Library. Rather, the grid of portraits is a geometric sea of dark brown, brown, tan, beige, and pink—a minimalist attempt to document only one hue present in the sitter's skin, usually taken from the underside of the arm or back of the hand. Gazing up at the grand terrain parceled into flesh hued swatches and knowing that these are skin portraits, the connections to race may seem obvious to a viewer. However, when Kim embarked on this now three-decade-long project, he was not thinking about how the paintings would engage race but rather modernist painting's fascination with pure color.[23]

The paintings are arranged in alphabetical order by the first name of the sitter. When displayed, there is an accompanying subtitle with their full names. At first, the field of variable brown rectangles challenges the idea that color and race are indivisible. Here is pure color. *Synecdoche* saturates the viewer in the emanating warmth of painted color on a sublime scale. And yet we know that this color is an extract from an intimate encounter—that of the relationship between painter and sitter. We can also see the names attached to each portrait, and with that comes all the racial associations that attend naming. If one were curious (and a bit creepy), it would be possible to find photographs of many of the sitters through an internet search and see for oneself if Kim's paintings are "accurate," letting a host of social information into the context of one's viewing (although in 1991, when the series began, this was not the case). Many of the sitters are celebrated artworld figures, their photographs easy to find.

In their grid presentation, the portraits also conjure up associations with racial pseudoscience. The grid invites categorical and comparative impulses. It opens the door to meditation on themes of division and equality, the insufficiency of color terminology in racial discourse, or relationships across racial difference. In his oral history interview with the Houston Asian American Archive, Kim tells the story of painting the skin of a security guard who worked at the National Gallery of Art in Washington, DC, where much of *Synecdoche* is held. The guard, who was extremely familiar with *Synecdoche*, was delighted to have her skin painted because after all her time spent with these panels, she had noticed that her skin color was not present.[24] That is, after more than five hundred paintings, there are still skin colors left to paint. This is all to say that although *Synecdoche* is an impressive experiment in modernist painting, its minimalism makes available a deluge of social and political interpretations rather than isolating "pure" color as an autonomous aesthetic experience.[25]

Even as *Synecdoche* remains profoundly interested in the transformative aesthetic experience of color, the metaphors and associations tied up with color spark like an electrified nest of wires. Like the skin hues in *Synecdoche*, chromatic black, particularly in color painting, is similarly overdetermined by social meaning.[26] Popularly, using chromatic black to discuss racial Blackness is a commonplace, what M. Ty has called a "riot of the literal" and Fred Moten has identified as a discourse of purity.[27] However, in art history, the racial meaning associated with chromatic black, particularly in abstraction, has been fiercely contested.[28] Throughout this chapter, I ask, What does it mean to say that "black is a color," as the African American abstract artist Raymond Saunders once did?[29]

Of course, chromatic black works by Black artists do not always contain symbolic evidence of the artist's racial Blackness, thereby, as Darby English has described, "installing a racial difference in an abstract work to compel it to function figuratively."[30] And artwork by Black artists does not always contain reference to their racial Blackness, nor is the role of the critic to reveal this obscured representation. The artworks explored in this chapter all use abstraction to directly engage questions of racial Blackness and chromatic black through titling (Whitten, Gallagher), related interviews (Whitten), obvious references to texts and events (Ligon), or an explicit engagement with the aesthetics of race-making (Hurston). They are actively questioning the historical relationship between chromatic black and racial Blackness and how Black artists might break out of this trap. However, not every artwork by a Black artist, including those making black monochrome work, makes race its subject or reveals the "truth" of the artist's Blackness as unavoidable autobiographical and representational content.

Black color abstraction shows us that color is always relational and contextual, a shifting convergence of matter and perception. This chapter explores the difficult entanglement of racial Blackness and chromatic blackness in (mainly) American abstraction. At stake is the possibility of the freedom to make as a central component of Black freedom struggles, the necessary pleasures of open interpretation, and the reductive violence of racism. My examination of this subject locates the color black as integral to visual discourses of purity, fixity, supremacy, and interpretation that are entwined historically with the logic of race. While many critics and abstract artists in the twentieth century have attempted to separate chromatic black and racial Blackness into fundamentally separate kinds of meaning, the case studies in this chapter demonstrate that chromatic black has been a ground on which racial thought is generated and articulated. Yet Black artists have also used the color black in abstractions that refute the fantasy of hierarchical separateness, purity, and negation. Throughout the case studies in this chapter, we see that chromatic blackness functions as a scene of aesthetic pleasure, a ground without figure, both deep and depthless, where racial meaning circulates and power is tensely negotiated.

This chapter is organized by a series of case studies in black monochrome. Each case study retells a canonical story of chromatic blackness, particularly within the history of black monochrome painting, and examines racial discourses of color as they are taken up by Black experimentalists, including Zora Neale Hurston, Ellen Gallagher, Glenn Ligon, and, of course, Whitten. These artists explore how racialization takes place through aesthetic abstraction, formal acts that sometimes articulate the ostensible boundaries of expression and sometimes break them open. Their work points to the ways that racist discourses of Blackness mark limits of possibility for Black creative making and interpretation. And yet they reach for abstraction, making those limits yield to a Black radical imagination. Whitten, Hurston, Gallagher, and Ligon explore how abstraction's universalism can be recalled from whiteness, how abstraction can be reclaimed from racial typing and racist stereotyping, and, finally, how the interpretative openness of abstraction can be recuperated for Black making and aesthetic pleasure.

Aesthetic pleasure, as we have seen, is not always characterized by the high-toned intensities of swelling, positive feeling—joy, cheerfulness, beauty, and so forth. Aesthetic pleasure is more often mixed, even contradictory, in its affective experience. The pleasure at the center of this chapter is often this way—the freedom to create is a good feeling that can also being attended by discomfiting, painful, or ambiguous feelings. This is the pleasure at the core of experimentalism, which is often accompanied by unpleasure—conceptualism's tedium, the provocateur's irritability, the deep grief of addressing an unspeakable loss. The great pleasure of experimentalism lies in the satisfaction of making freely, both on the part of the artist and the interpreter. The imaginative freedom of experimentalism is often linked to practices of building a world not structured by oppression and suffering, folding into itself the opalescent dreams of a just world. While the artworks under study in this chapter are not always obviously "about" pleasure or characterized by obviously "good" feelings, they protest that color cannot be owned, insisting upon their freedom to make.

A Living Form of Pure Color

In 1915, Russian avant-garde artist Kazimir Malevich revolutionized painting by creating the first monochrome, breaking with representational painting and thereby delivering the history of art into a new era of modernist nonrepresentational abstraction.[31] This painting, called *Black Square*, was first displayed in 1915 in the *Last Exhibition of Futurist Painting 0.10*, where it was hung in the top corner of the gallery, just beneath the ceiling, where Russian Orthodox icons were traditionally placed in a Russian home.[32] Combined with the painting's radical break from representation, *Black Square* garnered itself a respectable amount of scandal, opprobrium, and excitement during an already tumultuous time both aesthetically and politically.[33] Born in 1879 in Kyiv to an ethnically Polish family, Malevich went on to become one of the most influential artists of the modernist avant-garde. As art historian Aleksandra Shatskikh writes, while many other artists were experimenting with geometric abstraction during the period, "none of his contemporary revolutionaries created a manifesto, an emblem, as capacious and in its own way unique as *Black Square*, which became both the quintessence of the Russian avant-gardist's own art and a milestone on the highway of world art."[34] With *Black Square*, Malevich is credited with offering a truly new paradigm for painting.

The painting's subject is eponymous: a black square framed by a white square. Malevich would correct this last statement by saying that the painting has no subject, no object; rather, it is a "living form" of *pure color*, an attempt to radically sever art from known reality and, in this act, forge a new consciousness and form of life.[35] Malevich called this new style of painting dedicated to the purity of color and its dominance over all other elements of painting *suprematism*, a term that bears a tantalizingly close resemblance to *supremacy*, with which it shares a Latin root (*suprematia*).[36] Shatskikh explains that this term was indeed derived from the Latin *supremacia*, meaning "superiority" and "dominance."[37] Deeply influenced by cubism and both Russian and Italian futurism, Malevich provocatively framed his epoch-making break with representation as an evolution of human consciousness that previous art movements had presaged but failed to bring to fruition.[38]

In his 1915 manifesto "From Cubism to Futurism to Suprematism," Malevich theorized that pure aesthetic forms will lead to spiritual and, in fact, ontological purity in human beings. As he wrote, "I have transformed myself *in the zero of* form and have fished myself out of the *rubbishy slough of academic* art . . . only *cowardly consciousness* and insolvency of creative power in an artist yield to this deception and establish *their art on the forms of nature*, afraid of losing the foundation on which the *savage and the academy* have based their art."[39] Malevich went on to link this undeveloped representational artist to criminality: "To pronounce favorite objects and little nooks of nature is just like a thief being enraptured by his shackled legs."[40] The brisk transition from the savage to the criminal suggests a racial discourse in which representation, and an appreciative fascination with its imprisoning nature, limit the artist's ability to evolve and reach the apex of suprematism. At the end of the evolutionary line, with the savage as its starting point, there is an art of purity and independence, unbound and uninfluenced by external forces, a godlike ability to create. The suprematist artist is reborn in aesthetic freedom; they "emerge from the object and arrive at color as an end in itself, at the domination of purely painterly forms as ends in themselves over content and things, at nonobjective suprematism—at the new painterly realism, at absolute creation."[41]

According to Malevich's essay, any act of representation, however abstracted (as in cubism and futurism), was ultimately an imitation, timorous and without vision. Malevich portrayed his "transformation" from futurism to suprematism as an act of strength and "creative will," an action of self-determination that self-evidences superiority.[42] Malevich demanded a total rejection of realism, meaning any attempt to depict an object or "form of nature" perceived by the artist in the world, and an embrace of pure form—painting for painting's sake. In imagining the new world produced by suprematism, Malevich resorted to an imagistic repertoire full of savages and shackles, positioning himself against these metaphors as the champion of a new art consciousness.

Throughout the essay, Malevich describes art's previous modes in terms of slavery, imprisonment, and punishment. We might presume that he imagines as his audience—and target of critique—to be a group of white Russian and European modernist painters. However, the deployment of such imagery is not without racial meaning nor incidental to the manifesto's arguments. It is reflective of the progressivist and racial thinking that undergirds the essay.[43] To present himself as a truly "free" artist, Malevich recruited the language of colonialism and anti-Blackness, presenting figments of racialized unfreedom as the ground against that Malevich's summing freedom can be drawn.[44]

The evolution of art described by Malevich cannot be separated out from the racial thought that imagines the "savage" as the origin point of the human, the human being as a non-creaturely agent who progresses linearly along a path of cultural and technological advancement so that "The realist academics are the savage's last descendant."[45] While race, racism, and racial Blackness have their own contextual meanings within Russia and Eastern Europe in the early twentieth century, these concepts were not radically distinct from the racial thought, scientific racism, and fascism fermenting in Western Europe and the United States, what Denise Ferreira da Silva talks about as a global idea of race.[46] Malevich's statements were very much in line with modernist primitivism, and Malevich was up to date on avant-gardist interest in the "primitive" cultures of African and Asia in cubist and futurist artists in Italy and France.[47] The futurist Russian avant-garde, of which Malevich was a central member, was not isolated from the European Enlightenment or the developments in modernist art in Western Europe but deeply engaged in these issues of the day that were reshaping conceptions of the human on a global level.[48]

Malevich, of course, was not the only artist to explore how abstract shape and color could be utilized to reimagine the world. Geometric abstraction and color forms infiltrated the visual language of modernist painting as artists deepened questions surrounding the viability of representational art (whether representational systems could be depended on to communicate meaning), the desirability of representation (whether any kind of representation could meet the demands of modernist expression), and the value of spontaneity and intuition in making art.[49] However, I am not interested in making a claim about what a desire for abstraction might or might not mean. My focus is on how this particular discourse of color abstraction is also one of freedom, and what the intertwining of color and freedom means for the interrelationship of aesthetics and racialization across the twentieth century. As such, what is especially notable in Malevich's discussion of *Black Square* and suprematism is the language of dominance, purity, and progressive elimination: "Art advances toward creation as an end in itself and toward domination over the forms of nature."[50] Malevich's theory of artistic freedom depends on a colonial language of dominance shaded with suggestions of scientific racism.

This discourse of domination and supremacy so foundational to Malevich's theories of aesthetic evolution speaks to the sociality, historicity, and racialism of modernist abstraction. Lacking the primitivism of Picasso or Stein or the Orientalism of Pound or Matisse, key abstract painters like Malevich, whose subject was color itself, may appear to be operating in a world of "pure" aesthetics, unpolluted by social and political concerns. However, a closer analysis of modernist discourses of abstraction and color suggests otherwise. Malevich's discourse of dominance and supremacy reflects the global racial thinking made ubiquitous by the Enlightenment, racial capitalism, and the rise of racial science. In imagining that his intuition resulted in a kind masculine parthenogenesis, and that this genius was enacted through domination and conquest, Malevich espouses an aesthetic hierarchy of living things that is colonial and racial. Such ideas are constitutive of the suprema*cist* conceptualization of the human that Sylvia Wynter dubbed Man1 and Man2 and historicizes as the racial project of colonialism.[51] As Malevich proclaims, "I have transformed myself in the zero form and through zero have reached creation, that is, suprematism, the new painterly realism—nonob-jective creation. Suprematism is the beginning of a new culture, or perhaps species: the savage is conquered like the ape."[52] In this narrative of the conquest, Malevich brings together discourses of colonialism and social Darwinism, as well as the racial undercurrents of European totalitarianism that were rumbling in the First World War.

Artistic freedom, in this vein, is inseparable from domination and the obliteration of "affectable subjects," to use Denise Ferreira da Silva's term, who are marked using a discourse of scientific differentiation. As Silva writes:

> Scientific signification has deployed the racial to produce modern subjects that emerge in exteriority/affectability and exist between two moments of violence: (a) *engulfment*, that is, 'partial negation,' the productive violent act of naming, the symbolic appropriation that produces

them, inaugurating a *relationship* precisely because, in the regimen of representation interiority governs, it institutes unsublatable and irreducible subjects, and (b) *murder*, total annihilation, that which obliterates the necessary but haunting relationship between an I instituted by the desire for transparency (self-determination) and the affectable, always already vanishing others of Europe that the scientific cataloguing of minds institutes.[53]

The passages from Malevich's manifesto trace this dynamic exactly. The transparent, self-determined I ("I have transformed myself in the zero form") is created through the violent relationship of scientific naming, linking him to an affectable and irreducible subject (the "savage" who is almost the ape). This affectable subject is then annihilated through conquest, the "savage" destroyed through "the new culture" of suprematism.

Color was just as essential to Malevich's production of his free, self-determining, and transparent I—the artist who can create without being shackled by the world. Because color appears irreducible, it can serve as a powerful medium for the staging of the artist's interiority, a pure substance that allows the artist to directly convey their interior experiences unadulterated by the social. This perceived ability to directly transmit the artist's interiority is key to the portrait of the free artist articulated by Malevich and many of the modernists who would come after.

Color is an aspect of visual perception and meaning-making that can invite strong associative and symbolic interpretation and yet also consistently resists it. Although it feels universal, color is resolutely contextual and produced through interaction—"Blam-o!," as Whitten says. We cannot physically see color as it might exist independently, but we always perceive it in relation to other colors, which can dramatically affect color perception.[54] Color eludes every attempt to finally determine its meaning, to be nailed down or contained by a culture or a form. No wonder color has come to be seen as a portal to freedom.

The essentialism (aesthetic and racial) of "pure color," as seen in and around Malevich's suprematism and *Black Square*, sets up the monochrome as a site of circulation for higher feeling that transcends the social. Pure color is understood as free imaginative play, where individuals create meaning that circulates within color's fixed field. The act of interpretation that feeds our understanding of color often goes unrecognized, perceived as pure sensation or "intuition," arising from an exclusively internal place, disconnected from the environment and breaking from the historical.

Integral to Malevich's bombastic claims to freedom is a phenomenon that is perhaps so obvious that it is easy to overlook—by his account, it feels good to feel free. Malevich's text suggests that he finds it pleasurable to dominate. He finds supremacy satisfying. I have a sizeable quarry of objections to such statements. I might certainly object that this cannot be true freedom, as it is dependent on the unfreedom of others, that we ought to abjure a pleasure that is derived from the suffering of others, that the satisfaction of supremacy is a delusional and morally repulsive feeling.[55] Yet however objectionable on moral or philosophical grounds, there is nevertheless an unmistakable sense of glee that arises from Malevich's description of the freedom that he feels when making abstract color paintings. We see it in the insulting jokes lobbed at other painters, for example. A somewhat repetitive piece of writing, Malevich's piece seems particularly fond of unfavorable comparisons between non-suprematist artists and grandmothers. He taunts, "Why do you not put on your grandmothers' dresses, when you thrill to the pictures of their powdered portraits?"[56] The pleasure of the manifesto is also demonstrable in the soaring language throughout, which swells in crescendo at the end of the essay:

> I say to all: Abandon love, abandon aestheticism, abandon the baggage of wisdom, for in the new culture, your wisdom is ridiculous and insignificant.
>
> I have untied the knots of wisdom and liberated the consciousness of color! Hurry up and shed the hardened skin of centuries, so that you can catch up with us more easily.
>
> I have overcome the impossible and made gulfs with my breath. You are caught in the nets of the horizon, like fish!
>
> We, suprematists, throw open the way to you.
>
> Hurry!
>
> For tomorrow you will not recognize us.[57]

Malevich's orotund prose suggests that the artistic freedom wrought from color abstraction is a deeply pleasurable experience, a pleasure heightened by writing about it. As much as I disagree with Malevich's sentiments, I can still imagine that "From Cubism to Futurism to Suprematism" felt great to write.

"From Cubism to Futurism to Suprematism" is an important document for understanding the intertwining of racialization and radical abstraction in twentieth-century color abstraction not only because Malevich's essay is shaped by racial frameworks but also because it describes abstraction's freedom as a profound aesthetic pleasure. The pleasure of the freedom to create and its connection to the black monochrome becomes even more apparent as we dig deeper into the history of *Black Square*.

Square, Tunnel, and Cave

The story I have just told of Malevich's *Black Square* is a conventional origin narrative of monochrome painting, despite reframing Malevich's aesthetics via its racial logics of conquest and domination. However, like all origin stories, especially those of Great Men, this narrative is incomplete. Although *Black Square* is often referred to as the first monochrome painting, the credit may properly belong to a lesser-known poet and dramatist named Paul Bilhaud, a member of the ludic French art movement les Arts Incohérents, in English, the Incoherents. Incohérent artists, precursors to Dadaists and surrealists in some ways, were led by Parisian writer and publisher Jules Lévy and were active from 1882–89. As their name suggests, les Incohérents valued humor and anti-authoritarian art that would shock or bemuse, depending on who was looking. Despite their small number and the brevity of their movement, les Incohérents were fairly well known during their active years.[58] As proper bohemians thumbing their noses at academic art, they and their works trafficked in nonsense, juxtaposition, disjuncture, and the absurd. Visual puns were a particular favorite. Paul Bilhaud's 1882 painting *Combat de nègres dans une tunnel* (Negroes fighting in a tunnel) depends on such a device: the painting is simply a black rectangle (not unlike *Black Square*). Thus, an alternative genealogy of monochrome painting began with a racist joke, not the transcendent rupture for which one might have hoped.[59]

Bilhaud's early monochrome is consequential not only because it is a significant art-historical event gamboling about in racist muck but also because the joke was frequently copied and continued to circulate for two decades. The joke was reimagined by Alphonse Allais in his *Album primo-avrilesque* (April Fool's Day album, 1897), a portfolio of monochromatic visual jokes, including *Combat de nègres dans une cave, pendant la nuit* (Negroes battling in a cellar at night). The joke is picked up for a third time by Emile Cohl, referenced in his 1910 film, *Le Peintre néo-impressioniste* (The neo-impressionist painter), five years prior to Malevich's *Black Square*.[60] In the film, Cohl adds a variation on the theme, incorporating a lemon-yellow square animated with a sketch of an offensively rendered Chinese person who is carrying corn on the Yellow River.[61] The black square monochrome in *Peintre néo-impressioniste* remains the same: a black square featuring no animation and a caption that can be translated as "Negroes making shoe polish in a tunnel at night."[62]

These black and yellow monochromes represent racial difference as chromatic difference, reducing racial signification to hue. The saturation of the colors leaves no ambiguity and eschews contextuality; the black is solidly black, the yellow is solidly yellow, signifying race as a separate, empirical positive, as dense and certain as crushed pigment in its glass jar. The monochromes of the Incohérents imagine the racialized subject, particularly the Black subject, as an interpretive limit. The bluntness of "pure" saturated color lines up neatly with fantasies of racial purity and, adjacently, anxieties over mixing colors. The repetition of this aesthetic "joke" across two decades urges us to consider the relationship between the early beginnings of modernist radical abstraction and modernism's racial stereotypes.[63] Whereas we might think of racial stereotypes as a kind of wrongful figuration, for example in the grotesque or cartoonish representation of racialized bodies, we can also think of stereotype as an act of abstraction. The stereotype is always an attempt at conceptual reduction, even if its expression is elaborate.

As the text of the joke subtly shifts in each iteration, the image and logic of the joke remains essentially the same. The artist asserts a creative freedom to construct the events taking place within the black square's opaque field. The scene always plays out within a fixed range of possibility. This is reminiscent of Homi Bhabha's words on colonial discourse's production of racial stereotype in "The Other Question": "Despite the 'play' in the colonial system that is crucial to its exercise of power, colonial discourse produces the stereotype as a fixed reality that is at once an 'other' and yet entirely knowable and visible. It resembles a form of narrative whereby the productivity and circulation of subjects and signs are bound in a reformed and recognizable totality."[64] As Bhabha describes, while the white modernist artist may "play" with the circulation of racialized signs in the monochrome images, ultimately the images project a fixed reality, reproducing a racialized subject who is always already a known constant—an empirical Blackness. The Black figures pronounced to exist within the void of the painting are at once hypervisible in the blackness of the square and invisible within its darkness. Known and unseeable, the monochromes convey the uneasy tension in the stereotype's brittle elasticity, which is always about to snap.

Bhabha gets to what is pleasurable (for the stereotyper) about stereotype. These are abstractions that please through their recognition within a circuit of repetition, the childlike delight of predictable reappearance lightly seasoned by variety. Color is tied to a racial position through the monochromatic pun. It becomes stereotype or fixed abstraction, circulating in a carousel of cultural signification in which recognition is the aesthetic and affective reward. The interpreter is always guaranteed the pleasure of knowing the punch line, never undermined by the limits of his knowledge but buoyed by them. Thus, stereotype is not only an effective strategy of domination but also a way to manage the aesthetic disappointment that might shatter fragile claims to truth in a world where aesthetic judgment depends on mastery.

We might note that the term *color* as a metaphor for race is already a kind of abstraction—a phenomenon made visible in Kim's *Synecdoche*. This metaphor has been naturalized, but we might consider how an abstract representation of skin color stands in for the complexity of racial identity in a stylized and regulated way.[65] This abstraction works as a synecdoche replacing part for whole (skin color for the complex and variant signifiers of racial difference). In many cases, as in the work of les Incohérents, color works as the visual-linguistic emollient of racial stereotype. And according to recent research, the pranksters of les Incohérents were not the only ones who saw the potential for racist comedy in monochrome painting. In November of 2015, the State Tretyakov Gallery in Moscow, Russia, announced a curious finding from their art historical and technological study of Malevich's *Black Square*. A handwritten pencil scrawl previously assumed to be Malevich's disintegrated signature was revealed to read "Negroes Battling at Night," a clear reference to the earlier Parisian monochromes.⁶⁶

Reporting on the Tretyakov Gallery's findings dutifully observes that this discovery recontextualizes Malevich's suprematism within broader international developments in the visual arts; several journalists note that the joke is racist. Malevich expert Konstantin Akinsha said in an interview with the *New York Times* that "Malevich used Allais's prank, but turned it into the realm of high art," the scrawl thus demonstrates "how closely Russian avant-garde representatives were following the developments in France."⁶⁷ However, neither the Tretyakov Gallery nor journalists reflected on the ways that the content of the joke might be connected to modernist abstraction beyond a question of simple aesthetic influence. In a gymnastic attempt to avoid discussing the racism of the inscription, the *New York Times* went so far as to refer to it as a "mysterious message," as if the desired effect of this joke was somehow obscure, a puzzle left behind by an enigmatic genius.⁶⁸ The discussion of the racist joke stunningly fails to grapple with the obvious. Considering the role non-Western abstraction played in the "development" of Euro-American abstraction, from the influence of non-Western geometric forms on European and American painting, textiles, and sculpture to the minimalism of the haiku; considering Euro-American modernists' infatuation with primitivism and Orientalism, which produced some of the most iconic works of Euro-American modernist art, such as Pound's "In a Station of the Metro" and Picasso's *Les Demoiselles d'Avignon*; it seems not much more of a leap to argue that modernist color forms and monochromes were likewise entangled with the period's racial imaginary.

The reference to les Incohérents' monochromes found in Malevich's *Black Square* gives us insight into something more significant than an aesthetic genealogy of monochrome painting. More than this, it tells us something about the intimacies of abstraction, representation, and chromatic blackness as they intersect with a discourse of freedom and the pleasure to make. While at first it may seem that the crudeness of les Incohérents' joke distinguishes it from Malevich's high-art claims to creative transcendence, on deeper inquiry we can see that there are conceptual ties in addition to the obvious visual reference of the black square. Both present pure color as a racial form that marks an irreducible limit enabling the artist's free imaginative play, whether that be a series of oafish jokes or Malevich's more supernal claim that for the suprematist, "each form is a world."[69] In this consideration of the history of the black monochrome, questions of racial difference were central to the ways in which artists and consumers of art around the turn of the twentieth century were thinking about color, abstraction, and the pleasures of artistic and interpretive freedom. The new information about *Black Square*'s connections to les Incohérents' joke shows the ways in which abstract color can mediate power, where power is the freedom of creative expression and interpretation.

Color does not always "represent" race or racial stereotype. Nor is color as a metaphor for race always a cruelly reductive gesture. But anti-Black racism is demonstrably entwined with the history of chromatic black abstraction and its imaginative pleasures. The substitutive logic of the racist joke is reflected back by the substitutive interpretative play of the monochrome in a circulation of language and visuality that fixes racial difference. The pleasure of that play is inseparable from the discourses of artistic freedom associated with the black monochrome.

Reflect, Rub, and Run

As the case of *Black Square* shows, the complicated interfacing of abstraction and racialization in twentieth-century Western art defies an easy explanation or straightforward chronology. The free expanse of pure color that promises transcendence is yet bound to the coarse reductions of stereotype. Some might proffer realism as the cure to abstraction's ambiguities and how easily they can be capitalized on to further unsavory causes. However, realism can also serve projects of delimitation. As curator Adrienne Edwards parses this dilemma:

> In all instances, black representation has involved the confluence of an artist's individual perspective or desire for personal agency with the discourse of these movements circumscribing the parameters of blackness in art. There has been a tendency toward figuration and realism in these movements, which have operated on principles of transparency, immediacy, authority and authenticity. These well-meaning efforts ultimately reinforced a reductive notion of 'black art' or the idea of an essence locatable in works of art by black artists.[70]

In 2016, less than a year after the Tretyakov announced its *Black Square* findings, Edwards launched the exhibition *Blackness in Abstraction* at the Pace Gallery in New York City. In this show, Edwards selected a group of artworks representing a range of historical periods and aesthetic movements drawn from the collections of artists of multiple racial identities, including Sol LeWitt, Laura Lima, Ad Reinhardt, Glenn Ligon, Wangechi Mutu, Louise Nevelson, and Jack Whitten. The uniting feature of the show was that each work substantively explored the color black through abstraction, not to displace or reject the entanglement of racial Blackness and chromatic blackness but to stage new conversations about that relationship. In its selection of pieces, the show sought to interrogate art history's mainstream narrative of the black monochrome, which centers on a relatively small group of white Western male artists (Malevich, Ad Reinhardt, Mark Rothko, Robert Rauschenberg). *Blackness in Abstraction* suggested that questions of race had always been at the center of these projects and explored the social meaning and visual effects that might become available by placing a different set of artworks in conversation.

Included in this show was African American artist Ellen Gallagher's work *Negroes Battling in a Cave at Night* (2016), a group of four paintings that reference the Tretyakov Gallery's discovery of *Black Square*'s racist inscription. Throughout her career, Gallagher, born in 1965 in Providence, Rhode Island, has used a combination of painting, collage, and visual motif to tease out tensions between abstraction, figuration, and narrative through a practice that relies heavily on repetition and revision. In her work, Gallagher draws from a deep archive of art historical and popular visual references, from 1960s minimalism to oceanography to Black beauty magazines. She often defamiliarizes these references through a fluid reworking of repeated forms.

Gallagher's paintings included in *Blackness in Abstraction* are rendered in an extremely high-gloss black enamel, so that the viewer's image is reflected in the obsidian field of the painting. Within the black color field, Gallagher has created biomorphic shapes and raised, textured patterns using paper cutouts painted over with the enamel. These cutouts create edges within the glossy surface of the painting, so that the paint becomes a kind of skin that seems to stretch across and seal the whole canvas, giving the impression that the painting is simultaneously a container, a surface, and a field. The cutout shapes that press up against the reflective enamel skin look organic, morphological, in the process of formation. From this black reflective pool, the viewer can make out human eyes and 1960s bouffant hairdos that are sourced from vintage magazines such as *Ebony*. The eyeballs and hair float, unsettling in their disembodiment and with their suggestions of racist stereotypes and Black beauty culture, looking or witnessing, within the shiny black ground. Gallagher's *Negroes Battling in a Cave at Night* also appears to reference her own work, an earlier series of black monochrome paintings from 1998 that similarly employ a method of paper collage on canvas painted over with many layers of black paint to achieve a highly reflective sheen and textural complexity. Following this, Gallagher painted and stenciled a dense, angular arrangement of small silver lips, which reference the iconography of blackface minstrelsy. Of this earlier series, Gallagher has said that "the black paintings were in a sense a reaction to how people were reading and misreading the work" and "a kind of refusal."[71] In *Negroes Battling in a Cave at Night*, Gallagher extends this critique of racialized interpretations while exploring the interpretative possibilities of black abstraction.

As Edwards writes about the show, "Blackness in abstraction . . . shifts analysis away from the black artist as subject and instead emphasizes blackness as material, method and mode, insisting on blackness as a multiplicity. In this sense, we can think of what it does in the world without conflating it—and those who understand blackness from within a system that deems them black, that is black people—with a singular historical narrative or monolithic subjectivity."[72] As a result of Gallagher's formal choices and her titling, no one can look at the paintings and be outside of the racial imaginary it materializes. A critique of racialized interpretation bubbles in the reflective chromatic blackness, a play of sameness and unpredictability. A floating pool of black paint, hardened to a vinyl-like skin, incorporates the viewer's obscured image into its reflective surface. Thus, in *Negroes Battling in a Cave at Night*, black paint becomes a means of critiquing viewers' interpretive habits and assumptions of racial reduction while also exploring the nebulousness of black abstraction as an expressive material without clear boundaries or restrictions. Gallagher meditates on interpretation as an act of containment *and* expressiveness within and beyond the history of the black monochrome. Can a painting be an exorcism? Might black abstraction be recovered from structures of racist fixity, its potential for free play restored for Black artists? Probing the history of anti-Blackness tied up with chromatic blackness while executing an expertly compelling black monochrome, Gallagher presents an eloquent visual expression of these questions.

Gallagher was hardly the first to be intrigued by the potential of paint for critiquing and disassembling racist interpretation—or to explore its potential for the pleasures of boundless expressiveness. We can find an earlier iteration of this, a bit closer to the moment of *Black Square*'s creation, in writer and anthropologist Zora Neale Hurston's 1928 essay, "How It Feels to Be Colored Me." This classic piece is often read for its commentary on racial interpellation and self-reliance amid racial alienation, full of memorable and highly quotable, images, such as "No I do not weep at the world. I am too busy sharpening my oyster knife."[73] However, my reading of "How It Feels to Be Colored Me" takes a different tack, examining how Hurston's painterly metaphors of color unfold in complex interactions between race and aesthetics. In the essay, Hurston meditates on color abstraction as it facilitates feelings of racial difference and experiences of racism, lingering in a vacillation between color and "being colored," a movement between freedom, creative play, and racist fixity.

Having grown up in the Black community of Eatonville, Florida, Hurston characterizes her childhood self as gregarious, curious, and devoted to aesthetic pleasure. While adults in her community are wary of white Northern tourists who pass through town, Zora imagines the gawking procession as a drama acted out for her own enjoyment: "The front porch might seem a daring place for the rest of the town, but it was a gallery seat for me. My favorite place was atop the gate-post. Proscenium box for a born first-nighter."[74] In this period of her life when "white people differed from colored to me only in that they rode through town and never lived there," Hurston was not only an avid theatergoer; she was also a performer:

> [White tourists] liked to hear me 'speak pieces' and sing and wanted to see me dance the parse-me-la, and gave me generously of their small silver for doing these things, which seemed strange to me for I wanted to do them so much that I needed bribing to stop. Only they didn't know it.[75]

Here, Hurston explains the complicated relationship between creative expression and interpretation within the context of racial stereotyping. Young Zora understands aesthetic pleasure (as both viewer and performer) as an individual experience of free creativity and pure feeling.[76] She does not yet understand what the older residents of Eatonville perceive, which is the way in which her desire for, and pleasure in, creative expression can be read through racist stereotypes by the white visitors. Nor does Zora seem cognizant of the power structures in place that allow the white tourists to visit Eatonville as ethnographic tourists, as a site in which their expectations for Black performance, based in stereotype, might be realized. As Hurston paints her childhood self, Zora did not understand the racist misreadings in which she was being figured as a stereotype, although the adults in her community and the reader can (as can, of course, the adult Hurston writing retrospectively).[77] Her abstraction into stereotype is produced through the white tourists' interpretive failures. Hurston sketches the trap of racist stereotype that delimits Black creative expression via a poverty of interpretive possibility.

Leaving the sheltered world of Eatonville to go to school in Jacksonville, Hurston "suffered a sea change."[78] Hurston boarded the boat to Jacksonville as "Zora," but when she disembarked, "she was no more."[79] Hurston writes, "I was not Zora of Orange County any more, I was now a little colored girl. I found it out in certain ways. In my heart as well as in the mirror, I became a fast brown—warranted not to rub nor run."[80] Here, Hurston describes her coming to racial awareness as a loss, not only of individuality (the loss of the name) but of aesthetic possibility. The individual is replaced with a fixed abstract form—"a fast brown." This brown does not "rub," cannot be erased, smeared, or altered. It does not "run"; it cannot drip or change texture, becoming runny or liquid, and it cannot escape its fastened-ness. The power of Hurston's description of racial typing as an act of increasing abstraction and de-individuation lies in this sense of fixity and participates in a modernist discourse of painterly color forms. Diffused into pure color, this brown is fast as in fastened, fixed, unchanging, and unfree. According to Malevich, this pure color form would be pure feeling—a pre-social, embodied intuition. However, Hurston shows that the feeling of "fast brown" is not her own spontaneous feeling but one heaved upon her by racist interpretive frameworks.

Color abstraction continues to play a significant role throughout the essay, most memorably in the oft-recalled line "I feel most colored when I am thrown against a sharp white background."[81] As Barbara Johnson notes in her work on Hurston's essay, racial fixity is not a constant or stable experience (again, Bhabha appears); it is one that must be consistently reinforced and develops through social and linguistic interaction—the contextuality of color.[82] Hurston expresses this through the painterly image of stark contrast, color cut into a form by a sharp white edge (we recall the straight lines of the white border surrounding *Black Square*). Hurston depicts this transformation as a violent suddenness, the experience of being "thrown against" whiteness. This whiteness is "sharp," emphasizing that the process of racialized abstraction is aesthetic—that is, having to do with feeling—the form is a cut. Hurston explores the feeling of a racialized abstraction as an encounter with aesthetic form, being shaped by the white background and its geometric sharpness, an intensely alienating experience of observing your own misrecognition that results in a fragmentation of the self, prefiguring Fanon's stunning analysis of racial interpellation in *Black Skin, White Masks*. Hurston renders the process of racialization as the execution of an aesthetic form.

Hurston's "white background" also anticipates Toni Morrison's examination of Edgar Allen Poe's apocalyptic whiteness in the arctic landscapes of *The Narrative of Arthur Gordon Pym*. In *Playing in the Dark*, Morrison finds a blurring between racial and chromatic whiteness in Poe's imagery and in imagery of several other well-known American authors, including Herman Melville. She writes:

> These images of impenetrable whiteness need contextualizing to explain their extraordinary power, pattern, and consistency. Because they appear almost always in conjunction with representations of black or Africanist people who are dead, impotent, or under complete control, these images of blinding whiteness seem to function as both antidote for and meditation on the shadow that is companion to this whiteness—a dark abiding presence that moves the hearts and texts of American literature with fear and longing.[83]

The Africanist "shadow" projected against the snow-white surface of American literature is an image of contrast and constraint that recalls Hurston's "sharp white background."

Minimalist artist and writer David Batchelor likewise considers the associations between chromatic whiteness and colonial strategies of containment and power in his work on the fear of color, *Chromophobia*. Batchelor recalls the interior of a luxurious home he once visited decorated in an omnipresent, floor-to-ceiling white—an architectural apotheosis of modernist monochrome:

> There is a kind of white that is more than white, and this was that kind of white. There is a kind of white that repels everything that is inferior to it, and that is almost everything. This was that kind of white. There is a kind of white that is not created by bleach but that itself is bleach. This was that kind of white. This white was aggressively white. It did its work on everything around it, and nothing escaped.[84]

Batchelor's "aggressive" white rhymes with the painful sharpness of Hurston's white background, which similarly bonds whiteness to violent domination. Like Morrison, Batchelor turns to classic literature, Melville and Conrad in this case, to demonstrate chromatic whiteness's historic relationship to white supremacy. Via this literature, Batchelor argues that at the root of Western "chromophobia," or fear of color, is a desire for dominance. Color becomes associated with the "alien" and "dangerous," the childlike, trivial, and feminine; color is "routinely excluded from the higher concerns of the Mind. It is other to the higher values of Western culture. Or perhaps culture is other to the higher values of colour. Or colour is the corruption of culture."[85]

Anthropologist Michael Taussig corroborates these associations between color and subjugation, connecting these relationships more directly to colonialism while also explaining the seemingly contradictory colonial appetite for color that frequently attends chromophobia:

> Color for the West became attached to colored people or their equivalents, such as kids and the women of southern Italy with their brightly colored bodices and ribbons. This way the West could have its cake and eat it, could admire the Zouaves, sexually as well as aesthetically, while

standing in the darkness of war, the darkness of night, and the darkness of those dark overcoats, coats, trousers, socks, and shoes that men wore then in 1916, for centuries before, and to the present day.[86]

Morrison, Batchelor, and Taussig pick through the tangled mess of metaphor and abstraction that binds race and color into their unquiet affair. While these theorists of color offer truths about how color carries social meaning, a reader can quickly draw from their own repertoire of color experiences to offer counterexamples that would trouble an unnuanced engagement with these authors' arguments. Perhaps color's persistent connection to freedom has something to do with this dual desire both to assign meanings to color and yet insist on color's expressive openness. Colors hold associations beyond those identified in this chapter, including contradictory meanings. This does not mean that the above claims by Morrison, Batchelor, and Taussig are untrue, but it does suggest that color's meaning is prismatic, capable of holding many experiences at once. Ultimately, no one color exclusively *means* any one idea. Rather, color—including whiteness and blackness—is an abstract field where strategies of dominance come to be sorted, controlled, repaired, and undone.

Returning to Hurston's painterly invocation of color as an aesthetic form of race-making, the elisions between race and color are explored not only in the famous "sharp white background" moment of "How It Feels to Be Colored Me" but throughout Hurston's essay, which consistently returns to paint metaphors in order to analyze experiences of racialization and racial feeling. In a later scene, the adult Hurston visits a jazz club with a white acquaintance. Once again, color, both feeling chromatic color and feeling racially color*ed*, gives form to racial difference. While Hurston is intensely moved by the music in the club, the white visitor is apparently untouched. Listening to the music ignites Hurston's visual imagination. She writes, "My face is painted red and yellow and my body is painted blue."[87] In Hurston's recollection, to be moved by aesthetic pleasure is to become colored. When Hurston looks to her white companion, it seems that he is unmoved by the music: "Music. The great blobs of purple and red emotion have not touched him. He has only heard what I felt. He is far away and I see him but dimly across the ocean and the continent that have fallen between us.

He is so pale with his whiteness then and I am *so* colored."[88] The music is depicted as paint in its liquid representation as "blobs" of purple and red. But these colors have not touched Hurston's companion; his body remains pale as Hurston's metamorphizes into ecstatic red, yellow, and blue. In this scene, Hurston yet again describes an experience of racialization as an act of chromatic coloring, but this experience is markedly different from the brown and black color forms described earlier in the essay. The bright color forms of aesthetic pleasure are an expansive, mutable delight rather than a hard fixity. However, this moment quickly turns from ecstatic to alienating. The white acquaintance's failure of feeling marks a breakdown in interpretation; difference hardens between him and Hurston like drying paint. Once again, a flat white background becomes a site of painfully ossifying racial differentiation.

Feeling color leads to "feeling colored," illustrating how racial stereotypes restrict not only artistic expression but also reception. Moreover, it makes a direct connection between aesthetic pleasure (or its absence) and racialization. Hurston describes a transgressive aesthetic pleasure. More specifically, this is the pleasure of aesthetic identification within a collective tradition. A crucial element of Hurston's enjoyment is that the jazz invites her to take pleasure in Black collectivity and aesthetics, expressed here in a primitivist discourse of ecstatic belonging: "I follow those heathen—follow them exultingly. I dance wildly inside myself; I yell within, I whoop; I shake my assegai above my head, I hurl it true to the mark yeeeeooww! I am in the jungle and living in the jungle way."[89] Acknowledging the problematic primitivism of this jubilant description, the movement from "feeling color" to "feeling colored" is a movement from a vibrant collectivity produced through aesthetic pleasure to a position of fixed abstraction that alienates Hurston by discrediting the validity of her pleasure based on its associations with Blackness. This is important, not least because this shows us that aesthetic pleasure is a site of creation and play, as well as a scene of social regulation.

At the end of "How It Feels to Be Colored Me," Hurston continues to pursue the potentiality of radical color. Unlike the sharp, delineated contrasts of black and white that characterize the first half of the essay, Hurston's final exploration of abstraction lingers in the floppy, soft, lumpy, and overflowing—more similar to the red and purple blobs of music, than the "fast brown" or "sharp white background." Hurston writes:

> I feel like a brown bag of miscellany propped against a wall. Against a wall in company with other bags, white, red, and yellow. Pour out the contents, and there is discovered a jumble of small things priceless and worthless. A first-water diamond, an empty spool, bits of broken glass, lengths of string, a key to a door long since crumbled away, a rusty knifeblade, old shoes saved for a road that never was and never will be, a nail bent under the weight of things too heavy for any nail, a dried flower or two still a little fragrant. In your hand is the brown bag. On the ground before you is the jumble it held—so much like the jumble in the bags, could they be emptied, that all might be dumped in a single heap and the bags refilled without altering the content of any greatly. A bit of colored glass more or less would not matter. Perhaps this is how the Great Stuffer of Bags filled them in the first place—who knows?[90]

We might understand this shift in depiction as a transition from the painterly to the sculptural and as a relocation from a world of sharp, angular geometries to one of fluid, rounded softness. As opposed to being thrown against the sharp white background, the bag is casually propped against the wall. This position suggests a body in repose, in contrast to the violence of being thrown. Nevertheless, there remains a sense of objectifying arrangement by another, a disturbing immobility. In opposition to the painterly color form, the bag is three-dimensional—it has an inside. The bag gains its flexible shape not from cutting contrast but from what fills it. And what fills it is both arbitrary and exquisite.

Being able to dump out a person's contents, shuffle them around with someone else's, and then refill the empty container is a depiction of interiority that challenges the primacy of individual sovereignty. It is utopian and unnerving, especially in the explicitly cross-racial exchange. In some ways, the image follows the logic of color blindness or "it's what's inside that counts." However, the rest of the essay seems to contradict a color-blind reading. Considering the scene of Black aesthetic identification in the jazz club or the importance of Black communities like Eatonville to Hurston's life and work, it seems unlikely that Hurston is advocating for a rejection of racial identification or Black communality. Rather, this image of racialized bag people seems to explore a paradoxical fantasy of simultaneous radical sameness (everything is interchangeable) and radical difference (everything is unique). Abstraction makes coherent this ambivalent motion between sameness and difference. Hurston lingers in the lovely individuality of the fractured and discarded so that what is worthless and what is precious becomes impossible to determine—everything is valuable. Each item, while ordinary, seems laden with significance and even narrative: "a key to a door long since crumbled away" or "a nail bent under the weight of things too heavy for any nail." Yet while the poetic quality of these objects suggests a psychic and historical weight, broken glass and dried flowers refuse any deterministic relation to racialized identity or preconceived notions of it. There is also a suggestion of psychic nourishment in this image, a sense of being filled by beauty and complexity, as well as an uncertainty of what to make of it as Hurston's protagonist stands staring at this gallimaufry, holding the bag in her hand. The bag people are certainly a passive image of subjectivity that prompts ethical unease, but the image is perhaps also reminiscent of the kind of passivity that coincides with a sense of aesthetic satisfaction, of being replete with what is resplendent. This may or may not quell a reader's concerns. The bag imagery continues to depend on monochrome abstraction to represent racial difference (brown bag, white bag, red bag, yellow bag). However, it does so a bit differently by summoning an image of radical intersubjectivity rather than fixity. The confetti of peoples' lives travels fluidly, commingling and restructuring these bag people from the inside out in a way that is neither culturally determinant, nor biological, but aesthetic. The overall suggestion is that the aesthetic is a means of imagining alternative models of subjectivity and interrelationality. Here, Hurston imagines the pleasures of aesthetic free play as the substance of self.

While Hurston would not have seen Malevich's *Black Square* or the work of les Incohérents, she would have been aware of a range of modernist visual practices exploring color abstraction and blackness (racial and chromatic), for example, Aaron Douglas's work. Douglas and Hurston were both contributors to the sadly short-lived little magazine *FIRE!!* and generally a part of the same Harlem Renaissance milieu. For *FIRE!!*, Douglas created a compelling cover in the idiom of modernist color abstraction. Using geometric shapes and sharp, angular lines, Douglas's cover is dominated by a large Africanist head in profile. The profile is all the more striking with its black silhouette against a blaring crimson ground. At the bottom of the image is the red silhouette of a sphinx, whose expression mirrors the stoic mood of the human profile.⁹¹ *FIRE!!* was an attempt by a younger generation of Black Harlem Renaissance artists, including Wallace Thurman, Richard Bruce Nugent, and Langston Hughes, as well as Douglas and Hurston, to reject the perceived expectations and limitations placed on both the content and style of Black art by the established African American bourgeoisie, particularly its "deans" Alain Locke and W. E. B. Dubois. Thurman famously professed the hope that *FIRE!!* would be "burned in Boston" for its frank portrayal of taboo subjects like sex work, queerness, and colorism within African American communities and for the contributors' formal experimentalism that rejected the legibility of bourgeois realism. The magazine rebelled against the idea that limits could be placed on Black expressiveness by simultaneously centering social questions and aestheticism.

Douglas's use of chromatic black on the cover of *Fire!!* undermines assumptions about the stylistic range of Black aesthetic expression while also insisting on an historical particularity. In the black silhouette that boldly fills the cover, Douglas situates modernist geometric abstraction in relation to its African roots, a gesture of restoration and repair. Working as a critique of the whitening of abstraction, this move claims abstraction as part of a Black aesthetic tradition.

Smudge, Type, and Touch

In "How It Feels to Be Colored Me," Hurston's abstractionist color imagery dives into the knotty relationship between color abstraction, freedom, and aesthetic pleasure. It traces the complex imbrications of color and aesthetic racialization while also leaving the door open to the pleasure of color's expressive freedom. Beginning with color abstraction's role in hardening anti-Black stereotypes, Hurston ends with a scene of optimism for color's radical abstraction. More than half a century later, Hurston's painterly prose is picked up by the contemporary African American painter and conceptual artist Glenn Ligon. The Bronx-born artist's work often stretches the limits of medium and material to explore social meanings through conceptualism and abstraction. Ligon works across a variety of media, including neon, installation, photography, and silkscreen, however he first became well known for his series of text paintings from the 1990s quoting from Black literature, including Hurston's "How It Feels to Be Colored Me." Ligon has referred to abstract expressionist painting as "a touchstone for my painting practice," and we can see this knowledge in his painting *Untitled (I Feel Most Colored When I Am Thrown against a Sharp White Background)* (1990), which uses large amounts of color in a highly expressive way.[92] And yet Ligon also participates in a historical critique of modernist painting and the history of the color abstraction by engaging Hurston as a reader and fellow practitioner of Black modernism.[93]

Ligon's *I Feel Most Colored* quotes directly from Hurston's essay "How It Feels to Be Colored Me," hand stenciling the phrase "I feel most colored when I am thrown against a sharp white background" over and over again in black oil stick on a white ground. Ligon's process is methodical, messy, and repetitive. Working from left to right, top to bottom as Ligon "makes progress" across the painting, his stencil becomes encrusted with black oil, smudging the text so that the words become increasingly illegible as he approaches the bottom of the painting—finally becoming more of an amorphous black constellation of mackles than perceptible letters or words. The sense of progress (tentative to begin with) becomes more and more obscure; Ligon seems further away from any sense of completion as each line is completed. In Ligon's human printing press, text becomes texture, abstracted black feeling. This is color, contrary to Hurston's "fast brown," that *does* rub and we bear witness to the intimacy of Ligon's rubbing across the painting, the pressure of his hands and his tools, his commitment to a tedious practice reminiscent of punishment at the blackboard—remedial humiliation reclaimed as expressive remediation.

While it is not Ligon's first painting to incorporate text as its subject, *I Feel Most Colored* represents a breakthrough in his work, as Ligon developed his signature use of oil sticks and stenciling to create the smeared effect so powerfully deployed. This piece also initiates the use of recycled doors as the painting's "canvas," the door perhaps rematerializing Hurston's "door that has long since crumbled away." Hurston has the key and Ligon the door, it seems. As art historian Huey Copeland explains, as an abstract painter, Ligon was intrigued by language as an abstract form that enabled him to "address the demonization of black masculinity prevalent within American culture, allowing the black body to be disentangled from the graphic 'scenes of subjection' in which it is continually emplotted."[94] That is, "scenes of subjection"—such as Hurston's "thrown against a sharp white background"—are dislocated from the deterministic logic of racialized interpretive frameworks via Ligon's mechanical repetitions that make the text increasingly abstract and illegible.[95] *I Feel Most Colored* is a performed reading of Blackness, both racial and art historical, as well as a performance of Ligon reading Hurston. Ligon, who has a deep knowledge of the history of modernist abstraction, draws out the painterly abstraction of Hurston's prose, materializing the essay's reparative movements toward a Black abstract practice, wherein color makes possible, rather than forecloses, Black aesthetic pleasure.

As with the promise of the beautiful in chapter 1 or whimsy's appropriation of the criteria of judgment in chapter 2, with color abstraction we can see a recourse to recover aesthetic pleasure as a means of abolishing racism's unfreedom. All the Black artists discussed so far—Whitten, Gallagher, Hurston, Douglas, and Ligon—strive to find a kind of aesthetic transformation through abstraction that is not a denial of race and racism but a rejection of racial forms or race-making as fixed interpretation and stereotype. Ligon is an interpreter of Hurston, repetitiously performing his readerly encounter with the scene of subjection to dislodge it from a pattern of re-inscribed racial meaning. Hurston and Ligon are artists in conversation, attempting to solve the problems presented by abstraction and its associations with freedom. There is a mutuality between them, a structure of feeling—the meeting of sensibility and plasticity, Whitten might say.

As many scholars of Ligon's work have argued, the smudging of the black oil paint translates into a smudging of the legibility of racial Blackness as well as its accumulating stickiness.[96] Indeed, the tradition of modernist abstraction itself, and its relation to racial and racist reductionism, is also referenced in this smudging. While in one way the smudged text reads as the obfuscation of legibility, in another sense this is a reparative movement toward pure color that is neither separate from the visual overdetermination of race nor limited by stereotypes that foreclose the possibility of Black expression.

Ligon's use of literal "type" in the form of stenciled text signifies a history of stereotype and the process of being stereotyped as a kind of abstraction. In the early nineteenth century, stereotyping was a method of printing in which a mold (made of plaster or papier-mâché) was used to print text rather than *the form itself*.[97] This mold is taken from the *surface* of the original form. We have here, then, a process characterized by copying and superficiality. The stereotype is an act of reproduction based on an inexact or surface copy. This technical definition is now colloquially obscure, although the idea of reproducing superficiality remains. As if referring to this historical definition of stereotype, Ligon's text paintings explore racialization and racist typing as these things play out within the materiality of painted text. Ligon's choice of quotation frames the practice of racial stereotyping as a central concern of the work, while his repetitive stenciling evokes the mechanical nature of the archaic printing practice. Ligon draws a connection between the ideas and feelings expressed in Hurston's prose and the materiality that precedes the concept of stereotyping via the textured abstractions of chromatic blackness. Hurston's image of black on white suggests not only modernist color forms but also the printed page, drawing a connection between printed type and racial type, suggesting that the emotional and social experience of racial typing is like the physical machinations of printed type—a forceful, repetitious, and unthinking procedure. Ligon's Hurston painting draws together the practice of racial typing, textual mass production, and histories of modernist form.

Whitten's prismatic black resins explode a spectrum of color possibilities. Gallagher's glossy black refers the viewer back to herself, pushing her to reflect on the meanings she brings to the painting. The textures of Ligon's black painting are rough, smeared, thick, an uneven, dense surface that obscures as it accumulates. While at the top of the painting, Hurston's quote is perfectly legible and clear, as the thickly textured accretions build up on the painting's surface that clarity disperses into an abstraction that embraces opacity. Ligon's smudging suggests that while Hurston's pithy quotation may at first seem utterly straightforward, rendered starkly in black and white, Ligon's painting considers how abstraction opens interpretive possibility by engaging the vexed visual history of chromatic blackness, creating a powerfully inchoate density that is not easily parsed. The spread of color that refuses clear interpretation while marking a dynamic process (Ligon's active reading, his expressive copying of Hurston's text), recalling Édouard Glissant's "right to opacity," the right not to be transparent to the other—and for the other not to be transparent to you—as a foundation of ethical relations.[98]

In *I Feel Most Colored*, the pleasure of abstraction's freedom does not require Ligon to dispense with history and sociality. On the contrary, it is abstraction's ability to reference and engage the social while dispersing its fixity that makes Ligon's painting possible. Like the strange and optimistic ending of Hurston's essay, Ligon's use of abstraction critiques a fantasy of freedom based in asocial and ahistorical feeling while maintaining the potential utopianism of color's opacity. If the promise of color abstraction lies in its horizons of artistic and interpretive freedom, Ligon's black abstractions tread gently along their azimuth. Abstraction allows this wandering and wondering between the exultant possibilities of freedom and what might be lost in its pursuit. An engagement with color abstraction so preoccupied with justice suggests a notion of artistic freedom that is not purely individualist—the pouring of a single consciousness directly into the work—but one that considers how people are connected, how consciousness intermingles, and how interdependence can be a baseline for free making.

Artists like Whitten, Gallagher, Hurston, Douglas, and Ligon call our attention to the blurry materiality of racial abstraction and chromatic blackness. Chromatic blackness as an abstract form is neither ahistorical nor fixed by existing associative meanings. In its materiality, it is always relational, always contextual, always perceptual. We cannot see it separately from its saturation into textile, or the reflection of high gloss, the layering of historical meaning, or the built environment of the sentence. The history of the black monochrome shows a foundational entanglement with anti-Black racism, as expressed in a desire for imaginative artistic play that is based in principles of separatism and dominance. However, the examples of black monochromatic painting and color abstraction produced by the Black artists in this chapter demonstrate that the phenomenological and metaphysical aesthetic experiences attached to color—the color black specifically, in this case—have not and cannot be exclusively possessed by the racist logics that infused many twentieth-century approaches to "pure color." These examples of black monochromatic art and discourse by Black artists can even display an optimism, albeit a critical one, for the transformative pleasures of color abstraction as a "material, method, and mode."[99] Through their work, one finds a critical study of color and its promised aesthetic pleasures. In painted black, whether material as in the artworks discussed throughout the chapter or metaphorical as in Hurston's essay, boundlessness seems to become real. The pleasure of abstract black is a pleasure of materializing a yet undefined sensation, what it means to make freely.

The case studies in this chapter do not consider the relationship of the artist to their work in a vacuum but in acknowledgment that interpretive practices help shape the world in which art is made and received, highlighting the innate relationality of color perception and meaning. As with Edwards's show *Blackness in Abstraction*, curation can help up to recognize interpretive modes that have become naturalized and forge environments where a different set of meanings are available. In 2017, Ligon curated an exhibition titled *Blue Black* for the Pulitzer Arts Foundation in St. Louis, Missouri. Included in the show was Ligon's *Untitled (I Am Not Tragically Colored)* (1990), a painting that also quotes from "How It Feels to Be Colored Me" and follows the same painting procedures as *I Feel Most Colored*. The exhibition placed a broad range of aesthetic objects in conversation, from Carrie Mae Weems's blue-toned photograph of a young Black boy, *Blue Black Boy* (1997), to Derek Jarman's meditation on his approaching death from AIDS-related complications in his film *Blue* (1993), to Andy Warhol's black and blue print of Elizabeth Taylor, to Kerry James Marshall's *Untitled (Policeman)* (2015), a painting of a Black policeman resting on the hood of a police car against a slate blue ground, the hazy color of the light-polluted city sky at twilight. Ligon explains that the impetus for the exhibition was an encounter with Ellsworth Kelly's *Blue Black* (2000), a twenty-eight-foot-tall painted aluminum sculpture featuring a bright cerulean blue rectangle sitting atop a deep black one. As Ligon recounts the experience, when he stood in front of Kelly's *Blue Black*, he suddenly heard

> Louis Armstrong's gravel-strewn voice singing "What did I do to be so black and blue?" Given the title of the sculpture, that the Armstrong song would pop into my head was not so unexpected, yet I had to ask what the lyrics of a melancholy show tune about racial inequality had to do with Kelly's rigorous and elegant paintings, sculptures, drawings, and collages, part of an artistic practice that sought to "erase all 'meaning' from the thing seen" so that "the real meaning of it [could] be understood and felt."[100]

Conceptually and perceptually, the curation of the show induces simultaneous contrast—the effect of placing colors together so that the perception of those colors is altered, sometimes making them look radically different. At first, perhaps Ligon's show seems oppositional to Kelly's "rigorous" exclusion of meaning so that "the real meaning" of pure color can be experienced. The cohabitation of Weems's deeply sensitive conceptual portrait photography, Marshall's ambiguous portrayal the Black police officer, Jarman's elegy for his own life narrated against a Klein blue expanse, Warhol's pop iconography all cry out to be understood in charged arrangements of social meaning, spurning the idea that autonomy and purity reveal an essential the truth. But in another sense, Ligon is exactly performing the act at the core of Kelly's work: bringing elements into relation (black and blue) so that a truth previously unavailable might be perceived. The meaning dispensed with here, the meaning whose departure allows the truth to be seen, is the idea that "pure" color might exist at all.

Evocatively, Ligon explains that "in my ideal show, the artworks would physically touch—blue and black a shared identity prompting metaphoric backslapping and fist-bumping."[101] Ligon poetically imagines the ideal expression of the show as a series of celebratory physical intimacies, backslapping and fist bumping, which recall glad gestures in recognition of something shared. Of course, the preservative and proprietary procedures of museums forbid such affectionate touching. Yet the inching closeness of these objects produces the possibility of a revolutionary shared feeling, the felt possibility of social meaning that produces interpretive openness rather than foreclosure, and the pleasure of improvised and affectionate relations that might flourish in the clearing.

Color abstraction presents an unsolvable problem of interpretation. This is the source of its potentiality as well as its difficulty. As we saw in the recently revealed ignominious history of Malevich's *Black Square*, racism's logic lurks in modernist color discourse. The perceived freedom of color is often contingent on racist fixity—a delimitation of who can play and who is played with, of who can know and what is known, of who can make and what is made. Yet despite the risks, Black artists have explored color abstraction as an act of recovery, repair, and bold innovation, offering alternative visions of racialized collectivity and identification that refuse dominance, individuality, and separatism as the foundations of artistic and interpretive freedom. They reach for the pleasure of color as experiment, pulling it back from an aesthetic discourse entangled with racism, wherein the interpretation is already known, already in circulation, and needs only to be called to recognition through the act of stereotyping.

In the next chapter, I will continue to consider what can and cannot be shared in raced and gendered scenes of aesthetic pleasure. Turning to the work of writer and visual artist Theresa Hak Kyung Cha, I explore an experimentalist aesthetic of "dreaminess" as a process-based aesthetic method for sharing feelings and ideas that refutes conventional notions of empathy and identity, creating communal space based in difference rather than sameness. As I will argue, Cha's dreaminess is theoretically and materially linked to the reality-shaping technologies and aesthetics of projection and the cinema. Cha explores the notion of shared aesthetic experience as a shared dream using experimentalist techniques drawn from her study of film theory. Among the heightened affects and spectacle of the cinema, the sociality of aesthetic judgment becomes apparent. Rather than dissolve difference in the ether of shared experience, Cha employs experimentalist techniques that embed alienation and defamiliarization as part of the process of collective experience. Cha's expansion of the work that experimental forms might do within racial and gendered social arrangements laid the groundwork for a whole new generation of artists and writers of color seeking to expand the set of available practices and the visual and literary grammars of race.

4

Difficult Pleasures

When I had this dream I thought, *Here is the destroyed world,
and here—beyond the threshold—is the luminous world.*
—Jackie Wang, "The Coral Tree"

As in chapter 1, the final chapter of this book begins with the limerence of the cinematic close-up and what unspools between the viewer and the film in experimental projections, both technological and psychological. In this documentation photograph of her 1978 performance *Other Things Seen, Other Things Heard*, we see the performance artist, filmmaker, and writer Theresa Hak Kyung Cha kneeling to the left of a portrait-oriented closeup photograph projected on the wall. It is a still from Carl Theodor Dreyer's *The Passion of Joan of Arc* (1928), a tight shot of Renée Falconetti's face (who plays Joan of Arc), her shorn head, downcast eyes, parted lips, and two fat tears streaming down her face. In this image, which takes up the entire wall and part of the floor, the tears are the size of large lemons that could fill the palm of your hand. Cha is kneeling in the front corner to the left of the screen, her hands on her knees, back slightly rounded, her face turned away from the audience, watching Renée Falconetti cry as Joan of Arc awaits her death.

In another photograph from this performance, Cha stands in the far left third of a landscape-oriented rectangle of light, back against the wall. Her body faces the audience, but her face is turned in profile so that she appears to be watching the projected image. On the wall is a photograph of an empty movie theater, tall smooth columns flanking the theater screen, dark velvet curtains heavily frame the blindingly white light emanating from the center of the image. Cha's arms hang at her sides, her posture straight, languid but controlled. Her body merges with the projected photograph, becoming a screen herself. The movie screen in the photograph looks alive, as if Cha is meeting the gaze of some alien

Figure 4.1: Cha performing in front of Renée Falconetti. Theresa Hak Kyung Cha, *Other Things Seen, Other Things Heard (photographs)*, 1978. Twelve black-and-white photographs, 8 × 10 in. University of California, Berkeley Art Museum and Pacific Film Archive. Gift of the Theresa Hak Kyung Cha Memorial Foundation.

light-based creature. No images are visible on the move theater screen in the photograph, just the opacity of white.

In visual half-rhyme with Isaac Julien's affectively and historically layered portraiture explored in chapter 1, these images from *Other Things Seen, Other Things Heard* suggest an ambiguous relation between a minoritized viewer and the history of racial looking, playing out in aesthetic forms that circumvent realism, dislodging naturalized relations inherited through cinematic traditions. While Cha and Julien are quite different stylistically—Julien luxuriating in the silky density of high-contrast monochrome, Cha embracing the grainy, stippled textures of handmade paper, textiles, video, and film—both artists are interested in film's capacity to bring people together in acts of looking (for better or worse) and the alternative social formations that might be generated in this act. As we will see in this chapter, like Julien, Cha explores the political possibilities of aesthetic pleasure within ambivalent, risky conditions, opting for nonrepresentational and experimental forms that restructure relationships to race, pleasure, and belonging.

Cha was born in Busan, in what is now South Korea, in 1951, at the height of the battle period of the Korean War. Her childhood was shaped by this war, US occupation, and the Cold War devastation that followed. In 1962, Cha and her family emigrated to Hawaiʻi and then to San Francisco, California in 1964. Their exile was precipitated by a military coup led by General Park Chung-hee, which overthrew the brief Second Republic of Korea and ushered in an era of extreme repression. Coming of age in the Bay Area, Cha attended the Convent of the Sacred Heart, where she began studying French, a language that would come to play an important role in her life and work. She went on to study at the University of San Francisco before transferring to

Figure 4.2: Cha performing in front of the white screen. Theresa Hak Kyung Cha, *Other Things Seen, Other Things Heard (photographs)*, 1978. Twelve black-and-white photographs, 8 × 10 in. University of California, Berkeley Art Museum and Pacific Film Archive; Gift of the Theresa Hak Kyung Cha Memorial Foundation.

UC Berkeley, where she earned multiple undergraduate and graduate degrees in comparative literature and art. Cha cultivated a cerebral, atmospheric body of work, her art eventually taking her from the Bay Area to New York City in 1980. Then, in 1982, just as her artworld career was taking off and her book *Dictee* was published, Cha was raped and murdered by Joseph Sanza when she was only thirty-one years old. I invite readers to take a moment of pause before continuing with their reading to contemplate the preciousness of Cha's life and the ongoing urgency of ending the systemic racism and misogyny that precipitated her death.[1]

From the early 1970s until her death in 1982, Cha produced an impressive body of work that was conceptually rich and formally groundbreaking and explored a wide range of media, including ceramics, performance, artist's books, concrete poetry, film, video, sculpture, mail art, audio, and slide projection. She is perhaps best known for her full-length literary work *Dictee* (1982), which has made her a canonical author in Asian American literary studies and experimental literature. Those who experienced Cha's performances firsthand often describe a transformative quality to Cha's work and her capacity to create scenes of affective intensity that continue to resonate decades later. The Korean American artist Yong Soon Min, Cha's contemporary and fellow student at Berkeley, recalls that Cha used experimental forms, rather than realist or representational ones, to create her deeply affecting environments. Min notes that Cha's work often held particular sonority for Korean Americans impacted by the violent currents of global racial capitalism and empire.[2]

Although affective intensity and connection are more frequently associated with representational and realist aesthetic experiences, often understood as the result of identificatory responses that representation assumedly provokes, Cha's writing and art demonstrate that abstraction and experimentalism also carry a tremendous propensity for affective impact and meaningful social relations. This aptitude in Cha's work for generating feelings of "being with" seems only to have intensified over time. The New York–based multimedia artist Cici Wu, who was born in Beijing and grew up in Hong Kong, has discussed the continuing influence of Cha's art across generations. In an interview, Wu reflected on Cha's desire for Asian connections across cultural difference:

[Cha] has this really soft-hearted kind of perspective, of how she perceives cultural differences, where the end result of it is not to separate them, but to bridge them. From there, I think I understood that sometimes there might be no equivalents between cultures, and instead of trying to find equivalents, we may go to the bottom level of values, and seek what has been important to culture; the way of life and its enjoyment. When cultures find there are no equivalents, they can start learning from each other.[3]

In her description of connection without equivalency, Wu parses how Cha's experimentalism simultaneously expresses the untranslatability of what woman-of-color feminism names "difference" while also building meaningful connections across those differences.[4]

Drawing from her readings of Audre Lorde's use of the term, Grace Kyungwon Hong parses "difference" as "an epistemological position, ontological condition, and political strategy that reckons with the shift in technologies of power that we might as well call 'neoliberal'" and constituted by "material processes that protect some from death, disposability, and devaluation at the expense of others."[5] Difference is material in its production within racial capitalism and cisheteropatriarchy yet nearly infinitely variable in its iterations. Shaped by the Cold War racial capitalism that produced neoliberalism and arriving at the height of woman-of-color feminism in the late 1970s and early 1980s, Cha's work is historically poised to consider "difference" as Hong defines it. As Sunny Xiang points out, while Cha's work is frequently read through the historical trauma of the Korean War and Japanese colonization, *Dictee* arrived "at a time when Korea was becoming known as 'the miracle on the Han'" and a period of global economic restructuring at the end of the "American Century" that we now recognize as the early period of neoliberalism—one result being rapid economic growth in South Korea, fueled by its participation in the American war in Vietnam.[6] As scholars like Hong, Roderick Ferguson, Jodi Kim, Lisa Lowe, Jodi Melamed, and Dylan Rodríguez have observed in different ways, the sometimes contradictory desires of racial capitalism and the white supremacist US nation-state result in the strategic devaluation of groups of people who are then "pitted against each other in a desperate effort to deflect the precarious condition of 'surplus.'"[7] This is very much a part of the period of "Cold" War when so many proxy hot wars forced waves of people to leave their home countries in search of survival and security. To be surplus is to be disposable and vulnerable to premature death, with the state of surplus itself being unevenly inhabited. Navigating the differences produced in this deadly context is what woman-of-color feminism attempts to do.

More concretely, Cha's work was featured in an important 1982 issue of the feminist arts journal *HERESIES*, where the messy intricacies of difference were being hashed out in the wake of potent woman-of-color feminist critiques of white feminism in the art world. In 1977, when the all-white Mother Collective of *HERESIES* editors failed to substantively include women of color in its third issue focusing on "Lesbian Art and Artists," the Combahee River Collective wrote an open letter critiquing the Mother Collective on the point that "feminist and lesbian politics and creativity are not the exclusive property of white women."[8] The Mother Collective responded by publishing the Combahee River Collective's letter in the next issue of *HERESIES*, promising to make an effort to include more non-white women in its pages and editorial process and issuing two race-focused issues: "Third World Women: The Politics of Being Other" (1979) and then "Racism Is the Issue" (1982).[9] However, the implementation of these professed commitments was far from perfect, as reported by the women who edited those issues.[10] As the Black playwright, poet, and editor Hattie Gossett put it in her contribution to the editorial statement in "Racism Is the Issue," "The problem of broadening the participation in the women's movement is very real and will not be solved in any single or simple manner."[11] Cha's contribution to *HERESIES* appeared in the 1982 "Women's Pages" issue, which also included work by such heavy hitters as Adrian Piper, Lorraine O'Grady, Linda Nishio, Ntozake Shange, Tomie Arai, Faith Ringgold and Michelle Wallace, Jenny Holzer, Kazuko Miyamoto, and Thulani Davis.[12] Its placement in a publication with such great historical significance for issues of race and feminism in literature and the arts suggests that Cha's work has something to say about woman-of-color feminism beyond the blunt facts of her "identity"—a concept that Cha scholars have complicated in their engagement with her work.

Situating Cha within woman-of-color feminism as a series of historical events as well as a critical framework contextualizes Wu's observations on Cha's work. As Hong writes, only in culture do we find the "ability to maintain contradictory impulses at the same time without resolving them," what she calls "the impossible politics of difference."[13] Cha's writing and art exemplify how the particularity of difference need not be erased in order to participant in the collectivity of aesthetic judgment. I include Wu's words on the failure of equivalencies and the palpable presence of difference in Cha's work in part because in this chapter, Cha's legacy as an artist will be nearly as important to my analysis as her artwork itself. Cha provides models for new generations of artists on how experimental forms can restructure relationships to difference.

Cha has garnered a slow-growing but ardent iconicity among the generations of artists and writers who have come after her. At first largely ignored by literary scholars and art historians, since her "recovery" in the 1990s Cha has become a major figure of Asian American female experimentalism—and woman-of-color experimentalism more broadly. While it would be easy to become cynical about Cha's relatively newfound prominence, I take an optimistic view of Cha's popularity. Cha is a difficult writer and visual artist, bringing significant formal challenges to her readers and audiences. Yet although Cha's minimalist, conceptualist, poststructuralist, and woman-of-color feminist methods present audiences with quite a high bar for entry, in terms of both grappling with aesthetic difficulty and refusing the homogenization of difference, that audience has only grown over the past few decades.

In a belated 2022 *New York Times* obituary for Cha by Dan Saltzstein—part of the "Overlooked" series, which publishes obituaries for historical personages whose lives went uncelebrated in the paper at the time of their death—the bestselling Korean American realist novelist and National Book Award finalist Min Jin Lee says that she admires Cha's "sense of entitlement," adding, "I had never met anybody like me, who shared my biography, who felt a sense of entitlement to have that level of difficulty in her work."[14] Saltzstein also quotes from Korean American experimental poet and essayist Cathy Park Hong's essay on Cha in *Minor Feelings: An Asian American Reckoning*: "'I find her style, while not exactly pleasurable, to be liberating,' she wrote, adding that Cha had 'made the immigrant's discomfort with English into a possible form of expression.'"[15] Saltzstein pulls a line that emphasizes the formally challenging nature of Cha's *Dictee* and the intellectual and emotional labors of reading it, which can be discomforting. It is not entirely clear what Lee means by "difficulty," a word often associated with Cha's work. It might reference what Saltzstein calls Cha's "unapologetically avant-garde form," or it may be the suggested emotional difficulty of the "cultural history and inner experiences," referenced in the autobiographical *Dictee* especially. The overall impression given, however, is that Cha's work is not for a casual audience, requiring a kind of commitment or endurance from its readers and viewers.

The implication of being "unapologetic" is that someone somewhere thinks that you *do* have something to apologize for, in this case the trespass of "difficulty" by someone who doesn't automatically possess that "entitlement" or who takes it without permission. Whether that difficulty is located in content or form, the suggestion of the obituary is that there is traditionally little patience for difficulty from someone like Cha, a Korean American woman and immigrant. Like Lee, I am also in admiration of Cha's "sense of entitlement," the fierce curiosity and integrity of her work, which is uncompromising in its distinct intellectual and aesthetic vision. Hong's writing on Cha and the "minor" or "ugly" feelings (drawing from Sianne Ngai's term for socially spurned emotions) connected to Asian American literature and experience strikes the emotional tones appropriate to her project, filling an important gap at the intersection of Asian American studies and affect studies. But I wonder, is there room in remembering Cha and honoring the growing impact of her work to add to our understanding of her art's affective range, expanding the kinds of feelings associated with difficulty?

In addition to highlighting Cha's formal difficulty, it is common to approach Cha's art through its melancholy, specifically through the Korean concept of *han*, which Jennifer Cho defines in her important essay "Mel-*han*-cholia" as "an irreducible, intergenerational feeling of communal grief, suggesting that the pervasive memories of foreign invasion and colonization, civil war, and internal division in Korea continue to impinge upon and redefine the safe boundaries of the present."[16] Cathy Park Hong, who devotes a devastating chapter to Cha in her essay collection *Minor Feelings*, describes *han* as "a combination of bitterness, wistfulness, shame, melancholy, and vengefulness, accumulated from years of brutal colonialism, war, and U.S.-supported dictatorships that have never been politically redressed."[17] Emphasizing the heritability of trauma, Hong writes, "*Han* is so ongoing that it can even be passed down: to be Korean is to feel *han*."[18] The viciousness of centuries of military violence and political oppression in the Korean peninsula, never fully atoned for, is further exacerbated by the erasure of US responsibility for its part in this collective trauma.[19] As Cho argues in her important essay on *Dictee*, the political affect of the text that sutures the individual and collective, what she dubs "mel-*han*-cholia," "emerges as a subversive political practice" of collective grief denied by multiple former and current empires.[20] Melancholy—or mel-*han*-choly—is a major affective note aesthetically and politically in Cha's work. It is appropriate to read Cha in the affective and political context of the Cold War and emergent neoliberal violence and as someone who was directly impacted by the Korean War and ongoing violence. Such grief continues to aggregate with Cha's own death, a horror that is intimately connected to the racial and gender politics of US militarism in the Korean peninsula, and Asia and the Pacific more broadly. The political energy of such grief is evidenced by the reception of *Dictee*. However, melancholy or mel-*han*-choly is not the only affect within Cha's aesthetically adventurous body of work.[21]

In the past three decades, Cha has accrued an increasingly large and rhapsodic following, exactly because of her difficulty, in form and content, and not despite it. This excited following is a response to the aesthetic and affective complexity of the work. There are deep aesthetic pleasures available in Cha's art. In addition to melancholy, we find her unique sense of wit and humor that attends her word play, the immersive fascination of her self-designed rituals, the delight of surprise that accompanies aesthetic experimentalism, the knotty pleasures of working through her cerebralism, and the sensuousness of a body of work that is highly textured, a treasure box of finely ribbed creamy paper, gauzy muslins, dark glutinously printed inks, fuzzy videos, clear water, tenebrous film, and grainy photographs.[22] I am profoundly indebted to the body of Cha scholarship as it stands and do not wish to suggest that the general focus on melancholy, *han*, and obliqueness is off base. But in this chapter, I would like to bring to the fore other affective dimensions of Cha's work that are less frequently discussed in the criticism. Cha's experimentalism, rather than alienating readers as might be expected, draws people in. I have seen this firsthand in the undergraduate classroom. While students will be the first to admit that *Dictee* is unlike other books they have read, they are also deeply moved by its stories, excited by its linguistic puzzles, and fascinated by the patchworked, semi-annotated archive threaded throughout the book. In short, contrary to Cha's somewhat intimidating reputation, people with very little training in literary study reading *Dictee* are able to respond with appreciation, admiration, even love.

There is always a little tear in the completeness of your reading of *Dictee* once you have wrapped it up so tidily. And one of *Dictee*'s great pleasures is to pinch that little tear and pull, starting over again. These are the affective experiences of experimentalism that are less often discussed—not existential dread, fiery political righteousness, or absurdism but tender curiosity, a pull to keep going despite the confusion and disorientation. Cha teaches us that there is room for them all. The strange pleasures of difficulty do not necessarily derive from the act of overcoming or resolving difficulty but from learning to appreciate what it feels like to not fully understand, to not master. Cha must be recognized as an artist of affective breadth and depth and a theorist of experimentalism who understood how aesthetic interventions can help us imagine social arrangements that defy the habitual and expected. Cha's work *is* powerful, but this power does not come at the expense of aesthetic and affective variety, including aesthetic pleasure as it is defined in throughout this book.

Indispensable to Cha's continuing influence is a set of stylistic techniques and formal strategies that I call "dreaminess." In Cha's work, the dream is an experimental method for conducting attention, a method that undermines the primacy of liberal subjectivity in aesthetic judgment. Cha's aesthetic dreaminess is hypnagogically located between light and shadow, its representations moth-eaten and diaphanous, out of focus, or caught only peripherally at the edges of the frame. Dreaminess creates political textures that acknowledge asymmetries of power and the limits of comparison, an unevenness that arouses curiosity. This generates deeply immersive and affectively intense experiences that yet demand a kind of analytical participation from the reader or audience—a navigation of difference without false equivalencies. Difference is not a difficulty (formal or affective) to be overcome or surmounted. Formal difficulty and lack of understanding are not necessarily impasses to a meaningful aesthetic connection. Formal strangeness makes it challenging to restore a default realism, a world of the given that is formatively tied to white supremacist aspirations to mastery. The disorienting strangeness of Cha's work is not the titillation of the exotic, which is its own kind of justifying realism in that it restores desire structured by dominance over difference. Rather, Cha is skilled in suspending the fantasy of complete understanding while encouraging the audience to rise to the occasion of the work.

Cha's dreaminess is derived from the reality-shaping aesthetics of projection and the pleasures of the cinema. The cinema, as we will see, is a tenebrific space where the sociality of aesthetic judgment becomes heightened, shimmering in the romance of collective pseudo-sleep. Dreaminess offers a fresh surreality in which the relations between things have shifted so that new meanings and relations can come into being. As in a dream, the edges are blurred, magical change takes place. As we have seen throughout this book, aesthetic pleasure is a structure in which feeling and form come together in the social to negotiate meaning, value, and power. It is a particularly effective structure, if counterintuitive perhaps, for social and political formation, including racial forms. Experimentalism can interrupt, recircuit, and reimagine the relational structures produced and mediated by aesthetic judgment, thereby having the potential to create new worlds and ways of being in them.

Form is a method of directing attention. When we encounter what feels formally difficult, we are encountering the feeling of our attention being directed in an unfamiliar way, perceiving differently as a result. As aesthetic experimentalism restructures the relationships between racial meaning, aesthetic form, and feeling, it has the capacity to obscure race as an onto-epistemological structure. But it can *also* intervene in that structure by directing attention in unfamiliar ways. While aesthetic judgments and feelings can be deeply personal, quirky, and individually revelatory, they are never experienced in true isolation but as part of the political and social structure of aesthetic judgment. Thus there is a profound need to think about the ethics of attention and interpretation as *a social practice* in which the tether and tissue of being with others is made and remade.

So what is Cha's dreaminess like? As made famous by the 2001 exhibition of her work at the Berkeley Museum of Art and accompanying catalog, Cha once stated that she wanted to become "the dream of the audience."[23] Evidently, she was successful. As curator Constance Lewallen writes in her introduction to the catalog, Cha apparently excelled in creating the sensation of being in a shared dream.[24] Quoting from an unpublished review of *Other Things Seen, Other Things Heard*, Lewallen observes, "The critic Robert Atkins attests to the hypnotic power of Cha's performances: 'I left [*Other Things Seen, Other Things Heard (Ailleurs)*] feeling suspended between consciousness and unconsciousness, as if I had been dreaming someone else's dream.'"[25] In *Other Things Seen, Other Things Heard*, Cha manipulates words-as-objects in front of projected images—Falconetti, the glowing movie theater, a blurry face oriented horizontally and filling the entire screen, rocks stenciled with words like *abandon, redemption,* and *forbidden*. She drags rocks across a sandy floor amid the click and flicker of the familiar pedagogical tool of the slide projector in a darkened room. The environment hovers between the instructive and the otherworldly, drawing together the cinema, the lecture hall, and the home slideshow, defamiliarizing language and the audience's relation to space through a highly sensorial and immersive three-dimensional collage of image, sound, and movement. Through this recontextualizing praxis, sensation and affect are heightened as systems of meaning-making while conventional logic recedes. The naturalized relationships between these signs and their meanings become uncertain, working themselves free of their settings. In this dreamy space, new interpretations and associations become available as the grip of the normal is loosened in Cha's aesthetic solvent. In this way, Cha's performance *does* function like a dream, as Lewallen, Rinder, and Atkins emphasize, in that Cha creates environments that restructure the relationships between images, language, and meaning, articulating a different sense of reality in the process.

In the dream, meaning is surprising or withheld. "Rational" logics are suspended. Relationships of juxtaposition and association create unfamiliar shapes and new ideas. Cha's aesthetics push against the membrane of lucidity, cognition a fogged window, and yet there is a particular kind of *knowing* in a dream that dissipates upon waking. The dream is a temporary space that can hold a paradox, where you can drift through impasses like mist. Dreams beg for our interpretation; we cannot leave them alone, examining their incongruent details for the meaning that

Figure 4.3: Cha's heavy words. Theresa Hak Kyung Cha, *Other Things Seen, Other Things Heard (photographs)*, 1978. Twelve black-and-white photographs, 8 × 10 in. University of California, Berkeley Art Museum and Pacific Film Archive. Gift of the Theresa Hak Kyung Cha Memorial Foundation.

feels near. We call the things we want to happen most "dreams," especially if they feel impossible. Dreaminess conveys Cha's ability to loosen the audience's relationship to the given reality. It asks us to remember that even in texts shaped by trauma, there can be the pleasure of dreaming. Cha's experimentalism reimagines the practice of being with others, articulating a political desire, the eros of a collective yet to be.

Race and the Avant-Garde

As seen in *Other Things Seen, Other Things Heard*, the technology of projection and its reality-shifting aesthetics are vital to Cha's experimentalism. Yet Cha's repurposing of projection is not uncomplicated. As in Yoko Ono's whimsicality, Cha's dreamy aesthetics, silent cinematic looking, and radical interrelationality can raise specters of Asian feminine docility and submission. The centrality of film and video apparatus to Cha's art might also spark questions regarding techno-Orientalism, defined by David S. Roh, Betsy Huang, and Greta A. Niu as "the phenomenon of imagining Asia and Asians in hypo- or hypertechnolgical terms in cultural productions and political discourse."[26] One of the thorny questions presented by Cha's work and the reception of it is that as a Korean American woman, Cha can be subject to the audience's projections and fantasies of Asian femininity.[27] In this racial and gendered framework, Cha's invocation of the dream can be interpreted as an invitation to forget difference rather than a means of engaging it. Her sensuous linguistic play can be understood as apolitical mysticism rather than an abstractionism that ravels the political and the social.[28] In such misreadings, Orientalist notions of the submissive Asian woman or ascetic mystic not only cloud the audience's ability to properly interpret the art but also attend to the high ethical standards demanded by Cha's work. Viewers can fall back into the self-satisfying colonial pleasures of their dreams of the Orient.

In his classic *Orientalism*, Edward Said established how the perceived docility and feminization of the Orient is integral to its creation as an object of Occidental knowledge, the Western scholar "surveying as if from a peculiarly suited vantage point the passive, seminal, feminine, even silent and supine East."[29] Asian American studies has since offered decades of rich critique on the colonial constructions of Asian femininity. Asian American feminist scholarship has thoroughly catalogued and historicized the injurious stereotypes of Asian female docility (the geisha, the Madame Butterfly, the China doll, the "good" immigrant daughter, etc.) and their roots in empire and racial capitalism, as well as the historical minimization of women within Asian American studies, what Rhacel Salazar Parreñas and Winnie Tam call a "derivative status of Asian women" or "their use as a backdrop for the rite of passage to the masculinity of Asian and white male protagonists."[30] In critiquing stereotypes, diminutions, and other means of limiting possibilities for Asian and Asian American women, Asian American feminist scholars have emphasized the importance of agency and resistance.

This scholarship has so expertly explored these predominant stereotypes of Asian female docility that a recent branch of feminist and queer Asian American scholarship has sprouted in the other direction, investigating the power of apparent passivity and anti-sociality, a significant turn within a discipline that historically has been deeply invested in demonstrative critique and coalition. Scholars such as Summer Kim Lee, Vivian Huang, and Jack Halberstam have argued that Asian American refusals of sociality can be read through the lens of political abstention or escapism, as Lee puts it, refusals of "compulsory sociability" and the "burden of relatability."[31] As Halberstam writes, performed passivity has the power to act as a "critique of the organizing logic of agency and subjectivity itself."[32] Each of these scholars examines Asian American performances of radical passivity and asociality that critique liberal concepts of agency and subjectivity, arguing that certain forms of inaction have political and psychic value. Finally, Asian American studies scholars Leslie Bow, Anne Anlin Cheng, Celine Parreñas Shimizu, and Tan Hoang Nguyen have all explored how racial fetish and sexual objectification can complicate the application of a traditional ethnic studies framework to Asian identity, desire, and political resistance, offering examples of how Asian subjects have engaged stereotype and fetish from within, not necessarily undoing or reversing these asymmetrical power structures but forming self-knowing relations to pleasure, self, and desire within the context Asian racialization.[33] These trends at the intersection of Asian American studies, feminist studies, and queer studies reconsider a spectrum of pathologized behaviors associated with the "silent and supine East," generating often ambivalent analysis of the ethics and politics of living in relation to racial and gender stereotypes.

My reading of Cha's work considers how racial and gender stereotypes impact interpretation while staying open to forms of political resistance that do not rely on an agential liberal subject. Although dreaminess might at first seem a "passive" aesthetic, in fact its disorienting forms generate demanding, and in their own way pleasurable, challenges for the reader or audience. Although it is possible to argue that Cha's aesthetic difficulty is a kind of anti-sociality that enables autonomy or that her dreamy *perceived* passivity creates a scene of self-loving privacy, these artworks that paradoxically read as both difficult and passive are actually the result of a different mode of attention to aesthetic sociality. In the sociality of sharing an aesthetic experience, formal difficulty guides the reader or audience's attention toward the practice of being together in difference without equivalencies. Tonally, these pieces do not rise triumphantly, soaring with righteous social epiphany or political jubilation. But there is beauty here, a declaration of value that shuffles and sighs in the cinema's artificial darkness, reaching toward the other to see if, perhaps, they see it too.

Dreaming the Revolution

In linking aesthetic difficulty and alternative sociality through the structure of the dream, Cha references the history of the dream as an avant-garde and revolutionary form. Like the avant-gardists of the early twentieth century who looked to automatic writing and collage in attempts to access the hidden meanings of the unconscious, Cha utilizes the dream's juxtapositional surrealism to imagine new relations and realities. The quotidian materials of daily life are radically reorganized and presented in such a way that previously impossible meanings rise to the surface of immediate, at times inarticulate, understanding. The revolutionary potential of oneiric disorientation has roots in several nineteenth- and twentieth-century aesthetic traditions associated with modernism and the avant-garde, including symbolism, surrealism, and Dadaism. Many of these movements were deeply influenced by the early days of psychology and psychoanalysis and were fascinated by the possibility of tapping into the unconscious as a creative source of disruption within an oppressive ordinary reality. The difficulty of their formal experimentalism often reflects the difficulty of their political, social, and psychological challenges. Rendering a new reality is not an easy task. Situating Cha's dreaminess within the revolutionary politics of a global (and not only white and European) modernist avant-garde intervenes in pseudo-mystical, merely impressionistic readings of her work that decontextualize affect from its sociohistorical inceptions.

Cha was quite knowledgeable about European modernism, including the movements mentioned above. In particular, she enjoyed the symbolist poet Stéphane Mallarmé, the plays of Samuel Beckett, and the writings of Marguerite Duras. Artistically, her concrete poetry, experimental writing (especially her book *Dictee*), and her use of collage and other modernist techniques in her artist's books and mixed-media pieces relay her experience with earlier European avant-gardisms. In terms of formal education, Cha earned four degrees from the University of California,

Berkeley, between 1969 and 1978—a BA in comparative literature, a BA in art, an MA in art, and an MFA in art—and studied with scholars Bertrand Augst and Jean-Louis Baudry and the artist Jim Melchert. In 1976 she attended the Centre d'Etudes Americain du Cinema in Paris to study film theory. While in Europe, Cha traveled in the circles of the major European thinkers in film theory, psychoanalysis, feminism, and the avant-garde, including Ulises Carrión, Christian Metz, Raymond Bellour, Thierry Kuntzel, Monique Wittig, and Hreinn Friðfinnsson.[34]

While Cha was undoubtedly well informed of the aforementioned European avant-garde history, it is crucial to recognize that the aesthetic and politically revolutionary potential of dreams is hardly limited to European artists. The Black studies historian Robin D. G. Kelley has argued that the surrealist investment in reinventing reality through radical dreaming has decolonial, non-Western roots. Just as European modernism in literature and the visual arts was developed from primitivist and Orientalist understandings of abstraction in non-Western cultures, surrealists and other artistic dreamers were likewise strongly influenced not only by Black, Asian, and Indigenous aesthetics but also by the revolutionary politics of non-white colonized peoples. As Kelley argues, "Surrealism may have originated in the West, but it is rooted in a conspiracy against Western civilization."[35] In his study of artists associated with the Négritude movement and Black decolonization struggles, particularly the Black Martinican writers Aimé and Suzanne Césaire and Wifredo Lam, a Cuban painter of Chinese, African, Indian, and European descent, Kelley brings the non-Western origins of European surrealism into the foreground. While it is not clear that Cha's studies directly engaged the Black radical roots of European avant-gardisms, one could certainly argue that like the Césaires and Lam, Cha recognized in these experimental aesthetics a means of reconstructing social relations through the surreal dream of decolonial thought—the genuinely difficult project of imagining how a free world might feel if it were real.[36] Not only this, but scholarship such as Kelley's is important to cite because it reverses assumptions about lines of influence between European and colonial modernist experimentation. By engaging the avant-gardism of the dream, Cha is also accessing a tradition of decolonial aesthetic experimentation that is inseparable from revolutionary politics and its core mission of altering reality as we know it.

The history of the dream as a genre of anti-colonial politics and the avant-garde adds an important laminate to Cha scholarship, which in its early years tended to ignore the political aspects of Cha's experimentalism. At first ignored and now canonized by Asian American literary studies, Cha has been a complicated figure in a larger debate over the racial politics of realism versus experimentalism. While Cha scholars have since addressed the artificial bifurcation between form and politics that framed early critiques of Cha's work, the larger debate over the racial politics of the avant-garde continues. In the first twelve years or so from its initial publication, Cha's *Dictee*, a literary work of poetry, prose, photographs, film stills, and other ephemera, was rarely incorporated into discussions of Asian American literature. It had attracted a decent amount of attention in scholarship on avant-garde poetics, but this work tended to focus on the book's formal attributes while disregarding any notion that the form might have a political edge. This changed in 1994, when the literary scholars Norma Alarcón and Elaine H. Kim edited a book of scholarship, *Writing Self, Writing Nation*, exclusively on *Dictee*. The contributors to *Writing Self, Writing Nation*, including Kim, Laura Hyun Yi Kang, Lisa Lowe, and Shelley Sunn Wong, offered nuanced readings of *Dictee* that reimagined the text's relationship to Asian American subjectivity, Asian American feminism, and the gendering of nationalism. These scholars intervened in Cha scholarship and Asian American studies by rejecting the existing poststructuralist approaches to *Dictee*, which had declined to consider race, gender, ethnicity, or nation as major elements of the work. They argued that Cha's style, contrary to popular ideas about racial politics in the period, was politically revolutionary *because* of its refusal of representation. *Writing Self, Writing Nation* proposed that Cha's fragmentary, modernist style refutes the foreclosures of a single "authentic" identity and instead conceives of Asian female subjectivity as productively unstable and hybrid.[37]

Since the publication of that scholarly work, Cha's influence has exploded. *Dictee* is now a standard inclusion on American and Asian American literature syllabi.[38] Cha is embraced as a canonical example of an Asian American author who does not rely of realist and representational techniques to engage questions of race, identity, colonialism, and gender. *Dictee* in particular is held up as go-to evidence of a tradition of experimentalism within Asian American literature.[39] However, despite the prominence of *Dictee*, the persistent binarism of ethnic and racial content versus unraced, identity-less experimental style remains a significant framework organizing our discussions of form and race in American literature and art, as Cha's "Overlooked" obituary demonstrates.[40] While Cha herself may have approached avant-garde difficulty "unapologetically," her readers, even those who celebrate her work, often feel the need to steel audiences in preparation for its formal obliqueness specifically because such challenges are unexpected coming from a Korean American woman—or, indeed, any woman of color—within the naturalized binary of unraced experimentalism versus raced realism. And yet difficulty, as we will see, is also part of what draws audiences to Cha's work.

The Dream of Cinema

A dream resists translation, explanation, and recounting in its associative logic and generation of new meanings from a clutch of dislocated images. Upon waking from a dream, we often struggle to convey to others what was so important in the dream or to make sense of its idiosyncratic logic and imagery. Perhaps constructing a retrospective narrative structure, bestowing on the dream some semblance of rational direction, filling in the logical gaps with prosaic surmises. Yet while dreaming, each moment is intuitive, crystalline in the dream reality. In aesthetic experiences that feel like dreams or draw from the dreamspace, there is a similar rearrangement of the relationship between image and meaning, a sense of openness and possibility that feels removed from the ordinary world, a brittleness of narrative. Like the image-language of dreams, Cha's dreaminess relies on the slipperiness of recognitions, feelings, juxtapositions, and associations and the formation of new relations between these things. For Cha, it was the darkened, sleepy, and affect-saturated space of the cinema that especially informed her dreamy aesthetic.

The aesthetic and political potential of the dream was not an arbitrary touchstone for Cha but central to the cutting-edge theoretical projects in film, psychoanalysis, and semiotics in which she was embedded at Berkeley and in Europe.[41] While at Berkeley, Cha was a volunteer student usher at the Pacific Film Archive, where she had the opportunity to view avant-garde films from Europe and Japan and what was then called "Third World Cinema" or the Third Cinema.[42] As mentioned previously, she was a student of major French film theorists and studied film at the Centre d'Etudes d'Américain du Cinèma in Paris in 1976. However, Cha was not just a student but an active participant and theorist in these ongoing conversations on film. In 1980, while an editor at Reese Williams's now defunct Tanam Press, Cha edited a collection on film theory called *Apparatus: The Apparatus of the Cinema*. Cha's collection contained work by Jean-Louis Baudry, Thierry Kuntzel, Christian Metz, Roland Barthes, Dziga Vertov, Maya Deren, and Bertrand Augst. Importantly, she also included her own artwork in *Apparatus*, the poetic mixed-media text *Commentaire*, which invokes the forms and mechanisms of cinema by using alternating black and white pages, recalling the flicker of the movie screen.[43]

In this strain of film studies that rose to prominence in the 1970s, theorists drew comparisons between the cinema and the experience of dreaming, combining structuralist and psychoanalytic theories so that the cultural analysis of cinema became a kind of dreamwork. The dark, reclined space of the movie theater was likened to the relaxed environs of the bedroom. The enchanting images on the screen created an alternative and temporary reality similar to a dream, in which the logics of the real world are suspended. Latent to this criticism is an anxiety over the induced passivity of watching a film, the idea that narrative films have the capacity to inculcate the viewer with a dangerously false understanding of reality.

French film theory from this period fixated in particular on the film's "apparatus" or how the entire technological, formal, and environmental process of going to the movies affected audience perception and the ability to detect and analyze competing realities.[44] The sensual darkness of the cinema combined with the spectacular fantasies playing out on the screen easily lent themselves to comparisons to Plato's allegory of the cave.[45] Cha's teacher and intellectual collaborator, Jean-Louis Baudry, wrote that "the allegory of the cave is the text of a signifier of desire that haunts the invention of cinema and the history of its invention," calling the cave wall shadow-puppets cinema's "first ancestor" produced by "a desire inherent in our psychical structure" to turn away from reality.[46] Provocative comparisons were drawn between Plato's cave and the theater's darkened, cavernous space, its screen full of flickering light and shadow. The immersive sensations of the cinema exclude "reality" through artificial darkness and projected realism, seducing viewers into becoming passive receptacles for ideology, their capacity for critique dulled by the spectacle of cinema. Like the cave dwellers, the movie theater audience is so entranced by the shadow play that they forget that they are wearing chains. The ready metaphors of projection (the technical apparatus becoming metaphor for the psychological projection of our constructed truths), the tricks of darkness, the capacity of film editing to alter our sense of time and place without the audience ever noticing that a cut has been made, all contribute to the theory that in the cinema we mistake a dream for reality.

In his essay "The Apparatus," Baudry is concerned with a "forced immobility" created by the material conditions of the movie theater that distorts reality or reduces a person's ability to access it, entranced by the cinema's illusory reality.[47] These constraints are not so literal as the chains in Plato's allegory but "can also refer to the forced immobility of the child who is without motor resources at birth, and to the forced immobility of the sleeper who we know repeats the postnatal state and even inter-uterine existence; but this is also the immobility that the visitor to the dim space rediscovers, leaning back into his chair. It might even be added that the spectator's immobility is characteristic of the filmic apparatus as a whole."[48] Reclining in the darkened space of the cinema triggers the forced passivity of sleep, infancy, or even the womb. The enchantments of the dark cinema are fueled by the subject's desire, unknown to herself, to return to that state of swaddled tractability. The cinema thus triggers a "return towards a relative narcissism, and even more towards a mode of relating to reality that could be defined as enveloping and in which the separation between one's own body and the exterior world is not well defined." In the disorienting yet familiar darkness, the viewer is unable to disentangle the representations unfolding on the screen from reality, beguiled by the fetal comforts of a lack of separation between your body and the world.

We can see an engagement with Baudry's theory in *Other Things Seen, Other Things Heard*. The performance incorporates film stills and imagery of the cinema. To create the feeling of a shared dream, Cha uses the technology of the darkened room and projection to stage performances of minoritized looking, creating a mini-cinema in the gallery. However, it would be a mistake to interpret this performance as simply a dramatization of Baudry's theory or even an enactment of the sort of critical viewing that might disrupt the "regressive" absorption that Baudry argues takes place in the cinema. While *Other Things Seen, Other Things Heard* does perform critical looking, Cha is not so dependent on psychoanalytic theory's prioritization of the individual or so anxious over the influence of the dream. Instead, her non-narrative aesthetic experimentalism explores the dream as a shared space where reality is co-constructed through the communal, if uneven, practice of aesthetic judgment.

In Cha's edited collection of film theory, we also find Barthes's essay "Upon Leaving the Movie Theater," which theorizes that surreal sensation of stepping out into street after seeing a movie, when the world suddenly feels both more and less real after our duration in the darkened cinema. In "Upon Leaving the Movie Theater," Barthes idles in the soporific effects of the cinema created through its enclosed environment, the feeling of sinking into low plush (or once plush) seats, the soothing flicker of light that plays across the theater between projector and screen, amid the quiet, the whispers, the whirr of the projector, the immersive soundscape of the film, and the intimate sounds of the body shifting and dwelling. In the essay, Barthes loiters in the cinematic afterglow, associating the movies with the bedroom, not only because its cozy environs invite sleep but also because Barthes finds the cinema to be a quintessentially modern erotic experience. He refers to the medium of film as a "festival of affects," which are made more intense by the darkened theater that suspends the viewer in a solution of sleepy sensuality:

> Darkness is not only the very essence of reverie . . . it is also the color of a very diffuse eroticism. In its human condensation, its lack of ceremony . . . the relaxation of postures—how many spectators slip into their seat as they slip into bed, coat and feet on the seat in front of them—the ordinary movie theater is a place of disponibility (even more than 'cruising'), with the idleness of bodies that best characterizes modern erotics. . . . It is in this urban darkness that the body's freedom luxuriates. The invisible work of the potential affect proceeds from what is truly a cinematographic cocoon. The film spectator might adopt the silk worm's

motto: *inclusum labor illustrat*; because I am shut in I work, and shine with all the intensity of my desire.[49]

In Barthes's analysis, the medium of film and the environment of the cinema allow for a peculiar kind of bodily satisfaction in which the "work" of affect becomes available through idle repose and sensory saturation. The peculiar sensuality facilitated by the cinema enables the psychic work of "potential affect," a giving-in-to reverie as a kind of active relinquishment of agency, a dissolution into shared feeling guided by the aesthetic, a sensing of a powerful, temporary connection within the audience and the potential for some kind of shift in what the audience is able to feel, enabled by the "festival of affects" on the screen and the darkened theater's promotion of heightened sensation. Potential affect is like a suspension of the moment just before a proposition, or perhaps even the moment before that *awareness* of a desire for connection. It is the anticipation of a feeling.

The space of the cinema as the scene of drowsy erotic possibility is alluded to in Cha's mixed-media collage poem *Commentaire*, also included in *Apparatus*. *Commentaire* combines both text and images in a meditation on the cinema. In a photograph included in that work, a movie theater is captured from above, from what must be a back row of the theater's balcony. From this voyeuristic aerial view, six reclining or sleeping people appear arranged throughout the space of the theater. In the foreground of the photograph, a man, seemingly deep in sleep, lies across a row of balcony seats. His hands, fingers spread and relaxed, are delicately settled on his chest, with a ghostly third hand, barely perceptible, resting on his collar bone. The man's legs splay out, knees pointed in a frog-like shape so that the pelvis is turned up toward the camera. He wears no shoes, his feet sheathed in socks or perhaps bare. The phantom hand is likely due to the prolonged exposure necessary in such a dark space to take the photograph; the sleeping man would have moved his hand while the photographer was making his exposure, creating the ghostly third hand. And yet the third hand, once noticed, draws you in, searching the oil-slick shadows for a source. Could the sleeping man be resting in the lap of another figure, whose hand is placed gently on the man's chest just below his cheek turned in profile? This shadow figure is camouflaged by the darkness of the theater and of the photograph, a body made up of the absence of light, a negative of the bodies that flicker across a movie screen. The umbra of the third hand, composed in a gesture of tenderness suggests a second figure, there and not there, sharing rest in the Cimmerian balcony. Casting an otherworldly glow across the scene, the screen of the movie theater emanates bright white light. How can anyone sleep within such luminosity? This image from Cha's *Commentaire* not only comments on Barthes's claims regarding the cinema's erotic sensorium but situates the cinema as a site of barely perceptible intimacies, intimacies that require prolonged interpretation and a bit of wishful thinking, intimacies of potential affect.

Entering the Dream

Dreaminess: half-awake, associative, intuitive play, the awareness that there are experiences that escape language, the feeling tethered to the weight of an image, which keeps you from floating away. In her comprehensive and lyrical essay on Cha's body of work titled "White Spring," the experimental filmmaker and author Trinh T. Minh-Ha suggests that to encounter and be absorbed by Cha's art, one must relinquish themselves to the particularity of Cha's dreams: "One would have to enter the dream—even if one has only a shred of it to dwell in–and wait until it gives off words, like fragrances from burnt incense."[50] Here, it is not that Cha's body or writing works as a screen on which the reader or viewer projects their dreams, but it is the audience that must loosen themselves from the given reality to enter into the space of Cha's dream, waiting for her drifting words. The dream of the audience is not a total dissolution of the artist into the audience's fantasies; rather, it is the artist who builds a dream shared with her audience.

Referring to *Commentaire*, Trinh writes, "As with Cha's other works, reading is intimacy shared in night labor. . . . One follows, as with film, the effect of a variable flickering of light and the illusion of movement generated within the given space." "Night labor" invokes not only the range of situations in which reading must take place surreptitiously, signaling reading's history of anti-authoritarianism, something that must be hidden from the parent, the occupier, the censor, the master, because the act of reading can bring about intimacies between ideas and people that are dangerous to authority; it also invokes the night of the cinema.

What subversive ideas or acts might take place while reading at night? In participating in what Trinh calls the "intimacy" of the "night labor" and by agreeing to "enter the dream," the reader or audience labors to meet the beautiful difficulty of Cha's work in a highly constructed aesthetic space. This is a kind of dreamwork that is less about interpretation and the restoration of the real than a proliferation of realities: "Because I am shut in I work, and shine with all the intensity of my desire." In this manufactured space, like the artificial night of the cinema, enrapturing forms call attention to themselves, desire whirrs industriously. Trinh draws out the political aura of reading intimacies formed in night labor, a work of potential affect, whether natural or artificial darkness. The dream is not a symptom to be interpreted but a place to "dwell in," a text that is also a place to wait, to see who appears, to anticipate an exchange of meaning between people, which, like a fragrance, is sensed, material, but difficult to visualize.

We must be cautious of imagining that "the dream of the audience" is frictionless fusing of artist and audience. Cha's dreaminess demands attention to the ethics of aesthetic participation and a reckoning with the politics of difference conceptualized through woman-of-color feminism, an ethical relation that surfaces in Trinh's reading of Cha's aesthetic dreams. Through dreaminess, Cha's art invites certain kinds of participation in a shared aesthetic experience but thwarts the projective empathy often recruited by realism. Although Cha makes frequent use of projection, or references to it, even making her body into a screen, as in *Other Things Seen, Other Things Heard*, the immersion in projected light is far from a unifying experience—perceptual absorption need not result in linear completeness. The abstract forms that make Cha's work dream-like also make it difficult. They unsettle the dominance of empathetic projection in aesthetic experience through formal difficulty, enabling the sense of a shared experience wherein the ethics of relation must be parsed.

Interfusion of Things

This interest in what is and is not shared in the communal spaces of aesthetic experience is a frequent topic in Cha's writing. Reflecting on her artistic practice in her 1978 MFA thesis, "Paths," the same year that she performed *Other Things Seen, Other Things Heard*, Cha offers a variation of classical fourth-century BCE Chinese Daoist philosopher Zhuang Zhou's (romanized as Chuang Chou in the thesis) "Butterfly Dream," the most famous story from the *Zhuangzi*, one of the two foundational texts of Daoism:[51]

> Once I dreamt that I was a butterfly, fluttering here and there; in all ways a butterfly. I enjoyed my freedom as a butterfly, not knowing that I was Chou. Suddenly, I awoke and was surprised to be myself again. Now, how can I tell whether I was a man who dreamt that he was a butterfly, or whether I am a butterfly who dreams that she is a man? Between Chuang Chou and the butterfly, there must be differentiation. (Yet in the dream non differentiation takes place.) This is called interfusion of things.[52]

In relating this story, Cha frames her art practice as a kind of shared dream.[53] The artist, the artist's materials, and the audience are in a "covenant" wherein positions are interrelated: "The artist becoming object for the viewer, the viewer as subject, the artist as subject, and viewer as object."[54] Like the story of Chou and the butterfly, these aesthetic transformations offer a challenge to the notion of the self, the human, and a hierarchy of existence in which humans are at the top. Chou's dream destabilizes a hierarchy based on species or gender (the butterfly is gendered "she" in this version) in relation to knowledge or reality. Neither the butterfly nor Chou can know absolutely that they are "real" or that they are not—and this is what makes the story both beautiful and compelling in its decentering of the human, the importance of knowing, and the simultaneous coexistence of difference that seems contradictory. It delights in the pleasures of relinquishing human form in the fragility of the butterfly's near weightless body and the freedom of its movement, as well as the possibility of unexpected reversal, in which the butterfly dreams of being Chou. The dream is a beautiful and temporary existence with its own set of conditions and horizons that are no less real than the waking life.

The story of Chou and the butterfly is not a story of the erasure of material difference. In the "interfusion" of the two beings, their differences are paradoxically retained: "Between Chuang Chou and the butterfly, there must be differentiation. (Yet in the dream non differentiation takes place.)" Between the artist, the medium, and the audience, there must be differentiation, and yet, in the dream non differentiation takes place. I propose that Cha's interest in aesthetic experiences as a kind of shared dream is not only an existential or spiritual project but also profoundly connected to the anti-colonial feminism that unsettles Western notions of aesthetic judgment that depend on a singular, distinct, and rational subject. Her praxis investigates rich affective, cognitive, and sensorial "interfusion," using abstract aesthetic techniques to explore a new mode of being together not structured by the violences of cisheteropatriarchy, racial capitalism, and empire, if only briefly. Instead, Cha's experimentalism guides audience attention toward woman-of-color feminism's principle of living in difference.

However, with the radical ambiguations of self and other of the dream also come important ethical questions, particularly for a Korean American woman artist working in the 1970s, primarily in the United States, often in predominantly white spaces, whose art takes a postcolonial and woman-of-color feminist approach to questions of language, embodiment, and gendered and racial belonging.[55] By calling this relationship a "covenant," Cha suggests that something sacred and promissory is taking place. She is taking a risk but also raising the standard for the audience, asking that they rise to the occasion. It can be difficult to keep interrelationality from reproducing structures of dominance and submission, extraction, and abuse. Cha is not naïve to the power dynamics of race, gender, sexuality, and colonialism that shape the relationships between audience and artist—her work is entirely about how these political and social positions are constructed, managed, and resisted through everyday encounters with language and aesthetics. Yet she also refuses the clarity of didacticism or realist representation, placing the onus on the audience to show up for the work.

Aesthetic judgment prompts ethical questions because it asks us how we imagine ourselves in relation to others. Here, as I argue that form is an aesthetic method of directing of attention and that aesthetic judgment is a social relation as much as a perceptual one, I am reminded of anthropologist Tim Ingold's remarks on attention. Noting that the word *attention* is etymologically derived from the Latin *ad tendere*, "to stretch," Ingold goes on to suggest that attention is a kind of psychic stretching: "Reaching out beyond what is already to hand towards that which is now yet present or even conceivable, it forsakes the security of the fragile centre that we may have drawn around ourselves for an uncertain and unknown future."[56] Conceptualizing attention as a release of the liberal concept of self, Ingold reflects, "I have come to understand that paying attention is not about shining a spotlight on this or that object in the world, but about going along with things, opening up to them and doing their bidding. Intention is premised upon attentionality, not attention on intentionality."[57] This surrender to what is not the self, staying open and allowing oneself to be guided, is reminiscent of Trinh's description of what it is like to encounter Cha's work. It is a dream that the audience enters as Cha's words to waft over them, snagged by them as one is suddenly caught up in the invisible swell of a fragrance; it is a kind of night intimacy where, as in the cinema, one does not direct, but "One follows . . . a variable flickering of light and the illusion of movement."

The Theaters of *Dictee*

A mixed-media text alternatively referred to as a novel, autobiography, and epic poem, *Dictee* considers how the space of the cinema and aesthetics of projected image and light foment the political intimacies of the dream's "interfusion." Not coincidentally, the section of Cha's *Dictee* that most prominently experiments with the affective and political potential of cinema is called "Erato/Love Poetry." This section unfurls an ambivalent love of the movies as well as love at the movies. It follows up on Barthes's theorization of the cinema as sensual space, Cha's projection-based performance and slide art, and *Commentaire*'s flickering eroticism. The "Erato/Love Poetry" section is a love poem to the dreamspace of cinema and its political potential affects.

As the poet and Cha scholar Walter K. Lew has explored, the cinematic elements of *Dictee* not only suggest Cha's study of French film theory; it can also be read as a reference to the Korean art of "movietelling" or movie narrating. In the early twentieth century, Korean movie narrators, standing at the front of the theater to the side of the screen (not dissimilar to Cha in *Other Things Seen*), interpreted silent films (sometimes made silent by turning the sound off in later cinematic eras), often improvising and developing their own narratives to accompany the images of the film. They were like "pop stars" in the period of

Japanese occupation in the early twentieth century who also negotiated complex colonial power dynamics as their popularity crossed class and ethnic lines.[58] It is possible to read this section, as Lew's experimentalist tribute to Cha's *Dictee* EXCERPTS FROM: ΔΙΚΤΗ DIKTE 딕테/딕티 *for* DICTEE (1992) suggests, as a kind of movietelling or resistant narration of cinema.

The possible reference to movietelling in this section of *Dictee* speaks to the history of the screen as a colonial technology in the Korean peninsula—and beyond.[59] As Hamid Naficy writes in "Theorizing 'Third World' Film Spectatorship," while the cinema may have had a disciplinary function in colonized spaces, colonized people have not by any means been consistently docile viewers. Naficy's own autotheoretical recollections of the complex sociality in the Iranian cinemas of his boyhood are beautiful analyses of what he describes as the "hailing and haggling between self and other, real and fictional, and indigenous and foreign tak[ing] place in the moviehouse."[60] Rather than sitting silently in the dark theater, the movie houses of Naficy's childhood were noisy places, where audience members and student translators narrated the largely non-Persian language films and one could hear "the loud cracking of watermelon, pumpkin, and sunflower seeds" as audience members talked back to the film, yelling out, "'Oh, watch out, he is behind you;' 'Yeah, punch him hard in the stomach, hit him, hit him.'"[61] During the silent era, Iran's version of the movieteller, movie translators known as *dilmaj*, translated the films for the audience as they unfolded. As Naficy writes, although the screen is often wielded as a pedagogical tool to colonize the mind, viewers are far from being pliant audiences.

The cinema as a representation of Japanese cultural and technological expansion, controlled and distributed via Japanese colonial censors and administrators, could be a fraught space of political and cultural power struggle in Korea under Japanese colonialism. Movietelling was a popular folk art form beloved by colonizer and colonial subject alike, and some movietellers dared to use their celebrity as a shield for political critique. As Roald Maliangkay surmises:

> It may have been because they intended to expose the limits of the [Japanese] authorities' control that some narrators took great liberty in explaining a storyline as they risked arrest and torture in order to express

their political views. It is reported, for example, that Sin ch'ul was once arrested and beaten for improvising an anti-Japanese line while narrating a Japanese film in Pusan, while Sŏ Sangp'il famously used the galley slaves' revolt in *Ben Hur* as a metaphor for the Korean independence struggle. Interpretations such as these are likely to have been limited to occasions where the audience was predominantly Korean.[62]

The heyday of movietelling ended a decade or so before Cha was born, but one wonders if she could have heard stories of her family's favorite movietellers as a child. Perhaps the rebellious actions of Sŏ Sangp'il or Sin ch'ul made their way to Cha in the same way that other tales of Korean resistance were passed down through generations. Whether such conjectures have a grain of truth, the prominence of the movie theater and the projected image throughout Cha's work speaks to the role of a luminous screen, the techno-aesthetics of cinema in the history of colonialism in Korea and elsewhere, and anti-colonial struggle.[63]

Within the "Erato/Love Poetry" section, there are several subsections that describe an anonymous woman, who is sometimes read as a version of Cha, going to the cinema and watching a movie. Like a movieteller, Cha reframes the cinematic experience from the perspective of this critical and self-aware viewer, almost obsessively so. As with the voyeuristic perspective of the photograph in *Commentaire* and the performance of looking in *Other Things Seen, Other Things Heard*, the overall effect of the movie theater section in *Dictee* is a strange mixture of surveillance and erotic communality, harnessing the affective uneasiness and pleasure of "being seen."[64] We can draw a connection here between the innate voyeurism of cinema and the movie theater as a colonial and colonizing space, a space of watchfulness in every sense, and a scene of power negotiation where the most important actors are in the audience.

As "Upon Leaving the Movie Theater" and *Commentaire* suggest, the ambient desire of the cinema bestows on the theater the intimacy of cruising, a searching, heightened attention to ambient feeling. However, the surveillance narrated in this passage contains more anxious overtones than the scene of slumbrous eros found in *Commentaire* or Barthes's essay. The woman from *Dictee*'s "Erato/Love Poetry" section is clearly being watched, giving the text a noir-like tension:

The time is 6:35 p.m. She turns her head exactly to the left. The long hand is on 6 and the short hand on 7. She hands her ticket to the usher and climbs three steps, into the room. The whiteness of the screen takes her back wards almost half a step. Then she proceeds again to the front. Near front. Close to the screen. She takes the fourth seat from the left. The utmost center of the room. She sees on her left the other woman, the same woman in her place as the day before.[65]

In the next subsection, the point of view of the film camera becomes even more explicit as the language of the passage takes on the perspective of a screenplay using the language of filmmaking to re-narrate the same scene:

The theatre is empty, she is turning right into the aisle and moving forward. She selects a row near the front, fourth seat from the left and sits. Medium Close Up, directly from behind her head. She turns her head to the left, on her profile. Camera pans left, and remains still at the profile of another woman seated. Camera pans back to right, she turns her head to the front. The screen fades to white.[66]

These passages narrate two perspectives within a film about going to the movies. Both emphasize the gendered vulnerability of being watched as a source of narrative tension, creating a palpable atmosphere of disquiet and anticipation. The protagonist is being watched by the narrator as well as the reader. However, she is also a watcher, as a moviegoer and by virtue of her awareness of the "other woman" seated nearby. Unlike Baudry or Barthes who presume a universal experience of the cinema determined by its apparatus, Cha contemplates a cinematic space striated by perspectival difference and anxious awareness of the environment. These passages present a heightened alertness to the ways in which a simultaneous experience—as in the bathetic darkness of the theater's spectacular alternative reality—can yet be experienced from markedly different points of view.

The political and aesthetic potential of the cinema for the cinema's excluded subjects is suggested by the presence of the second woman in the movie theater who toggles the positions of "other" and "same."[67] The repetitious presence of the second woman ("the *other* woman, the *same* woman in her place as the day before") suggestively sets up the cinema as a scene of potential collectivity; a kind of cruising is enabled by the dreamy eros of the movie theater. The first woman notices the second woman. Is she noticed back? Like the barely perceptible shadow of a second figure in *Commentaire*, the lap across which the sleeping man languidly strews his limbs, the registration of a second figure in *Dictee* issues an ambience of social and affective possibility. Undermining the default gendering of the cinematic gaze, the "Erato/Love Poetry" section offers scenes of women watching other women—on the screen as well as in the seats—staging minoritized looking as a scene weighted with possibility. Drawn back to the theater again and again, it is like a reoccurring dream in which the dreamer continually returns to the same place, attempting to work out a problem that will not satisfactorily resolve.

As Trinh argues regarding Cha's work, "Reading is intimacy shared in night labor." In this episode of *Dictee*, Cha draws out the affective labor of the silkworm, the screen's soft pulsing beacon startling her "back ward," asking the reader to imagine the intimacy of sitting together in the dark, shining not just with erotic potential but with political potential. This scene of women watching other women proposes a desire for shared relation amid the colonial technology of cinema. As in Barthes's "Upon Leaving the Movie Theater," there is "potential affect" in this sequence taut with suggestive recognition without a clear resolution, a sense of what might be seen if one knows how to look. The movie theater is a space of possibility in which spectatorship is the basis for spontaneous and unexpected connections.

The art historian Jill Casid has argued that projection holds a colonial pedagogical function. Like dictation, Casid identifies projection as a "pedagogical setup that operates across a range of sites as an 'influencing machine' of persistent training and repetitive exercise," citing the importance of the apparatus of slides, magic lanterns, cinema, and other "scenes of projection" in shaping subjectivities during the heyday of European colonialism.[68] Like Baudry, the assumption of colonial administrators is that the environs of projection soothe the subject into a passively receptive state, absorbing the content that will produce her, as in an artificial womb or a prisoner in a cave. Yet Naficy paints quite a different picture of the cinema as a more chaotic space, almost like a party, where influences are certainly exerted but also subverted—these social aspects are all a part of the mixed pleasure of the movies. Filmmakers like Trinh and Isaac Julien are critical of film's coloniality yet remain enchanted by the medium, examining what is so enticing about this vexed art form. They experiment with how to direct the viewer's attention toward the process of filmmaking itself, encouraging a more participatory and analytical spectatorship that is still highly pleasurable. In this context, *Dictee* models a resistant looking attuned to the disciplinary procedures of the cinema without submitting to them. Although the dominant conventions of narrative cinema and its apparatus function pedagogically to reproduce oppressive structures, *Dictee*'s spectator-protagonist generates something else within the cinema between the screen and the other woman. The potential affect of cinema, a kind of reading at night, is suggested as a possible foundation for political intimacy between women. In the cinema, there is a light toward which the protagonist and the *other* woman might stretch. Whatever its content or disciplinary structures, the movie theater nevertheless makes available the potential affect of attention between minoritized subjects.

So often, the content of the cinema is the white face of the actress, a drama of race, sexuality, and gender that holds the audience in rapture. As mentioned previously, the "Erato/Love Poetry" section also features the figure of Joan of Arc, a character who is performed in photography, diary fragments, and film across the chapter.[69] Most prominent is a full-page film still from *The Passion of Joan of Arc* (1928) by Carl Theodor Dreyer, a close-up of Falconetti's face in fervid disconsolation (very similar to the one used in *Other Things Seen, Other Things Heard*). In her staging of the emotional and erotic intensity of Joan of Arc performances, Cha asks us to think carefully about circuits of racial and gendered meaning within systems of domination and what alternative formations might be made available under such conditions. We might draw a comparison to Sŏ Sangp'il's movietelling of *Ben Hur*, a *reading against* that film's conscription of classical history to white American notions of masculinist liberty for the project of Korean freedom. Similarly, something is raised in Cha's appropriation of the Joan of Arc imagery, like goose flesh arching in the dark chill of the theater.

Dreyer's closeup of Falconetti's face performs what Laura Marks calls "haptic visuality" that is "the way vision itself can be tactile, as though one were touching a film with one's eyes."[70] Giving its attention, the eye reaches out to touch the luxuriously textured skin of Joan's face, which is also the skin of the film. Marks argues that "to think of film as a skin acknowledges the effect of a work's circulation among different audiences, all of which mark it with their presence" Film has a "tactile and contagious quality," which "we viewers brush up against like another body."[71] Marks argues that the haptic quality of film holds political potential in particular for "intercultural cinema," which, as in *Dictee*, or Trinh and Julien's work for that matter, "challenge[s] the separateness of culture and make visible the colonial and racist power relations that seek to maintain this separation. . . . Intercultural cinema builds up [audience] impressions like a palimpsest and passes them on to other audiences. The very circulation of film among different viewers is like a series of skin contacts that leave mutual traces."[72]

The fascination with texture, the uneven grain of film and its reproductions, which is so similar to the seductive irregularity of skin, is found throughout *Dictee* and Cha's other experiments with projected media, performance, and artists' books. The grain mesmerizes as it denies our predictions, eschewing regularity. In photography, the quality of graininess is the result of the film's sensitivity to light. Elsewhere I have written on Eve Kosofsky Sedgwick's remarks on texture, which she develops in conversation with an essay by Renu Bora.[73] Sedgwick argues that our psychic experience of texture stimulates our curiosity. She writes, "To perceive texture is never only to ask or know What is it like? nor even just How does *it* impinge on *me*? Textural perception always explores two other questions as well: How did it get that way? and What could I do with it?"[74] The grainy skin of the film, reproduced on the skin of the book, piques our interest and sense of touch without necessarily touching, inviting further investigation. Texture in Cha's work sensuously befuddles logic, whispers disruptively, perforates the smooth contiguity of linear narrative. In film, as Marks argues and Cha's work actuates, this skin or textured surface enables the unpredictable circulation of affect and curiosity between parties whose interests, let alone identities, do not perfectly align. The results are often ambivalent, entwining violence and pleasure.[75] While texture often refers to the raised, uneven surface, we might also recall the silky textures that Julien cultivates in *Looking for Langston*—an excellent example of how visual texture can work as an affective circuit through which both harm and delight are carried.

The close-up of Falconetti's face merges the texture of her skin with the grain of the film. This texture of historical, political, and aesthetic feeling then becomes actually tactile on the page of *Dictee*. The historical fiction of Joan of Arc becomes available through the touch of cinema and of reading, providing the imaginary and affective grounding for different formations of political intimacy through a collusion of cinematic, photographic, and literary textures. In reproducing the still, *Dictee* does not perform an identification with white womanhood or an uncritical valorization of Joan of Arc's martyrdom repurposed for modern nationalistic and colonial enterprises. Rather, Cha uses the Joan of Arc image to build textures, stippling the text to prime the circulation of political affect.

Recalling the image of Cha kneeling in front of Renée Falconetti's weeping face in *Other Things Seen, Other Things Heard* and staring up into the larger-than-life drama of white female martyrdom, we are pushed to situate the specificity of Cha's viewership, abolishing the idea of the universal (white male) cinematic viewer who simply absorbs (or is absorbed into) the immersive drama of Falconetti's face or his own narcissistic pseudo-infancy. Cha positions herself just outside the rectangular frame of the projected image, seated almost demurely. And yet she is there, and her gaze, her response to the film, unknown to the audience behind her, reframes the entire context of the scene. By staging the colonial subject's gaze in the glow of the movie screen, recontextualizing the film within relationship to her own body, Cha creates an opportunity for disidentification. As José Esteban Muñoz famously theorizes disidentification:

> To disidentify is to read oneself and one's own life narrative in a moment, object, or subject that is not culturally coded to "connect" with the disidentifying subject. It is not to pick and choose what one takes out of an identification. It is not to willfully evacuate the politically dubious or shameful components within an identificatory locus. Rather, it is the reworking of those energies that do not elide the 'harmful' or contradictory components of any identity. It is an acceptance of the necessary interjection that has occurred in such situations.[76]

Disidentification takes places in the potential affect of critical cinematic eros. In a sense, it is a staged interpretation where the audience is drawn into a collective practice of critical reading, within the "festival of affects" of the "cinematographic cocoon." The shared dream produced by the projected image and its apparatus is not homogenous but collectively produced in the friction of difference. As such, the shared experience of looking creates a differentiated communal experience that has the capacity to hold a range of feelings and meanings and a spectrum of mixed identification and alienation.

Dreaminess becomes an aesthetic for thinking through an ethics of interrelationality and shared political futures that is not smooth but textured. In the work of reading at night, Cha makes available feminist intimacy and collectivity within a history of looking dominated by cisheteropatriarchal whiteness. She visualizes the unstable minoritarian disidentifications (of gender, race, ethnicity, or relationship to colonialism) taking place in the literal and figurative dark. In the cruising that takes place not only in the cinema among women but also in the text among readers, Cha claims the pleasure of cinema and of night-reading for minoritized subjects.

Upon Leaving *Dictee*

While the "Erato/Love Poetry" section of *Dictee* feels out the potential of political sensibility within a colonial cinematic dreamspace, Cha's treatment of the Korean revolutionary hero Yu Guan Soon expands on these interpretative intimacies formed in the glow of the screen.[77] At sixteen years old, Yu Guan Soon was a leader in a national movement against Japanese occupiers in 1919, later known as the March First Movement. As Kun Jong Lee recounts, Yu Guan Soon "was advised not to participate in the March First demonstrations in Seoul by her teachers because of her gender and age. After her return to her hometown, village elders also tried to dissuade the sixteen-year-old girl from organizing a popular demonstration, since her public display of patriotism was not in accordance with the gender code of Korean society."[78] In 1920, Yu was captured by the Japanese colonial administration and imprisoned. During her time in prison, she was tortured for refusing to reveal the identities of other members of the revolution and died as a result of her injuries in September 1920. Remembered as a nationalist martyr, Yu Guan Soon became known as "Korea's Joan of Arc."

Yu Guan Soon first appears in *Dictee* in the "Clio/History" chapter, perhaps the most frequently discussed chapter in the critical literature on *Dictee*, in part because it is the section of the book where *Dictee*'s feminist and anti-colonial politics emerge most obviously. Yu Guan Soon's prominence as a revolutionary foremother acts as a beacon in a text that consistently complicates identification and representation. Throughout the "Clio/History" section, Cha includes biographical narratives recounting aspects of Yu Guan Soon's life, emphasizing her resistance to the Japanese colonial administration and her nationalist representation as a martyr. The section opens with a close-cropped photographic portrait of Yu Guan Soon. This portrait has an official look to it, reminiscent of an identification photo in its tight framing of Yu's face, her neutral expression, forward-facing stare, and her body cropped just below the shoulders. The formal appearance of the photograph recalls the composition of photographs developed in the late nineteenth and early twentieth century for travel and immigration documents, a photographic composition still used today. In a text about Korean history and diaspora, the photograph of Yu Guan Soon refers to a history of photographic looking and circulation directly connected to the control of the movements of racialized and colonized peoples, immigration policy as a tool of racialization, and Cha's own history of migration and exile.[79]

Although it is easy to hold up the Yu Guan Soon references as evidence of a strong Korean and female historical protagonist within *Dictee*, as Anne Anlin Cheng points out, the fragmented and decontextualized forms of *Dictee* continually undermine seemingly straightforward feminist and racial iconography, such as Yu Guan Soon's photograph. As Cheng argues, "*Dictee* is not interested in identities, it is profoundly interested in the processes of *identification*."[80] *Dictee* does not perform a politics of representation. Yet the text remains interested in the promise of political feeling through collective aesthetic experience. This reproduction, like the Joan of Arc/Falconetti still, is also highly textured. The grain of the copy—perhaps a copy of a copy—obscures through a soft fuzz of mildewy grays. It does not show Yu Guan Soon clearly, despite the cropping that aims to pin down a representative, identifiable image; texture prompts a different relation to the image and questions about how it came to be.

By the end of the book, we realize that the portrait of Yu Guan Soon is not actually a photograph of an individual but cropped and magnified from a group photograph. Yu is to the far right on the upper row, among eight other young women—perhaps they constitute the nine muses referenced in Cha's choice to title each of *Dictee*'s chapters after a Greek muse (with a fictional tenth representing her mother? Herself?). The faces of the women are difficult to discern with the photograph's somewhat overexposed look. Perhaps it is an effect of the reproduction process.[81] But we can see the outlines of arms chummily embracing, a chain of connection across the two rows of young women. The movement from the cropped photograph (appearing relatively early in the book) to the group photograph on the book's final page resembles the cinematic cut from close-up to long shot, relating the flick of the page to the flicker of cinema. The organization of *Dictee* mimics the editing of an avant-garde film. Finally, centered in the middle of all-black pages, the photograph appears like an illuminated screen in a darkened movie theater. At the end of *Dictee*, Cha asks the reader to consider where they sit in relation to the text and who else might be in the audience. Look around. Where is the other woman? The same woman?

Upon leaving *Dictee*, we are asked to consider how the reader's gaze enables or disables different political intimacies, as in the photo of Yu Guan Soon, whose heroic single portrait is complicated by the political promise of female affection that drifts from the group photograph and the Joan of Arc performances and the several other examples from the book that encourage a revolutionary feminist reading. The reader has a role to play in the dream of Cha's paper cinema. Cha's tactical cropping of Yu Guan Soon and then revelation of the full photograph highlights the apparatus of the material book and Cha's process—cutting, editing, and framing are engaged in the construction of *Dictee*. By formally mimicking the isolating cut of national martyrdom, which artificially extracts the heroine from the context of her movement and communities, and then restoring Yu Guan Soon to a collective space, Cha critiques the individualism of the martyr narrative through reparative editing. As *Dictee*'s parting image, the group photo activates the desire to read anti-colonial feminist meaning into this group photograph and to imagine Yu Guan Soon's bravery as a part of a revolutionary collective that might be newly formed through reading intimacies. And yet there are still questions to be asked and answered. The reader leans into the dark space of the paper cinema. I ask, "How did this image come to be?" and "How can I attend to it?"

A dream is being summoned in these cinematic cuts and sutures enacted within the bound pages of the book. The reader traces her fingers across the grain, creamy and chiffonous gray, and pauses to wonder at a question. *Dictee* offers a dream of feminist anti-colonial desire, suggesting that the organization of anti-colonial feminist collectivity is, at least in part, an aesthetic question to be realized through the anticipatory connections developed in the darkroom of aesthetic judgment. The work of political desire that, like the silkworm, shines more brightly within the space of the cinema, enclosed both in the gendered and racial patterns that keep repeating, as well as in the dark, sensorially saturated enclosure of the theater. Reaching out in the dark, *Dictee* feels out political intimacies: textured, fictive, historical, imminent, and immanent.

Dreaming of Theresa Hak Kyung Cha

Cha's staging of critical feeling, affective reading, and the eros of cinematic communion is evident not only in her work but also in her legacy as a recovered foremother of a woman-of-color avant-garde. Especially since Kim and Alarcón published *Writing Self, Writing Nation*, Cha's work has been discussed as an anchor point for Asian American artists and other artists of color and an example of the illegitimacy of racial boundaries placed around experimental artistic praxis. Cha's work, particularly *Dictee*, has been cited as an influence or point of comparison for generations of artists resisting racialized limits on the form that their art takes, including Elaine Castillo, Don Mee Choi, Renée Green, Cathy Park Hong, Alexandra Kleeman, Sally Wen Mao, Lara Mimosa Montes, Suiyi Tang, Cecilia Vicuña, Ocean Vuong, and many others.[82] Cha's legacy is transformative, and the continued impact of her work enacts the feminist, anti-racist, and anti-colonial collectives that are proposed and imagined in her dreamspaces.

For example, in 2020, the Whitney Museum of American Art held an online exhibition, in collaboration with Artist's Space (the gallery where Cha was due to exhibit at the time of her death), called *After La vida nueva*. Curated by the Whitney Independent Study Program's 2019–20 curatorial fellows Weiyi Chang, Sofia Jamal, Colleen O'Connor, and

Patricio Orellana, *After La vida nueva* refers to a 1982 performance in which five decommissioned World War II planes departed from Flushing Airport in Queens, New York, to spell out the artist Raúl Zurita's poem "La vida nueva" in puffs of white smoke. The performance memorialized the 1973 US military-sponsored coup in Chile against the democratically elected socialist government of Salvador Allende, precipitating an era of harrowing, bloody dictatorship under Augusto Pinochet. The Whitney exhibition explores the historical, affective, and aesthetic moment surrounding this artwork, which Zurita dedicated to the "minorities of the world."[83] The curators describe this era of the early 1980s in New York as "one that was once full of the promise of the new and a period that followed various Third World liberation movements," yet as neoliberalism emerged as a dominant global ideology, through which racialized military violence was rationalized via the just cause of economic "freedom," the dreams of those movements would soon seem very fragile.[84] A connection between Zurita's work and Cha's, in addition to their interest in text-based art, conceptualism, and the ability to work across both literature and the visual arts, is that both were pushed to migrate to the United States as a result of US anti-leftist militarization in their countries during the Cold War. The curators cite 1982 in particular—the year of publication for *Dictee* and Cha's death—as a singular moment of felt political and aesthetic potential, produced by global decolonial resistances that sought intervention in the aesthetic-political power structures that organize colonialism and white supremacy. In Zurita's poem, its conceptual execution, and its coalitional dedication we can hear a revolutionary call to redefine reality through the decolonial dream. Written across the sky like a sign from heaven, each line except for the final line begins with the phrase "MI DIOS ES" (my god is): "MI DIOS ES HAMBRE / MI DIOS ES NIEVE / MI DIOS ES NO." My god is hunger, snow, no, disillusionment, carrion, paradise, pampa, Chicano, cancer, emptiness, wound, ghetto, pain, and a blank space. Zurita ends the poem by reversing the syntax of the line: "MI AMOR DE DIOS" (my love of god). In puffs of cloud-like exhaust, exhaled from planes built by the military that backed the Pinochet coup, Zurita's words bring a new reality into being with each emission, realities that dissolve into air and the memories of the readers below.

Cha is central to *After La vida nueva*, not only because her video *Mouth to Mouth* (1975) was included in the exhibition but also because several of the artworks also featured in the exhibit reference Cha's work, including pieces by Renée Green, Caroline Key, and Cici Wu. Cha was selected by the curators as a key figure in the affective and political currents of 1982, which continued to swirl with possibility in 2020. As the curators explain, Cha finds the "impasse" of difference to be productive for, rather than obstructive to, social and political transformation: "The impasse reached when one attempts to bridge the space between languages should not, in that sense, be considered a failure of translation, but rather an opening to the horizon of relational possibilities in which one's sense of language is not subsumed to the logic of universal communicability."[85] *After La vida nueva* thus demonstrates how Cha's formal difficulty conducts audiences toward a reconsideration of difference, and that this aesthetic method brings in audiences, rather than rebuffing them.

With Cici Wu's *Foreign Object #1 Fluffy Light* in particular, we see an artist from a younger generation building upon the models found in Cha's work to produce new aesthetic experiences, ideas, and relations. *Foreign Object#1 Fluffy Light* is a device to record changing brightness of a film and ambient light of cinema in twenty-four frames per second. The light fluctuation data is stored in a mini memory card and can be rendered into a digital video. Its smooth light-pink-hued opalescent glass casing is oblong with ergonomic depressions for resting a thumb or fingers and perfectly sized—at 4.5 × 4.5 × 4.5 inches—for holding in one's hand or lap. Without any writing or symbols to indicate how it works or what it does, just two indicators vaguely reminiscent of eyes, *Foreign Object* has a science-fiction visual appeal, seeming both manmade and organic. In the *After La vida nueva* exhibit, *Foreign Object* was displayed on the armrest of a repurposed cinema chair.[86]

In 2017, Wu used a prototype of *Foreign Object* to record Cha's unfinished film, *White Dust from Mongolia* (1980), at a screening at the Museum of Art and Design in New York City. Cha's film, which was to be accompanied by a novel, comprises footage fragments that were shot during a highly anticipated return visit to South Korea in 1980, where Cha and her brother James stayed for three months. Cha's written film scenario suggests that she had additional plans for editing and expansion

Figure 4.4: Cici Wu, *Foreign Object #1 Fluffy Light*. Photography by Joerg Lohse. Courtesy of the artist and 47 Canal.

of this footage, but this was not realized before her death.[87] The footage that constitutes *White Dust from Mongolia* is very rarely screened publicly, making Wu's bootleg copy a special artifact. However, as mentioned, the device records only light. In Wu's copy, Cha's film exists only as the imprint of the play of light at that specific screening, without sound.

The titling of *Foreign Object #1 Fluffy Light* does quite of bit of work in this piece. It conjures the idea of "perpetual foreignness," a concept theorized in Asian American studies that describes the perception that Asian and Asian American subjects in the United States can never "truly assimilate" into the national body. Calling this futuristic looking device a "foreign object" also suggests an alienness—both extraterrestrial and national—that links the "object" to a dehumanizing racial history of US immigration policy and enforcement, as well as the fascination reserved for the interstellar objects that sometimes pass through the earthling skies or land smoldering on the pock-marked ground. Here, the whimsical turns a term of degradation and fixity into one of wonder and opacity. Finally, a "foreign object" can refer to an unwanted stray fleck or particle that finds its way into the eye, where it does not belong, creating discomfort or pain and obscuring vision. In this understanding of the title, the same device that captures and reproduces Cha's film is also the source of an irritation or obstruction in the vision of the viewer. We cannot see the film except through the obfuscation of its medium. The metaphorical elements signaled in Wu's titling create an assemblage of associative meanings connected to identity, movement, belonging, and the visual, a lens that shifts slowly across the work allowing its complexity to grow as the viewer continues to sit with it.

In naming the device *Foreign Object #1 Fluffy Light*, Wu also tethers this enchanting object to a repertoire of political affects through texture. In describing its light as "fluffy," Wu heightens the creaturely aspects of the sculpture, which are suggested by the eye-like buttons squinting at the viewer and biomorphic roundness. This choice also calls attention to the cuteness of this small, pink, squishy-looking expressive object with differently sized "eyes."[88] "Fluffy" does not describe the texture of the object itself, which is smooth and pearly, but seems to refer the quality of the light that it consumes, digests into binary code, and regurgitates as digital video. Calling the light data "fluffy" perhaps describes the texture of projected light, which can have a soft or "fluffy" appearance due to the dance of particulates in a white beam shining across a dark room. The "fluffy" light takes on a quality of animal liveness, nestling in the code inside the machine.

The bootleg video of Cha's *White Dust from Mongolia* was also included in Wu's installation *Upon Leaving the White Dust*, exhibited at 47 Canal in 2018 and again in 2020 with additional pieces—drawings by Wu of Cha's storyboards for *White Dust from Mongolia*.[89] In this installation, the recording of *White Dust from Mongolia* is seen as a white rectangle of projected light, which is recorded by *Foreign Object #1 Fluffy Light*, pulsing and flickering in the form of abstracting film in pure light.[90] Against the white wall of the darkened gallery, the installation recalls photographs from Cha's performances of the 1970s, which made frequent use of projected images and light. Arranged in a grid pattern on the floor in front of the projected video is an array of handmade light-colored objects that reach no higher than a foot or so off the ground and cast shadows against the white video, the surreal skyline of a distant city. The objects reference shots from Cha's planned film, either from the footage or surviving storyboards, and are made from a range of materials, including ceramic, clay, handmade glass, silicone, plaster, white fabric, and rice paper. We see toy trains, half a mop posed in mid-swipe, light-emitting globules, a plaster cast of manicured hands posed elegantly on a rectangle of Styrofoam with a small brown pebble resting against the knuckles, model airplanes, and an array of highly textured sculpted, cast, and blown abstract sculptures. Everything is colored in very light hues: white, pale aquamarine, a translucent topaz, dusty gray, a wispy lavender.

Upon Leaving the White Dust references both Cha's film and Barthes "Upon Leaving the Movie Theater" included in Cha's *Apparatus*. In the press release for the exhibit, Wu poetically expresses the longing and eros of cinema within the context of Cha's work and Asian diasporic art history. The text recalls both Barthes's theory of potential affect and Cha's own lyrical prose style, theoretically exacting yet evocative: "In the darkness, I see the look of myself leaving. I bring both of my bodies out of the

Figure 4.5: Cici Wu, *Upon Leaving the White Dust*. Photography by Joerg Lohse. Courtesy of the artist and 47 Canal.

Figure 4.6: Cici Wu, *Upon Leaving the White Dust*. Photography by Joerg Lohse. Courtesy of the artist and 47 Canal.

white dust. A narcissistic body of being loved by you which is looking, lost in materializing the structure of the film through gazing into the mirror, and a perverse body of loving you, ready to contain and absorb not the image of the film, but precisely that which exceeds it: grain of sound, sign of subtitles, and rays of light."[91] Wu's prose is lucent and dreamy, piercing in its emotive clarity and misty in its syntactic abstraction. This "I" and "you" who meet in the filmic space of *White Dust from Mongolia* are reminiscent of the two women from *Dictee*'s "Erato/Love Poetry" chapter, their elliptical exchanges of love conveying intimacy and distance simultaneously. In Wu's use of the first person, her writing suggests that she sees a visualization of her own departures in Cha's film—"I see the look of myself leaving." This sense of personal connection is part of what makes the press release so moving. Yet Wu complicates the apparent transparency of that tricky pronoun *I*, cautioning us against easy assumptions and at-hand narratives about Cha's work or *Upon Leaving the White Dust*, writing, "*Upon Leaving the White Dust* is a situation created by distance, my last temporary state of being with the unfinished film *White Dust from Mongolia* (1980) by artist Theresa Hak Kyung Cha (1951–1982).

It perhaps will always stay at the 'temporary state of being with', crude and open, as if the moment of leaving a movie theater could actually be pulled very very long."[92] Instead of settling into the certainty of knowing, Wu describes a sense of *being with* that resists the straightforwardness of fixed identification. *Upon Leaving the White Dust* suspends that feeling of leaving the movie theater, focusing on what "exceeds" the film itself, the feeling that pulls like taffy, stretching out time. In the installation, we can feel the dreaminess of remembering being in another world, the body stubbornly slow to awaken to "reality." Sitting with *Upon Leaving the White Dust* and its paratexts, one wonders, What could be made by staying with the dream remembered upon waking?

It is no surprise that Wu is also an archivist. The attempt to preserve a particular feeling through meticulous care materializes in Wu's reproductions of the film—the plaster casts and ceramic models of objects found in Cha's footage, the copying of the film through *Fluffy Light*, the drawings reconstructing Cha's storyboards. In a sense, these are all failed reproductions because they cannot exactly duplicate Cha's work, but as the curators in *After La vida nueva* write and Cha's own work suggests, such impasses need not be obstructions but can be openings. Reproduction as a sign of both affective attachment and critical distance is a technique used throughout *Dictee* and Cha's other works. It marks the desire but cannot reproduce its object perfectly, instead offering the cord of love itself as something to be looked at and tenderly preserved. A new dreamspace thick with potential affect comes into being as Wu performs connections to Cha's work through her own "difficult" aesthetic forms.

The dedication of other artists, writers, and readers to Cha's work is lasting testament to the brilliance of Cha's "difficulty" and its ability to generate interrelationality through critical feeling. Like all the artists and authors in this book, Cha's experimental forms may alienate conventional interpretive practices, but they create new spaces of belonging and possibility for readers and audiences looking for something else. Cha has now influenced multiple generations to reconsider the potential of difficult experimental forms for living in difference. In becoming the dream of the audience, Cha has not dissolved into passivity but reshaped the work that experimental aesthetics might do. She has provided the aesthetic forms for building a new ethics of social arrangement that reimagine the role of political feeling in diasporic and American art and literature.

Conclusion

Being Moved

Experimental art and literature prompt us to consider, What does reality feel like? Experimentalism asks us to consider the moment of aesthetic judgment itself and how it participates in the institution of norms and a shared sense of what is given and real. Experimental forms alter our sense of what is possible. As experimental forms depart from convention, they expand our understanding of how art can be made, what it looks like, and the range of intellectual and emotional experiences associated with it. By cuing the reader or viewer to reflect on the practice of interpretation and aesthetic judgment, experimentalism makes available different arrangements of the social, different notions of value, and the awareness that reality can be altered.

Aesthetic judgment brings together sensation, emotion, and knowledge in a mode of address that makes a claim about value. Our aesthetic pleasures always take place in the social, in the imagined or actual presence of others. As such, aesthetic pleasure is a structure for building the social, not merely as a series of mechanisms but as textured, sensorial experiences that inform the parameters of reality: how we relate to others and what is of value in this world. Aesthetic pleasure is a place where social meaning is made and where it circulates.

In *For Pleasure*, I have focused specifically on how aesthetic pleasure produces and circulates racial meaning and how experimental artists and authors of color have used form to redirect our attention. To depart from conventions in aesthetic form is to direct attention to unconventional and unexpected possibilities for thought, feeling, and relations with others in the sociality of aesthetic judgment. Such formal inventiveness makes available different perspectives on race, especially in regard to how race becomes imbued with the aura of the real (normative, natural) and how a restructuring of knowledge and feeling might lead to different understandings of value not defined by hierarchies of racial domination.

In chapter 1, I looked to the history of Black aesthetic theory and Black experimentalism to argue that Black artists have produced an alternative and antagonistic theory of the beautiful in response to the inherent anti-Blackness of Kantian aesthetic theory. W. E. B. Du Bois, Nella Larsen, and Isaac Julien show us that beauty judgments can be conceptualized as political demands. The demands of the beautiful have the power to redefine aesthetic collectivity and value, and Black experimentalism is especially poised to perform this recalibration. In chapter 2, I continued to examine how critical theories of race can help us address what is oppressive in the Kantianism that has become common sense. Through Yoko Ono's understudied conceptualism from the 1960s and 1970s, we see that that the aesthetic category of whimsy radically shifts the criteria of aesthetic judgment, and with it, the given terms of reality. The "rationalism" of racialized and gendered state and military violence might be reconsidered through Ono's topsy-turvy irrationalism. In the third chapter, I turned from the subject of aesthetic categories such as beauty and whimsy to the aesthetic and affective experiences particular to experimentalism, that is, the freedom to make art and interpret it. By tracing the racial history of black monochrome painting, we can see that for the white avant-garde, freedom has often been conceptualized against the ground of Black unfreedom and racial fixity. However, the freedom promised by color's affective richness and superfluity of meaning ultimately refuses to be captured by whiteness's proprietary grasping. In work by Jack Whitten, Ellen Gallagher, Zora Neale Hurston, and Glenn Ligon, the creative freedom promised by monochrome abstraction has been reclaimed against anti-Blackness and in service of a kind of freedom that does not depend upon others' fixed unfreedom. Finally, in the last chapter, I sought to theorize how experimental art and writing can offer alternative forms of interpretative interrelationality within the space of aesthetic pleasure. Theresa Hak Kyung Cha's performance art and writing and Cici Wu's multimedia installations use form to direct audiences toward ethical relations within aesthetic judgment. While conventional Western aesthetic theory has depended on the idea of a normative aesthetic subject, who is inseparable from whiteness, to determine what is a "proper" aesthetic judgment, Cha emphasizes the social relations within aesthetic judgment as a kind of covenant that rejects exclusive individualism and creates a model for ethical judgment. In each of these chapters, I have tried to situate how racially minoritized authors and artists living in the United States have approached fundamental questions related to the sociality of aesthetic pleasure. By contextualizing each artwork historically and framing my analysis within a critical study of race, I hope that I have shown that experimentalism uniquely presents answers to the urgent ethical and political questions at the intersection of race and aesthetics.

Working in a US context around the mid-twentieth century, I have focused on Black and Asian American artists in particular. As a whole, the artists and authors in this book are rarely spoken of together. W. E. B. Du Bois and Theresa Hak Kyung Cha can seem like people from entirely different planets. However, I propose that this perception of extreme distance is a reflection of disciplinary boundaries rather than actual life. This book locates authors and artists not typically thought of together as collaborators in an interrelational and heterogenous project of aesthetic and political freedom. I hope that the selection of texts expands our understanding of who practices aesthetic theory and experimentalism. The differences between these artists are important and real, but they are not an insurmountable boundary. I do not wish to artificially transplant ideas from one specific context to another, but I do think that reading across racial difference can help to break down the institutional boundaries that produce conceptual rigidity, making it difficult to see beyond habituated modes of thought and reified identities.

To be clear, I offer my full-throated support of ethnic studies disciplines such as African American studies, Black studies, and Asian American studies. These disciplines are important both for political reasons and because the depth of study cultivated in those fields is profoundly necessary. I certainly do not mean to suggest that ethnic studies disciplines reinscribe separatist and rigid ideas of racial identity. Indeed, this book would be impossible without those disciplines. Rather, I think it is important for us to remember that while our objects of study are often framed through the lens of similarity and commonness, seemingly disparate events do happen in the same world. As Grace Kyungwon Hong and Roderick Ferguson write in their introduction to the edited collection *Strange Affinities: The Gender and Sexual Politics of*

Comparative Racialization, "The stakes for identifying new comparative models are immensely high, for the changing configurations of power in the era after the decolonizing movements and new social movements of the mid-twentieth-century demand that we understand how particular populations are rendered vulnerable to processes of death and devaluation over and against other populations, in ways that palimpsestically register older modalities of racialized death but also exceed them."[1] Direct lines of influence may not be present, but they are also not necessary for mutually informing impact to take place.

In this way, my focus on Black and Asian artists and authors is meant to restore *some* of the context that is missing from our common understanding of US experimentalism. Experimentalism cannot be properly understood without considering race. By placing Black and Asian authors in conversation around questions of experimental form and aesthetic pleasure, this book argues that we must understand experimentalism as emerging in the afterlives of slavery and global anti-Blackness, colonialism, war, shifting racialized demands for labor, and immigration policy as a tool of racialization. Traditions of Black and Asian cultural expression in the United States are meaningfully interconnected through what Lisa Lowe has dubbed the "intimacies" of four continents and by way of an intertwined history within US racial politics.[2] As Joan Kee argues regarding the concept of "Afro Asia" in art history, these interrelational cultural formations offer an alternative to additive diversity and inclusion models, which aim to correct injustice simply by adding more art by minoritized groups, without enacting any structural changes. Kee writes, "Addition proceeds on the assumption that there is an existing body to which units can be added depending on whether they can affirm what has already been deemed central—hence the use of terms like *noncanonical* or *underrecognized*, or the co-optation of words like *inclusion* or *diversity* that are hollowed out as quickly as they are deployed by a structure that relentlessly feeds on division."[3] By contrast, Kee argues that the concept of Afro Asia "is a project of value creation that extends well beyond calls for prioritizing non-Western or non-white artists and certainly beyond efforts to render Euro-American and/or white artists as morally suspect. While plurality might be fruitfully construed as a vital form of multiplication, quantity and volume are insufficient to bring about the kind of structural overhaul needed to put life rather than death at the center of discussion."[4] Experimental artistic production by racially minoritized authors ought to be considered as complexly interrelated as part of heterogeneous projects seeking to produce societies not built on racial domination. This experimentalism offers alternative models for understanding the aesthetic and its role in the production of shared realities. The Black and Asian aesthetic histories, theories, and texts examined in this book look to create new forms of value rather than to merely complement existing standards. As I said at the outset of this book, I am in no way aiming for a comprehensive or chronological overview of the racial history of experimentalism. I hope that despite the many gaps, this book can provide a methodology portable enough to be of use to a wide array of projects.

In the final moments of this book, I would like to take the opportunity to reflect on the title: *For Pleasure*. This book is "for" pleasure, as in I am enthusiastically in favor of aesthetic pleasure as something necessary for the soul, for a life that is more than survival, and as a mode of social and political connection and invention. I hope it serves a functional purpose "for pleasure," helping to cultivate aesthetic pleasure and our understanding of its importance. The title also has an obscured interrogatory valence: What is pleasure for, if anything? What would it mean to be "for" pleasure—and is this even a needed stance to take? Is anyone actually against pleasure? And if we enact something, attend something, perform something, make something "for pleasure," what are the ethics of that experience? As I have tried to show throughout this book, the answer to all these questions is: It depends. Aesthetic pleasure is exactly what we make of it.

As I explained in the introduction and tried to demonstrate in each of the chapters, aesthetic pleasure is not a one-dimensional experience. Not only does it exist within a wildly various tonal range, from the ecstasies of the sublime to the mildly amusing, but pleasure is rarely experienced on its own as *just pleasure*. Human experience is too diverse for me to claim that a single kind of feeling can exist entirely on its own. We have feelings about our feelings, thoughts about the feelings we have about our feelings, feelings about our thoughts. And on it goes. Among all this mess, I contend that pleasure has an ethics, which is not so much about cataloguing good pleasures and bad but understanding aesthetic pleasure as a social relation. As a social relation, aesthetic pleasure necessitates our contemplation of how we impact others in the world and how others impact us. As with any social relation, finding ethical alignment is not very often a process of prohibition but more frequently one of relearning, adjustment, and invention. Sometimes pleasure comes at the expense of others in utterly heinous and devastating ways. Sometimes it is a banal kind of violence, cancerous and quiet. As much as I would have loved to write only about the joyous, the rapturous, and the healing kinds of aesthetic pleasure, much of the time I found myself writing about the relationship between pleasure and pain, freedom and unfreedom, living in the gnashing tension between them.

However, at the end of this book, I would like to give just a little space to pure, unqualified, borderline uncritical aesthetic pleasure. If aesthetic pleasure is a social relation, then what would it mean to truly feel such joy? In this sense, the bliss of aesthetic pleasure might be what Ruth Wilson Gilmore has called a rehearsal for living.[5] Thought of another way, aesthetic pleasure might be a little sliver of actual freedom—temporary, protected, and slipping through our fingers. Because what is the difference, truly, between practicing a thing and doing the thing? The experimental can prepare us for the kinds of joy that do not depend on domination, the kinds of value that are not extracted through violence. But what if experiences of aesthetic pleasure can also just *be those things*? Who is to say that it isn't real just because it doesn't last and it is not enough? This is what minoritarian aesthetics can provide: an understanding that the aesthetic is a social relation, a deep knowledge of unfreedom, and the desire to end it through the social enactments of being together in aesthetic experience. It carries the historical, whispering the future in your ear along the present corridor. It tries to find the forms that make the most possibility out of the least possibility. It hates the police and loves the wildness of imagination.

As a final example of an experimental text that embraces pleasure against racist unfreedom, I look to Félix González-Torres's conceptualist sculpture *Untitled (Passport)* (1991). In 1992, the Cuban-born conceptual artist González-Torres wrote the following letter to his friend Andrea Rosen, the gallerist who showed his work and, after his death of AIDS-related complications in 1996, became the co-executor of his estate. In this letter, González-Torres is thinking about *Untitled (Passport)* (1991). *(Passport)* is composed of a stack of white 23 5/8 inch × 23 5/8 inch pieces of paper, four inches high at its ideal height. Visitors are invited to take paper from the stack, which is continually replenished. González-Torres writes:

> The other day I was still thinking about this piece and how it fulfills me now even more. You know, the title: *(Passport)* is very crucial and significant—a white empty blank uninscribed piece of paper, an untouched feeling, an undiscovered experience. A passport to another place, to another life, to a new beginning, to chance; to the chance of meeting that other who makes life a moving force, a chance to alter one's life and future, an empty passport for life; to inscribe it with the best, the most painful, the most banal, the most sublime, reasons for being. A simple white object against a white wall, waiting.[6]

(Passport) creates the possibility of delight, generosity, and creativity, within a form—the passport—which exists to control the global flow of people along lines of social desirability and political power. In the United States, the passport impedes the mobility of some groups while increasing the mobility of others and is a prized instrument in the nation's race-making toolkit. Yet in contrast to the typical spaces of waiting associated with migration (detention centers, courtrooms, borders, application processes) this *(Passport)* waits for the audience, blank and unassuming, resting on the floor. The piece is performed through the participant's feeling, perhaps unexpressed, private, or precognitive. It is not bestowed on one as a birthright or hard-won sigil. *(Passport)* exists as a play on what it means to "be moved." In his titling, González-Torres converts a scene of management into a scene in which *to be moved* means allowing oneself to be changed by feeling. Literal passports (if you have the right kind) supposedly support unfettered movement, the fantasy of a liberal subject who moves through the world at will. In actuality, this movement is all about the state taking choices out of peoples' hands. The document issued by states enables or disables individuals' abilities to move through the world, subject to a calculated hidden ruleset. But with this *(Passport)*, to be moved means tapping into experimentalism's capacity to make available different experiences of the world. Through González-Torres's formal choices (titling, large size, color and blankness of the paper, placement of the paper and the need to bend, stoop, or

crouch to pick it up or to have it handed to you, constant replenishment that simulates infiniteness), *(Passport)* directs the participant to reflect on the moment of aesthetic pleasure itself and their role in making it. The feelings of the participant move them, give them access to a world that González-Torres insists is *new, another,* or *altered,* as they consider all the ways that normative passports function in relation possibility and its foreclosure. Here, "having papers" is a different kind of talisman. González-Torres does not attempt to predict how anyone might be moved by the conceptual passport. It stands waiting as "an untouched feeling, an undiscovered experience" for the participant to enact.

ACKNOWLEDGMENTS

I'd like to start by thanking the editors of the Minoritarian Aesthetics series: Uri McMillan, Sandra Ruiz, and Shane Vogel. It is an honor to be part of this series, and I still can't quite believe it. My sincere thanks to Eric Zinner, Furqan Sayeed, Martin Coleman, Ainee Jeong, Richard Feit, and everyone else at NYU Press for seeing this project through the publication process. I also extend my gratitude to the anonymous readers for this book, who gave wise advice and helped shape the final form of the book. My deepest thanks to you all.

I really can't express how thankful I am for the support of Leslie Bow, an intellectual powerhouse who let me know it was okay to be a "quirky" thinker. I am grateful for the generosity of Ramzi Fawaz, whose enthusiasm and infectious energy kept me motivated and focused. Cherene Sherrard-Johnson is a model of scholarship, creativity, and grace. Brian Glavey's mentoring and friendship has been a lesson on the impact that teaching can have on someone's life (mine!).

It is impossible to write a book without material support, and I am appreciative of the fellowships that allowed me to finish this work. I was honored to join Rutgers University as a postdoctoral research associate in African American literature in the English Department in 2018–19. During my time there, the incomparable Cheryl Wall passed away. Dr. Wall was instrumental in creating the fellowship that helped me write this book, and I wish to honor her essential contributions to the field of African American literature here. She leaves behind a superb legacy. My sincere thanks to the American Council of Learned Societies and the University of Illinois, Urbana-Champaign, for the generous opportunity of an ACLS Emerging Voices Fellowship. With the support of this fellowship, I was able to complete the final manuscript.

I must also offer my gratitude to Cici Wu for additional clarification on her work, as well as for the permission to include images. My love and thanks to Beverly Acha for her painterly insights on color. Additionally, I thank the University of California, Berkeley Art Museum, and Pacific Film Archive for permission to use documentation photographs of Cha's performance of *Other Things Seen, Other Things Heard*. This book is the product of many years of research and writing. An early version of the Isaac Julien section of chapter 1 was published in *Criticism*.

To friends and family: Sunny, I love you a completely normal amount. Sarah, always my truest reader, dearest friend, and favorite Taurus. V.v.V. To Paul, the ultimate father figure and comedian with the kindest heart. To Marissa, a new friend and a cherished one. Jack and Chloe, thank you for inviting us into your town and your home, and to Wren, thank you for the lessons on the joys of wildness. To Emily, Bennett, Mom, Harold, Mom, Dad, and MJ: unconditional love. To Alex, what can I say? You only live once, probably.

NOTES

INTRODUCTION

1 This is a reference to Jenkins's earlier video *Mass of Images* (1978).
2 I use the term *racial capitalism* as it is deployed by Cedric Robinson in *Black Marxism: The Making of the Black Radical Tradition* and as it has been popularized in such works as Gaye Theresa Johnson and Alex Lubin's edited collection *Futures of Black Radicalism*. As Robin D. G. Kelley summarizes in his foreword to *Black Marxism*, "Robinson explains, capitalism emerged within the feudal order and grew in fits and starts, flowering in the cultural soil of the West—most notably in the racialism that has come to characterize European society. Capitalism and racism, in other words, did not break from the old order but rather evolved from it to produce a modern world system of 'racial capitalism' dependent on slavery, violence, imperialism, and genocide" (Kelley, "Foreword," xiii). This is to say that "racial capitalism" can also be called just plain "capitalism," but it is important to always keep present the ways that race and capitalism are inseparable social orders.
3 Although Kraft's 1967 composition predates it, it seems very possible that Jenkins at least in part chose Kraft's *Contextures* as a reference to the 1978 show *Contextures* at Linda Goode Bryant's Just Above Midtown Gallery in New York City. The show included work by one of Jenkins's important collaborators, the conceptual and performance artist Senga Nengudi.
4 Hong, "Delusions of Whiteness."
5 Hong, "Delusions of Whiteness."
6 For example, the term *study* as it is used in Moten and Harney, *The Undercommons*.
7 De Duve, *Aesthetics at Large*, 22.
8 Chuh, *The Difference Aesthetics Makes*, 19.
9 Chuh, *The Difference Aesthetics Makes*; Silva, *Toward a Global Idea of Race*; Lowe, *The Intimacies of Four Continents*; McKittrick, *Sylvia Wynter*.
10 Rodríguez, *White Reconstruction*, 8.
11 Rodríguez, *White Reconstruction*, 7, emphasis in the original.
12 A reference to Ruth Wilson Gilmore's well-known definition of racism: "Racism is the state-sanctioned and/or extra-legal production and exploitation of group-differentiated vulnerabilities to premature death, in distinct yet densely interconnected political geographies" (Gilmore, "Race and Globalization," 261).

13 Ngai, *Theory of the Gimmick*, 51.
14 De Duve, *Aesthetics at Large*, 18, emphasis in the original.
15 Ahmed, *The Cultural Politics of Emotion*, 10.
16 Chaouli, *Thinking with Kant's Critique of Judgment*, 12, emphasis in the original.
17 Aubrey, *Guilty Aesthetic Pleasures*, 2.
18 Aubrey, *Guilty Aesthetic Pleasures*, 1.
19 Scarry, *On Beauty and Being Just*, 57.
20 Scarry, *On Beauty and Being Just*, 58.
21 "Killjoys" is a concept drawn from Ahmed, *The Promise of Happiness*.
22 On experimentalism and value, see Cecire, *Experimental*.
23 Ganeri, *Attention Not Self*, 15.
24 Ganeri, *Attention Not Self*, 11.
25 Ganeri, *Attention Not Self*, 12.
26 Ingold, *Imagining for Real*, 3, emphasis in the original.
27 Ingold, *Imagining for Real*, 128.
28 Odell, *How to Do Nothing*, 102.
29 Odell, *How to Do Nothing*, 102.
30 Odell, *How to Do Nothing*, 103.
31 Odell, *How to Do Nothing*, 104, 107–8.
32 Wang, *Thinking Its Presence*, 17.
33 Cecire, *Experimental*, 46.
34 Cecire, *Experimental*, 2.
35 Cecire, *Experimental*, 4. Cecire finds several issues with this historicity, which tends to look to history to affirm what she calls the "epistemic values" of the present in ways that rely on unreliable notions of progressivism and objectivity.
36 Weheliye, *Habeas Viscus*, 13.
37 Cacho, "Racialized Hauntings," 27.
38 Robinson, *Black Marxism*, 28.
39 Muñoz, *Disidentifications*, 189.
40 Chambers-Letson, *After the Party*, 15–16.
41 Táíwò, *Elite Capture*, 120.
42 Táíwò, *Elite Capture*, 121.

1. WHAT CAN BEAUTY DO?

Epigraph: Hartman, "Venus in Two Acts," 3.
1 Richard Dyer points to the way that lighting and the manufacturing a "glow" of white heterosexuality around the face of the Hollywood female film star in *White*. Dyer, *White*, 1997.
2 Such as George Platt Lynes. Lynes is mentioned by Julien as an influence in *RIOT*. In *Disidentification*, José Esteban Muñoz explores Julien's references to Harlem Renaissance photographer James Van Der Zee's *Harlem Book of the Dead*, which consisted mainly of deathbed and funeral photography.

3 The concept of social death is also an important presence in this shot. "Social death" refers to Orlando Patterson's greatly influential *Slavery and Social Death*. Patterson's concept of social death has had an enormous impact on twenty-first-century debates in Black studies around ontology, politics, and Afropessimism, as theorized by scholars such as Frank B. Wilderson III, Saidiya Hartman, Jared Sexton, Christina Sharpe, and Calvin Warren, among others. See Wilderson, "Afropessimism and the Ruse of Analogy." On gender, politics, and Afropessimism, see Day, "Afro-Feminism before Afropessimism." On queering social death, see Bost, *Evidence of Being*.

4 Cheng's particular concern is the impasse beauty presents for women of color, asking, "Between a feminist critique of feminine beauty and a racial denial of non-white beauty, where does this leave the woman of color? Can she or can she not be beautiful? Is her beauty (or potential for beauty) good or evil?" (Cheng, "Wounded Beauty," 192).

5 The ambivalence between liberatory desire and fetish, especially in interracial relationships, is also taken up in Julien's other films, including *The Attendant* (1993) and *The Long Road to Mazatlán* (2000). Julien also addresses this directly in his essay "Confessions of a Snow Queen," and these themes are taken up in Elizabeth Freeman's essay on race, queer temporality, and sadomasochism, "Turn the Beat Around."

6 Cheng, "Wounded Beauty," 208.

7 See Elaine Scarry's *On Beauty and Being Just*. Scarry also offers a theory of the beautiful as a means of achieving justice. However, Scarry's arguments maintain the centrality of sameness and symmetry, while my arguments here emphasis the importance of difference.

8 Bost, *Evidence of Being*, 2018.

9 Cecire, *Experimental*, 4.

10 Cecire, *Experimental*, 4.

11 In an interview with the poet Essex Hemphill, Julien explains that the research process took several years and included meetings with the photographer Roy DeCarava and the family of James Van der Zee. See Hemphill and Julien, "Looking for Langston."

12 Cecire, *Experimental*, 8–9.

13 According to Black studies scholar and political theorist Cedric Robinson, the Black radical tradition is "an ongoing 'revolutionary consciousness that proceeded from the whole historical experience of Black people and not merely from the social formations of capitalist slavery or the relations of production of colonialism" (*Black Marxism*, 169). As Erica Edwards writes, "The Black Radical Tradition is the history of 'a whole other way of being,'" which Robinson argues grants "supremacy to metaphysics, not the material" ("Foreword," xix; *Black Marxism*, 69). See also Johnson and Lubin, *Futures of Black Radicalism*.

14 Ngai, *Our Aesthetic Categories*, 38.

15 Kant, *Critique of Judgment*, §7, 55–56.

16. Kant, *Critique of Judgment*, §7, 55–56, emphasis in the original.
17. Kant, *Critique of Judgment*, §15, 73.
18. Kant, *Critique of Judgment*, §22, 89.
19. Kant, *Critique of Judgment*, §19, 86. On reason and aesthetic subjectivity, see Chuh, *The Difference Aesthetics Makes*, especially chapter 3, "Making Sense Otherwise."
20. Kant, *Critique of Judgment*, §48, 179, emphasis in the original; §50, 188.
21. Kant, *Critique of Judgment*, §50, 188.
22. Kant, *Critique of Judgment*, §41, 163, emphasis in the original.
23. Kant, *Critique of Judgment*, §40, 162.
24. Kant, *Critique of Judgment*, §41, 163–64.
25. Silva, *Toward a Global Idea of Race*, 2007.
26. Taylor, *Black Is Beautiful*, 2016.
27. Roelofs, "Racialization as an Aesthetic Production."
28. Kant, *Observations*, 2:244.
29. Kant, *Observations*, 2:253.
30. Bernasconi, "Who Invented the Concept of Race?," 26.
31. Bernasconi, "Who Invented the Concept of Race?," 29.
32. Bernasconi, "Who Invented the Concept of Race?," 29.
33. Cervenak, *Wandering*, 56.
34. Moten, *Stolen Life*, 2–3.
35. Moten, *Stolen Life*, 29.
36. The raised fist in Moten's essay belongs to a Black male juror who reportedly raised his fist at the reading of the O. J. Simpson criminal trial when the jury was dismissed after the reading of the verdict. But Moten's poetic riff extends beyond this historical event. Moten, *Stolen Life*, 96.
37. Moten, *Stolen Life*, 111–12.
38. Moten, *Stolen Life*, 113.
39. Hartman, *Wayward Lives*, 33, emphasis in the original.
40. See Denise Ferreira da Silva's "In the Raw" for an analysis of the despotism of the Kantian aesthetic judgment and an alternative methodology for understanding aesthetic experience.
41. See English, *Unnatural Selections*; Gilmore, *Defying Dixie*; Goldsby, *A Spectacular Secret*; Hughes, *The Fight for Freedom*.
42. Wispé, "History of the Concept of Empathy," 19, emphasis in the original.
43. Wispé, "History of the Concept of Empathy," 20, 19.
44. Martha Nussbaum makes the liberal argument for empathetic reading in her advocation of social realist literature in *Upheavals of Thought*. Paul Bloom has made the case against empathy (and for compassion) in his book *Against Empathy*.
45. Moten, *Black and Blur*, 257.
46. Rankin, *Letters on American Slavery*, 56.
47. Hartman, *Scenes of Subjection*, 19.
48. Hartman, *Scenes of Subjection*, 20.

49 In *Sensational Flesh*, Amber Jamilla Musser offers additional perspectives on empathy, in conversation with Hartman's critique, but ultimately offering an alternative construction of empathy that attempts to preserve difference without resorting to identity. Musser's method of reading empathetically is based in identifying structures of embodied knowledge and exploring what can be shared in the "simultaneous internality and externality of sensation." In chapter 4 in this book, on the art and legacy of Theresa Hak Kyung Cha, I explore similar analytical methods that seek to find spaces of social simultaneity without erasing difference. However, I do not find *empathy* to be the most useful term for describing the experiences of connection and collectivity found in relation to Cha's work (Musser, *Sensational Flesh*, 23).

50 See Kelley, *Freedom Dreams*.

51 John Keene—writer, translator, professor, artist, and MacArthur Fellow—has written a short story imagining the parallel lines of sight between Du Bois and Santayana in "Persons and Places," found in his collection *Counternarratives*. It is very much worth a read for those interested in the connection.

52 Appiah, *Lines of Descent*, 38.

53 See Saidiya Hartman's chapter on Du Bois in *Wayward Lives, Beautiful Experiments*.

54 See, for example, Johnson and Johnson, *Propaganda and Aesthetics*; Baker, *Modernism and the Harlem Renaissance*; Smethurst, *The African American Roots of Modernism*; Wall, *Women of the Harlem Renaissance*; and Vogel, *The Scene of Harlem Cabaret*, among many, many other sources.

55 For example, famously in 1926, the same year that "Criteria of Negro Art" was published, the *Crisis* published a "Symposium" called "The Negro in Art: How Shall He Be Portrayed?" The Symposium published the answers from a questionnaire sent to a variety of artists, publishers, and public figures, including Langston Hughes, Jessie Fauset, Carl Van Vechten, and Alfred Knopf. Locke, *The New Negro*.

56 Chandler, *Toward a New History*, 23.

57 Castronovo, *Beauty Along the Color Line*, 1444, 1448.

58 Du Bois, "Criteria," 328.

59 Du Bois, "Criteria," 328.

60 Du Bois, "Criteria," 325.

61 Du Bois, "Criteria," 325, emphasis added.

62 Hartman, *Wayward Lives*, 33.

63 Sherrard-Johnson, *Portraits of the New Negro Woman*; see chapter 1, "A Plea for Color."

64 Irene's narrative perspective is famously "unreliable," and its psychological complexity keeps the reader on their toes throughout the novel. See Butler, "Passing, Queering"; Carr, "Paranoid Interpretation"; Tate, "Nella Larsen's *Passing*"; Wall, "Passing for What?"

65 Cheng, "Ornamentalism," 443.

66 McMillan, *Embodied Avatars*, 7.
67 Moten, *In the Break*, 1.
68 Larsen, *Passing*, 182.
69 Larsen, *Passing*, 143.
70 See Carr, "Paranoid Interpretation." In invoking paranoid reading, I am thinking of Eve Kosofsky Sedgwick's "Paranoid Reading."
71 Larsen, *Passing*, 239.
72 As Cherene Sherrard-Johnson has established, artists and activists of the Harlem Renaissance were fascinated by the character of the mulatta, her political potential, and the pleasures of sensationalism and sentimentality that were her constant attendants. These projects were inseparable from an ambivalent relation to racialized discourses of beauty and respectability. The mulatta figure was meant to provoke (white) readers' (voyeuristic) empathy for Black subjects through the artist's portrayal of elegant, virtuous, and pale women. See also Tate, *Domestic Allegories of Political Desire*.
73 Larsen, *Passing*, 148, 161.
74 Larsen, *Passing*, 194.
75 Keeling, "Looking for M," 570.
76 Allen, *There's a Disco Ball between Us*, 9.
77 Hong, *Death beyond Disavowal*, 117.
78 Hong, *Death beyond Disavowal*, 117.
79 Diawara, "The Absent One," 108.
80 This detail about the club is mentioned by Julien in the DVD commentary.
81 Mercer, *RIOT*, 59.
82 Gilroy, *RIOT*, 39.
83 Stuart Hall wrote in response to the 1985 Tottenham Broadwater Farm Riots, "The plain truth is that, in the black communities, policing is now 'out of order.' . . . [Police] appear to have forgotten any other means of entering a black person's home than breaking down the door." Hall, *The Hard Road to Renewal*, 77. The riots began after Cynthia Jarrett, an Afro-Caribbean woman, died of heart failure when police burst into her home during a raid. This came only weeks after the Brixton Riots, which began in response to the police shooting of Dorothy "Cherry" Groce, who was paralyzed by her injury.
84 Crimp, "AIDS," 7.
85 Watney, *Policing Desire*, 8.
86 Miller, *Slaves to Fashion*, 227.
87 Morrison, "James Baldwin."
88 I will use upper case *Beauty* to refer to the character and lowercase *beauty* to refer to the aesthetic concept. However, since Beauty works as a metaphor for beauty, sometimes this distinction is beside the point.
89 Producer Nadine Marsh-Edwards explains in the DVD commentary that the film uses a combination of slowing down the film and directing performers to move slowly in order to achieve this effect.

90 Cheng, "Wounded Beauty," 202.
91 Lorde, "Uses of the Erotic: The Erotic as Power," in *Sister Outsider*, 53–59.
92 For an analysis of race, the gaze, and the struggle of (mis)recognition in *Looking for Langston*, see David Marriott's chapter on Julien's *Looking for Langston* and *The Attendant* in *Haunted Life*. Julien also discusses "the silence of whiteness in black queer film practice" in "Confessions of a Snow Queen," qtd. 125. Julien and Kobena Mercer discuss the racial politics of Black and racially minoritized cinema in the late 1980s in "De Margin and De Centre."
93 Michael Oreskes, "Senate Votes to Bar U.S. Support of 'Obscene or Indecent' Artwork," *New York Times*, July 27, 1989.
94 See, for example, Tucker, *The Moment of Racial Sight*; Roelofs, "Racialization as an Aesthetic Production"; Bindman, *Ape to Apollo*; Painter, *The History of White People*; Tibebu, *Hegel and the Third World*.
95 The song is "Can You Party (Club Mix)" (1988) by Royal House, which samples Larry Heard's "Can You Feel It?" (1986). An early innovator in the house music genre, Heard's "Can You Feel It?" was often mixed with recordings of Martin Luther King's "I Have a Dream" speech. Julien notes in the DVD commentary that "Can You Feel It?" was a kind of anthem for queer Black sociality at this moment in the 1980s.
96 See Tate, *Black Beauty*; Ongiri, *Spectacular Blackness*; and Taylor *Black Is Beautiful*. GerShun Avilez's *Radical Aesthetics and Modern Black Nationalism* also offers important theorizations of what Avilez calls "aesthetic radicalism" in relation to post-civil rights era Black nationalisms, "a method that acknowledges the value of political frameworks rooted in collectivity (i.e. common racial circumstances) while also recognizing fragmentation within that collective" (12).
97 Laclau, *Emancipation(s)*, 28. I acknowledge that Laclau's definition of universalism is crucially different from Kant's. Although in *Contingency, Hegemony, Universality*, Slavoj Zizek accuses both Judith Butler and Laclau of being "secret Kantians," so perhaps for some readers, these differences are less disruptive (Zizek, *Contingency*, 111).
98 Silva offers an important critique of Laclau's work on contingency, with Chantal Mouffe, and their silence on race:
> I could not locate racial subaltern subjects in their portrait of the social. Would they be "moments" (discursively instituted subject positions) or "elements" ("antagonistic parts") in their reframing of the social as a contingent "structured totality"? Under what conditions, what sort of "partial fixations," do they move into (as a "moment") and/or out (as an "antagonistic part") of this discursive field? Or is raciality a "total" fixation, that is, the sole always already feature of the field itself, which in this case would contradict their account of the social or force them to name it racial? (*Toward a Global Idea of Race*, 4)
99 Zerilli, "This Universalism Which Is Not One," 15, emphasis in the original.
100 Laclau, *Emancipation(s)*, 27.

101 In invoking "beside," I am thinking of Eve Kosofsky Sedgwick's parsing of "beside" as a critical relation:
> *Beside* is an interesting preposition also because there's nothing very dualistic about it; a number of elements may lie alongside one another, though not an infinity of them. *Beside* permits a spacious agnosticism about several of the linear logics that enforce dualistic thinking: noncontradiction or the law of the excluded middle, cause versus effect, subject versus object. Its interest does not, however, depend upon a fantasy of metonymically egalitarian or even pacific relations, as any child knows who's shared a bed with siblings. *Beside* comprises a wide range of desiring, identifying, representing, repelling, paralleling, differentiating, rivaling, leaning, twisting, mimicking, withdrawing, attracting, aggressing, warping, and other relations. (*Touching Feeling*, 8, emphasis in the original)

102 Muñoz, *Cruising Utopia*, 35, emphasis in the original.
103 Moten, *Stolen Life*, 111–12.
104 Alex is Beauty's love interest in this scene and the protagonist in Nugent's "Smoke, Lilies and Jade." He is also styled with a pencil mustache recalling Langston Hughes, and some critics refer to him as "Langston," although he is referred to as "Alex" in the credits.
105 For a history of how fatness became stigmatized and associated with Blackness, see Strings, *Fearing the Black Body*, 2019.
106 Allen, *There's a Disco Ball between Us*, 5.
107 In the DVD commentary, Julien reveals that this sequence was filmed at a real gay club called—appropriately—Heaven. Julien notes that this sequence refers to the many closures of gay clubs in the UK during this period.
108 Langston Hughes, "Night and Morn," in *The Dream Keeper and Other Poems* (New York: Alfred A. Knopf, 1994), 11–12. On the soundtrack, this track is credited as "Hey!" Langston Hughes with Jazz Quartet from the NBC documentary *The Subject Is Jazz*, *Looking for Langston*, the Vinyl Factory, 2017, vinyl record.

2. YOKO ONO'S WHIMSY

Epigraph: Briante, Defacing the Monument, 16.

1 Ono, *Grapefruit*, np.
2 Kant, *The Critique of Judgment*, trans. Pluhar, §54 207. I take the term *whimsy* from Werner S. Pluhar's English translation of the *Critique of Judgment* from Hackett Press. Other translators take a different approach to translating the German term *launig/launicht*. The Paul Guyer and Eric Matthews translation from Cambridge University Press, another prominent English-language edition, translates *launig* as "caprice": "Someone who is involuntarily given to such alterations is **subject to caprice**, but someone who can assume them voluntarily and purposively (for the sake of a lively presentation by means of a laugh-provoking contrast), such a person and his performance are called **capricious**" (*Critique of the Power of Judgment* §54 211, bold emphasis in the original). Meanwhile, James

Creed Meredith translates this term simply as "humor" in the Oxford edition (*Critique of Judgment*, §54 164). It can also be translated as "wit." I have selected *whimsy* not necessarily because I believe it is the most accurate translation, but because I think this English term more perfectly captures the affective and social qualities that I am interested in theorizing. *Humor* is extremely general, wit is also quite broad, and *capriciousness* can suggest a dissatisfied moodiness. *Whimsy* conveys unpredictability while also being associated with femininity, cuteness, and mischievousness. On the whole it is more pleasure-oriented than *capriciousness*. I refer to the Hackett/Pluhar translation throughout this book for consistency.

3 See Berlant on humorlessness in "Humorlessness (Three Monologues and a Hairpiece)" and also Fred Moten on the administrator in the chapter "The Touring Machine (Flesh Thought Inside Out)" in *Stolen Life*.
4 Reddy, *Freedom with Violence*, 37.
5 Reddy, *Freedom with Violence*, 38.
6 See Perée, *Cover to Cover*. The category of artist's book can include works ranging from illustrated books, such as William Blake's *Songs of Innocence and Experience* (1789), books of images (such as photographs or collages), like Edward Ruscha's *Various Small Fires and Milk* (1964), to Dieter Roth's *Literature Sausage* (1969), a sausage casing stuffed with fat, gelatin, spices, and ground-up books and magazines.
7 While many art historians trace the invention of the conceptualist instruction to John Cage's *4'33"*, Midori Yoshimoto has shown that Ono actually came to this form independently in the mid-1950s. There are important differences between Cage's text compositions, which favor chance operations, and Ono's emphasis on the performer's or reader's imaginative experience. See *Into Performance* for more on the history of Ono's instructions.
8 Yoshimoto, *Into Performance*, 81.
9 Alexandra Munroe has suggested that Ono's instructions are influenced by Japanese literary and philosophical forms like the haiku and koan, both of which share the brevity of Ono's instructions, which are always very short, sometimes as short as a single word, and also contain the riddle-like quality that can be found in some of Ono's instructions. See Munroe, *YES Yoko Ono*.
10 Through her famous Chambers Street salons—organized by Ono at her apartment on Chambers Street—Ono created a space for avant-gardists to experiment and present their work, fomenting the Fluxus and conceptualist movements in the 1950s (Yoshimoto, *Into Performance*, 85).
11 Theoretically, at least. Conceptualism's "failure" to resist commodification and absorption into the elite heights of the art world is well known.
12 Yoshimoto, *Into Performance*, 30.
13 Perreault, "The Art Cops Return."
14 Rei Terada writes compellingly on this facet of the Given in *Looking Away*. "The given," a concept that Terada derives from Kant, is the absolute most basic foundation that allows daily social life to proceed according to the status quo.

Although things that are given are technically only appearances, they are part of a host of normed agreements that organize what we recognize as the "real world."

15 Terada, *Looking Away*, 4.
16 Here I refer to Ono's "Bed-In for Peace," performed on her honeymoon with John Lennon in Amsterdam and Montreal in 1969. In "Bed-In for Peace," Ono and Lennon famously invited fellow celebrities and the media into their hotel room as they sat in bed for peace. Many expected to find a more lascivious display than the white-pajama-clad couple campaigning for world peace, especially after the nude cover of *Two Virgins*. Despite (or maybe because of) the chaste presentation, Ono and Lennon—especially Ono—received some rather vicious criticism from some of their visitors, notoriously from conservative satirist and cartoonist Al Capp.
17 Ono has more often been the punchline of a joke than appreciated for her punchlines since her relationship with John Lennon became public, although respect for Ono as an important and influential figure in the avant-garde has grown especially since her 2015 retrospective at the Museum of Modern Art in New York. See Leslie Bow's *Betrayal and Other Acts of Subversion* for more on the ways that Ono's notoriety is part of larger racial and gender stereotypes of Asian women. See also Joseph Jonghyun Jeon's *Racial Things, Racial Forms* for the ways in which the racist and sexist animus toward Ono connects to her avant-gardism.
18 Yoshimoto writes that the instructions were developed not only from Ono's study of literature and music but also from meditative rituals that she created to soothe herself (Yoshimoto, *Into Performance*, 83).
19 Following the work of Sianne Ngai and her theorization of "minor" aesthetic categories, as well as Ngai's work with Lauren Berlant on comedy and aesthetic judgment in the Critical Inquiry special issue "Comedy Has Issues."
20 *Critique of Judgment* §54, 207, emphasis in the original.
21 Patterson, "Notes on PETS," 49.
22 You can see a full performance of *Pond*, including the lesson teaching the performers how to perform the work, in this recording from the 2013 Performa 13 biennial: The Studio Museum Harlem. "Benjamin Patterson: Pond (1962)," April 4, 2014, YouTube video, 16:53, www.youtube.com/watch?v=DoDfaRQH8mk&list=PLQpCqdEzX6b6JoNLDwbeAU1rExwiNMugZ&index=4. This performance by a group of children also captures the spirit of whimsy quite wonderfully: Weston Art Gallery, "Ben Patterson—'Pond' FLUXUS Performance," March 13, 2016, YouTube video, 3:21, www.youtube.com/watch?v=peenNjL_c8c&list=PLQpCqdEzX6b6JoNLDwbeAU1rExwiNMugZ&index=5.
23 See Yoshimoto, *Into Performance*; and Munroe, "Spirit of Yes: The Art and Life of Yoko Ono," in *Yes Yoko Ono*, 18.
24 Yoshimoto notes, "Ono conceived most of her works in English in the United States, but she often worked directly in Japanese while living in Japan" (Yoshimoto, *Into Performance*, 96). Additionally, the 1964 self-published first edition of *Grapefruit* was bilingual; "about one-third of its 150 works were accompanied by Japanese versions." Yet these were not literal translations, Yoshimoto explains: "In

general, the Japanese texts were more abstract in terms of wording while the English versions had more specifications. Some of the Japanese pieces had different titles from the English versions" (ibid.).
25 Javadizadeh, "The Atlantic," 476.
26 Javadizadeh, "The Atlantic," 476.
27 Graeber, *Utopia of Rules*, 17, 18.
28 Graeber, *Utopia of Rules*, 32.
29 Graeber, *Utopia of Rules*, 73.
30 This is an example that Graeber gives in *The Utopia of Rules* (72–77).
31 Ono, *Grapefruit*, n.p.
32 Ono, *Grapefruit*, n.p.
33 See Concannon, "Yoko Ono's *Cut Piece*"; Huang, "Inscrutability, Actually"; and Wilson, "Remembering Yoko Ono's *Cut Piece*."
34 Benjamin Buchloh argues that conceptual art differentiates itself from pop art, Dada, or other art movements that wrangle the ordinary, mass-produced, or industrial into the realm of art by depending on legalist and linguistic definitions of art. Conceptualism thus reflects back, or is perhaps contiguous with, the administrative state and its informational aesthetics. As Buchloh writes, "Conceptual Art came to displace even that image of the mass-produced object and its aestheticized forms in Pop Art, replacing an aesthetic of industrial production and consumption with an aesthetic of administrative and legal organization and institutional validation" ("Conceptual Art 1962–1969," 119).
35 Contemporary poets such as Jennif(f)er Tamayo and Susan Briante have also recently turned to immigration paperwork as a means of exploring how people, their identities, their bodies, and their mobility are administered in cruelly racial and violent ways. Conceptual and multimedia artists Collective Magpie, led by Tae Hwang and MR Barnadas, also explored the creative potential of the administrative aesthetic in their project *Who Designs Your Race?*, an online survey presented as "a poetic exploration of race" and distributed at the 2021 La Trienal with El Museo del Barrio. The survey asks participants to identify themselves in relation to different ethnic and racial categories but also to describe when and where they "feel" most like that category and how much. The "Poetic Exploration of Race Survey" can be found at the Collective Magpie website, www.collectivemagpie.org.
36 Munroe, "Spirit of Yes," 14.
37 Munroe, "Spirit of Yes," 16.
38 See Leon Wilde's *John Lennon vs. the U.S.A.*
39 See Ngai, *Impossible Subjects*.
40 As Jodi Melamed has written, the "antiracism" of liberalism at mid-century, such as the end of explicit racial quotas and establishment of "equal" quotas, was vital to the functioning of racial capitalism and US nationalism as it entered the Cold War era. Melamed writes:

> For racial liberalism the incorporation of antiracism into state governmentality (the production of official antiracist discourse), with the interjection of U.S. geopolitics into fields of racial meaning was decisive. Whereas earlier antiracisms connected to the heterogeneous struggles of people of color often linked racial and economic justice, racial liberalism sutured an official antiracism to a U.S. nationalism that bore the agency for transnational capitalism. This suture produced a liberal nationalism that normed and restricted the field of race politics to the point that antiracist discourse itself came to both deflect counternationalisms (especially in the context of early Cold War Americanism) and mask the workings of transnational capitalism. (Melamed, *Represent and Destroy*, 54)

41 See Lisa Lowe's *Immigrant Acts*.
42 Bow, *Betrayal*, 4.
43 Bow, *Betrayal*, 7.
44 See Bhabha, "The Other Question: The Stereotype and Cultural Discourse," in *The Location of Culture*, 94–120.
45 Huang, "Inscrutably, Actually," 191.
46 See Ngai, *Impossible Subjects*; Lowe, *Immigrant Acts*; Lipsitz, *The Possessive Investment in Whiteness*; and Shah, *Contagious Divides*.
47 Ono, *Grapefruit*, n.p.
48 Ono, *Grapefruit*, n.p.
49 Ono, *Grapefruit*, n.p.
50 Ono, *Grapefruit*, n.p.
51 Ono knew Kate Millett personally. Millett was a sometime associate of Fluxus (she considered herself a member, although Fluxus membership is always a topic of debate), and Ono knew her socially as well. Millett and Ono both left the United States to join the Japanese avant-garde in Tokyo, and their time there overlapped between 1962 and 1964. For a detailed history and analysis of Millett's time with the Japanese avant-garde in the early 1960s, including her relationship with Ono, see Fredrickson, "*Trap*."
52 As Kate Millett writes of Freud in *Sexual Politics*, "In America, the influence of Freud is almost incalculable, and America, in many ways the first center of the sexual revolution, appears to have need of him. Although generally accepted as a prototype of the liberal urge toward sexual freedom, and a signal contributor toward softening traditional puritanical inhibitions upon sexuality, the effect of Freud's' work, that of his followers, and still more that of his popularizes, was to rationalize the invidious relationship between the sexes, to ratify traditional roles, and to validate temperamental differences" (*Sexual Politics*, 178).
53 Ono, "The Feminization of Society," 41.
54 Ono, "The Feminization of Society," 41.
55 Foucault, *Discipline and Punish*, 135.

56 Ono, *Grapefruit*, n.p.
57 The Japanese artist Yayoi Kusama was part of the cohort of postwar Japanese women who traveled to New York in the 1960s seeking artistic freedom and resources. Kusama's happenings were ludic and usually nude (Kusama herself very rarely partook of the nudity). One of her most famous happenings was "Grand Orgy to Awaken the Dead," held (without permission) at the Museum of Modern Art in New York (the *Mausoleum* of Modern Art, Kusama called it). During the happening, Kusama choreographed a bacchanal of nude performers who traipsed through the sculpture garden as a clothed Kusama painted polka dots all over their bodies—until removed by security. See Yoshimoto's *Into Performance* for more on Kusama's time in New York City.
58 Espiritu, "About Ghost Stories," 1700.
59 Nguyen, *The Gift of Freedom*, 2012.
60 Of course, while ideologically an American military presence was linked to whiteness, the American soldiers fighting in the war in Vietnam were often people of color. Both antiwar movements and US antiracist movements linked the domestic oppression of people of color to racial capitalism and colonialization. This was an important point of galvanization for the Asian American movement in the United States, which understood the war as yet another iteration in the history of colonization and imperialism that had produced the diasporas to which they belonged. Asian American organizers and community leaders also recognized the intensification of anti-Asian prejudices and violence in the United States as a result of racist military propaganda. Civil rights and Black nationalist leaders and organizations such as Martin Luther King Jr., Malcolm X, Muhammed Ali, Kwame Ture, and the Student Nonviolent Coordinating Committee all spoke critically about the war in Vietnam and drew connections between the experiences of the Vietnamese and the conditions experienced by Black Americans in the United States. The Third World Women's Alliance, comprising activists like Gwen Patton, Frances Beal, and Mae Jackson, believed racial, gender, and class oppression to be inseparable from each other and the imperialist project. They found inspiration in images and narratives of female Vietnamese freedom fighters. In the Chicano movement, groups such as the Brown Berets and the Chicano Moratorium organized coalitions against the war and disproportionate drafting, wounding, and killing of Chicano soldiers. The American war in Vietnam served as a reference point for "Third World" coalition building, mobilized under a shared goal of global decolonization. See Westheider, *The African American Experience in Vietnam*; Maeda, *The Chains of Babylon*; and Ishizuka, *Serve the People*.
61 Chong, *The Oriental Obscene*, 2.
62 *Film No. 4*. 1966–67, 16 mm film (black-and-white, sound), 80 min, private collection.
63 To recruit performers, Ono advertised in London newspapers looking specifically for "intellectual bottoms" (Yoshimoto, *Into Performance*, 108). According to Yoshimoto's research on the film,

As soon as the news spread over London through mass media as well as the mouths of participants, a curious crowd consisting of actors, artists, businessmen, and others gathered in a house temporarily lent to Ono by a patron for the film's shooting. Over two hundred people's bottoms were taken within ten days. After editing, the film became nearly ninety minutes long, consisting of about a twenty-second sequence for each person's bottom. The repetitive sequences of the close-up view of the bottoms were accompanied by an unsynchronized sound recording of the people being interviewed about their bottoms while they were being filmed. (*Into Performance*, 108)

64 Ono, *Grapefruit*, n.p.
65 Ono, *Grapefruit*, n.p.
66 Ono, *Grapefruit*, n.p. The insect-like "swarm of exposed bottoms" may reference Ono's earlier film *Fly*, which features a naked woman lying prone as flies cover her body and likewise teases an aesthetic tension between freedom and vulnerability.
67 MacDonald, "Yoko Ono," 4.
68 Ono, *Grapefruit*, n.p.
69 Ngai, *Our Aesthetic Categories*, 64. It should be noted that the concept of the commodity and capitalism's reifying power are also integral to Ngai's analysis of the cute.
70 Ngai, *Our Aesthetic Categories*, 64.
71 Ono, *Grapefruit*, n.p.
72 Muñoz, *Cruising Utopia*, 97.
73 Muñoz, *Cruising Utopia*, 1.

3. PURE COLOR

Epigraph: Walker Arts Center, "Jack Whitten on Mapping the Soul," *Smarthistory*, September 10, 2021, https://smarthistory.org., video transcribed by the author.

1 Greenberger, "An Old-School Painter Adapts to a New World Order."
2 For more on the pleasure of color as paint specifically, as well as color's associations with freedom, see Amy Sillman's essay "On Color," in *Faux Pas*, 47–73.
3 Nevelson qtd. in Danto, "Black, White, Gold," 39.
4 Sexton, "Basic Black," 76–77.
5 Hurston, "How It Feels to Be Colored Me," 154.
6 Darby English's *1971: A Year in the Life of Color* offers a clear description of this impasse that Black modernists encountered in the 1960s and 1970s. Although I find that English's arguments pit individual expression (as enabled by radical abstraction) against the promises of Black collectivity (here aligned with representation) too starkly, English nevertheless powerfully explains an enduring logic of racial fixity and separatism that shapes Black art history. As he writes in response to criticism on Edward Clark's color painting, "The urge for symmetry between biography and picture-effects is so strong in black art history that the turbulent color work in the art is impotent next to the sureness that it, or *something* in the picture, reflects back on all the unassailable epistemological stability of Clark's

racial blackness. . . . The fact is, abstraction has always been political precisely in its *opposition* to the fetish that the figure becomes in circumstances of unremitting spectatorial narcissism" (1971, 68, emphasis in the original). Margo Crawford's *Black Post-Blackness* is a valuable interlocutor here for her arguments on seeing "black abstraction in black representational space" (48).
7   Harper, *Abstractionist Aesthetics*, 2.
8   See art historian and critic Darby English's *How to See a Work of Art in Total Darkness*, as well as Kobena Mercer's *Welcome to the Jungle*.
9   Wang, *Thinking Its Presence*, x.
10 Wang, *Thinking Its Presence*, 10.
11 See Kandice Chuh on undisciplining scholarship in the humanities as a response to the exclusion of minoritized authors and artists from the aesthetic in *The Difference Aesthetic Makes*.
12 See Sammond, *Birth of an Industry*, for a history of the relationship between blackface minstrelsy and American animation.
13 This is seen in cartoon minstrelsy and racist kitsch in particular, where racist figurations play out through abstraction and a reductionist, often minimalist, approach to form. A few precisely executed lines become an instantly recognizable racist image.
14 Art21, "An Artist's Life: Jack Whitten."
15 Whitten credited Du Bois as a forerunner of Black aesthetic theory, saying in an interview with the Crystal Bridges Museum of American Art:
    The legacy of W. E. B. Du Bois is founded on the necessity of aesthetics. With a firm structural construction of aesthetics, anything is possible. There would not be "the artist Jack Whitten" without the benefit of Du Bois' legacy. All Black artists are aware of the impact of slavery on our culture. Slavery destroyed our culture. I believe that Black artists can reconstruct our culture. Not only can we reconstruct our culture, but we are in a position to exert influence on a global scale. Art is organic and therefore it operates within the same principles of evolution: it evolves like all organic structures." We can see that organicism in the unregulated form in this painting. (Whitten, "An Interview with Artist Jack Whitten")
16 Here I am also thinking alongside Margo Crawford's conceptualization of "black light" in her readings of work by Faith Ringgold, Sun Ra, Glenn Ligon, David Hammons, and Amiri Baraka in *Black Post-Blackness*. As Crawford argues in that work, "Black light, as figured during the BAM, is a rethinking of what it means to become a subject. Instead of the subject entering into light (imagined as whiteness), the movement imagines subjects enter in into illuminated darkness (imagined as blackness)" (65).
17 Whitten, "Jack Whitten," 1994.
18 Whitten, "Jack Whitten," 1994, 41.
19 Whitten, "Jack Whitten," 41.
20 TateShots, "Jack Whitten—'The Political Is in the Work.'"

21 Jennifer Chu, "MIT Engineers Develop 'Blackest Black' Material to Date," *MIT News*, September 12, 2019, https://news.mit.edu. See Sexton, "Basic Black," on such technological and artistic innovations in relation to Black studies.
22 Kim, "Byron Kim Oral History Interview," transcript p. 10.
23 Kim, "Byron Kim by Adam Simon"; Min, *The Unnamable*, 50–52.
24 Kim, "Byron Kim Oral History Interview," transcript p. 10.
25 Kim's commentary on this work adds an additional, and tender, laminate of meaning. Kim has said across multiple interviews that what is most important and interesting to him about the project is the encounter that he has with the sitter. The painting at the end of the process holds little meaning for him. In this sense, *Synecdoche* is a highly conceptual work; the meaning is derived from the process of making the painting, the intimate exchange between painter and sitter that the viewer will never have access to. The painting is just the record of the art event (see Kim, "Byron Kim by Adam Simon").
26 Kim has made a related work with his friend and sometimes collaborator Glenn Ligon, whose art is discussed in depth at the end of this chapter. In their collaborative painting *Black & White* (1993), Kim and Ligon painted thirty-two panels arranged in an 8 × 4 grid, each artist painting sixteen 10 × 8 inch panels. As a commentary on the limited range of skin tone paints available in art supply stores, Kim painted his panels each in a different brownish flesh-colored hue, from a yellow-tinted ivory to ruddy mauve to woody brown. Ligon painted sixteen panels using all-black pigments. While the distinctions between Kim's panels are obvious at a glance, the different hues in Ligon's black panels require a much more careful examination of the work to discern.
27 See Ty, "The Riot of the Literal." See also chapter 3, "Chromatic Saturation," in Moten, *The Universal Machine*, 140–246.
28 An example of a controversy that has had a much longer career than the actual artworks or artist at its center is the 1979 Artists Space exhibit of a series of drawings by Donald Newman, a white artist who went only by Donald, entitled *The N****** Drawings* (original title not redacted). This is a perfect example of how chromatic black and the materiality of black color became entwined with racial Blackness in modernist abstraction in racist ways. The drawings are triptychs featuring a plexiglass center panel and charcoal abstract drawings on either side. While the center drawings are at times representational, they do not contain representations of Black people as the title slur brutally suggests. Rather, the slur references the materials (charcoal), the black monochromatic nature of the drawings, and their radical abstraction. The exhibit has lingered in art historical memory mostly because of the protests that emerged rebuking the racism of Donald and Artist's Space, led by the arts activist group the Black Emergency Coalition, whose membership included artists and curators such as Janet Henry, Lowery Stokes Sims, Linda Goode Bryant, and Howardena Pindell. The anti-racist protests then became the target of counter-protesters who saw protests against the exhibit as censorship and an attack on public arts funding. These counter-

protesters included artworld luminaries such as Douglas Crimp, Laurie Anderson, Rosalind Krauss, Roberta Smith, and Craig Owens. We will see that this is a recurring arrangement in the history of monochromatic black abstraction. White supremacy and artistic freedom are tied together, anchored by racist chromatic black abstraction. Anti-racism is presented as a threat to the freedom of the white artist. For more detailed histories of the Artists Space exhibit and the protests, see Chang, *Who We Be*.

Another instructive example is unpacked in the third chapter of Fred Moten's *The Universal Machine*, where Moten unwinds a strange conversation on the color black between a group of artists in 1967, hosted by *arts/canada*. The interlocutors included Stu Broomer, Harvey Cowan, Ad Reinhardt, Arnold Rockman, Michael Snow, Aldo Tambellini, and Cecil Taylor. The highlight of the conversation is a tense debate between Reinhardt and Taylor on the social meaning of black and the impact of the social and political on both the conditions of art making and the meaning of a work of art. Reinhardt is adamantly against the porousness between art making and the social. He imagines the color black as the ultimate negation of art's sociality. These are sentiments that he expressed at length in his writings (see especially the section on "The Black Paintings" in *Art as Art*). Meanwhile, Cecil Taylor repeatedly pushes back on Reinhardt's claims—a sense of real exasperation palpable even in the transcript:

> Don't you understand that every culture has its own mores, its way of doing things, and that's why different art forms exist? . . . Don't you understand that what artists do depends on the time they have to do it in, and the time they have to do it in depends upon the amount of economic sustenance that allows them to do it? You have to come down to the reality. Artists just don't work, you know, just like that—the kind of work, the nature of their involvement is not separate from the nature of their existence, and you have to come down to the nature of their existence. (Broomer, "Black," 13–14)

Reinhardt refuses to acknowledge not only the social conditions that shape art, but the racial politics of chromatic black that hover in the periphery throughout the conversation. Questions of race are only addressed, still somewhat indirectly, through Taylor's insistence on the inevitable sociality of art and the conditions of artistic freedom. It is a revealing conversation on the embeddedness of a kind of compartmentalism that is necessary to sustain a strain of white modernism that we can trace to Malevich. Moten offers a distinct illumination of this conversation that shouldn't be missed:

> To insist on the distinction between the canvas as scene and the canvas as thing is to detach oneself from the scene as much as it is also to represent the scene. It is to establish something like a freedom from the community in the most highly determined, regulative, legal sense of the word, in the sharpest sense of its constituting a field in which the human and the (dis-

orderly) thing are precisely, pathologically, theatrically indistinct. Let's call this community the black community, the community that is defined by a certain history of blackness, a history of privation (as Taylor points out) and plenitude, pain and (as Taylor points out) pleasure. It is from and as a sensual commune, from and as an irruptive advent, at once focused and arrayed against the political aesthetics of enclosed common sense, that Taylor's music emerges. (*The Universal Machine*, 167)

29. "Black Is a Color" is Saunders's heated response to a 1967 article written by Ishmael Reed (see Reed, "The Black Artist").
30. English, *1971*, 61.
31. Malevich originally claimed that *Black Square* was painted in 1913, coinciding with a rise in anti-tsarist political activity. Although this narrative benefited Malevich's claims to total revolution through aesthetic production, scholars later confirmed that *Black Square* was painted in 1915 (Shatskikh, *Black Square*).
32. Kazimir Malevich, *Black Square*, 1915, oil on linen, 79.5cm × 79.5 cm, Tretyakov Gallery, Moscow.
33. See Crone and Moos, *Kazimir Malevich*.
34. Shatskikh, *Black Square*, x.
35. Malevich, "From Cubism," 123.
36. The OED dates the first instance of the phrase *white supremacy* in English to 1824. *Oxford English Dictionary Online*, s.v. "white supremacy," Oxford University Press, www.oed.com.
37. Shatskikh, *Black Square*, 54.
38. In *The Futurist Manifesto*, F. T. Marinetti writes, "We will glorify war—the world's only hygiene—militarism, patriotism, the destructive gesture of freedom-bringers, beautiful ideas worth dying for, and scorn for woman." Marinetti's framing of war as "hygiene" conveys his fascism that would emerge more clearly in the coming years, particularly as co-author of *The Fascist Manifesto* (1919), and links *the Futurist Manifesto* to a discourse of eugenics.
39. Malevich, "From Cubism," 118, emphasis in the original.
40. Malevich, "From Cubism," 119.
41. Malevich, "From Cubism," 131.
42. Malevich, "From Cubism," 121.
43. This thinking is itself a reflection of the racial and eugenical thought circulating in Russia, Europe, and the United States during this early twentieth century period. Law, *Red Racisms*; Wolff, *Inventing Eastern Europe*.
44. Lest one wishes to give Malevich the benefit of doubt that the "savages" in his essay are only importune references to an ancient European past, Malevich also uses the term to refer to people whose lifetimes overlapped with his own, as in his critique of Gaugin, of whom he writes, "Gauguin, fleeing from culture to the savages, and discovering more freedom in the primitives than in academism, found himself subject to intuitive reason" ("From Cubism," 132.) Here Malevich refers to

Gaugin's time spent in Tahiti and the Marquesas Islands, where he did not arrive until 1891, only twenty-five years prior to Malevich's essay.

45 Malevich, "From Cubism," 124. Sylvia Wynter's theorization and critique of Man1 and Man2 (the latter produced very much from the Darwinian discourses intertwined with colonialism) is a helpful framework for understanding this aspect of Malevich's manifesto. See Wynter "Unsettling the Coloniality of Being/Power/Truth/Freedom."

46 Silva, *Toward a Global Idea of Race*, 2007. Malevich was strongly influenced artistically by F. T. Marinetti, who brought Italian futurism to Russia in 1914, an influence for Russian futurism. (Crone, *Kazimir Malevich*, 70; Milner, *Kazimir Malevich*, 119). See also footnote 47.

47 Malevich made an important trip to Paris in 1912, where he absorbed many of the lessons of cubism and also showed at the Salon des Indépendants in Paris in 1914. While Rainer Crone and David Moos have observed that there were important differences between Italian and Russian futurism, portions of "From Cubism to Futurism to Suprematism" read as if they could be excerpts from Marinetti's "Futurist Manifesto," a document fixated on the machine and technological advancement as signs of racial and masculine power: "Gigantic wars, great inventions, conquest of the air, speed of travel, tele-phones, telegraphs, dreadnoughts are the realm of electricity. But our young artists paint Neros and half-naked Roman warriors. Honor to the futurists who forbade the painting of female hams, the painting of portraits and guitars in the moonlight. They made a huge step forward: they abandoned meat and glorified the machine" (Malevich, "From Cubism," 125). Ultimately, though, Malevich rejects futurism, and we can see between the two manifestos an active and ongoing conversation on the relationship between the European avant-garde and the future of the human.

48 On this topic, Denise Ferreira da Silva's *Toward a Global Idea of Race* is indispensable.

49 See Gibson, "Color and Difference in Abstract Painting"; Buchloh, *Neo-avantgarde and Culture Industry*; and Folgarait, *Painting 1909*.

50 Malevich, "From Cubism," 119.

51 See Wynter, "Unsettling the Coloniality of Being/Power/Truth/Freedom."

52 Malevich, "From Cubism," 133.

53 Silva, *Toward a Global Idea of Race*, 29.

54 Josef Albers's classic instruction manual *Interaction of Color* continues to be an insightful and practical resource for understanding how the relationship between colors impacts our perception of them.

55 In recent criticism theorizing freedom, collectivity/interdependence, and care, see Anker, *Ugly Freedoms*; Moten, *Consent Not to Be a Single Being*; and Nelson, *On Freedom*.

56 Malevich, "From Cubism," 125.

57 Malevich, "From Cubism," 135.

58 A *New York Times* reviewer on November 21, 1886, commented, "I cannot see where art is to find much progress in this kind of wild improvisation, and the best way to consider the matter is to deem it a colossal farce, one of those many things

that Paris needs to make up its Winter amusement" ("Incoherent Art in Paris," *New York Times*, November 21, 1886). An 1883 exhibit drew twenty thousand visitors over the course of a month, and prominent artists such Manet, Renoir, and Pisarro attended their exhibitions (Gluck, *Popular Bohemia*, 117).

59 A much earlier engraving by Paracelsian physician and occultist Robert Fludd is yet another earlier example of the monochrome. His engraving of the darkness of the world prior to creation in his masterwork *Utriusque Cosmi* (1617) is a similarly proportioned black square within a white border. Within the white border, Fludd has written "*Et sic infinitum*," or "and so on to infinity."

60 Cohl is considered one of the fathers of animation. In *Emile Cohl, Caricature, and Film*, Donald Crafton also demonstrates how caricature (as opposed to the physical, slapstick comedy of vaudeville) was essential to Cohl's work. In *Colored Pictures*, Michael Harris has shown how caricature, especially racist caricature, is also linked to the visual grammar of scientific racism from this same early-twentieth century period.

61 Elcott, *Artificial Darkness*, 2.

62 Elcott, *Artificial Darkness*, 2.

63 Of course, there are many ways that jokes and humor have been used to define (or destabilize) racial difference in visual culture. See Carpio, *Laughing Fit to Kill*, Lott, *Love and Theft*; Goings, *Mammy and Uncle Moses*.

64 Bhabha, *The Location of Culture*, 101.

65 Irene Tucker traces the binding of race to skin color to Kant in *The Moment of Racial Sight*; see especially chapter 1, "Kant's Dermatology."

66 Nechepurenko, "Examination Reveals." It ought to be noted that although the staff members of the Tretyakov Gallery have asserted that they believe the inscription is in Malevich's hand, Aleksandra Shatskikh, an authority on Malevich's work, has strongly argued that the inscription is vandalism and not Malevich's doing. However, my arguments do not hang on Malevich's authorship of the inscription. Rather, I am interested in the ways that the painting engages with a global modernist discourse of abstraction and race in which the vandal's interpretation of the work is just as meaningful as Malevich's authorial intent. See Shatskikh, "Inscribed Vandalism."

67 Nechepurenko, "Examination Reveals."

68 Nechepurenko, "Examination Reveals."

69 Malevich, "From Cubism," 134.

70 Edwards, "Blackness in Abstraction."

71 Gallager quoted in Morgan, *Ellen Gallagher*, 26–27.

72 Edwards, "Blackness in Abstraction."

73 Hurston "How It Feels," 153.

74 Hurston, "How It Feels," 152.

75 Hurston, "How It Feels," 152-3.

76 Adrienne Brown examines Hurston's capacity for play and appreciation for aesthetic pleasure in her wonderful essay "Hard Romping."

77 This scene performs an additional function as Hurston also potentially addresses her adult public image as a person who is thought to perform stereotypical Blackness for white consumption, profiting from this relationship at the expense of other Black people by perpetuating stereotypes. For instance, Langston Hughes's representation of Hurston as "the perfect 'darkie,' in the nice meaning [white people] give the term" in *The Big Sea* or Richard Wright's famous critique of *Their Eyes Were Watching God* as "not addressed to the Negro, but to a white audience whose chauvinistic tastes [Hurston] knows how to satisfy" (Hughes, *The Big Sea*, 185; Wright, *Critical Essays on Zora Neale Hurston*, 75).
78 Hurston, "How It Feels," 153.
79 Hurston, "How It Feels," 153.
80 Hurston, "How It Feels," 153.
81 Hurston, "How It Feels," 154.
82 See Barbara Johnson's "Thresholds of Difference," in *A World of Difference* (1987).
83 Morrison, *Playing in the Dark*, 33.
84 Batchelor, *Chromophobia*, 10.
85 Batchelor, *Chromophobia*, 23.
86 Taussig, *What Color Is the Sacred?*, 16.
87 Hurston, "How It Feels," 154.
88 Hurston, "How It Feels," 154, emphasis in the original.
89 Hurston, "How It Feels," 154. The use of primitivist imagery here to summon a sense of Blackness is too complex for me to fully do justice to in the brief space I have here. Suffice it to say that Hurston's idiosyncratic racial politics are present in this essay, as discussed especially in Black feminist scholarship on Hurston in the 1980s and 1990s, including in work by Hazel Carby, Alice Walker, and Deborah Plant. As many scholars have observed, racial primitivism was a common feature of Harlem Renaissance aesthetics. Alain Locke, Langston Hughes, Nella Larsen, Claude McKay, Aaron Douglas, William H. Johnson, Josephine Baker and many other artists, writers, and performers incorporated primitivist tropes into their work. More recent scholarship on race and desire in this period, notably Anne Anlin Cheng's work on Josephine Baker, has deepened the ambivalence surrounding primitivism in Black modernist expressive culture. See Cheng *Second Skin*; Carby, "The Politics of Fiction"; Walker, *In Search of Our Mother's Gardens*; and Plant, *Every Tub Must Sit on Its Own Bottom*.
90 Hurston, "How It Feels," 155.
91 Amy Helene Kirschke has detailed Douglas's rich knowledge of both Western and non-Western art traditions, including modernist abstraction, especially cubism and primitivism, as well as ancient Egyptian and "African folk aesthetic" visual vocabularies (Kirschke, *Aaron Douglas*, 44).
92 Ligon, "Glenn Ligon Speaks."
93 Ligon, "Glenn Ligon Speaks."
94 Ligon, *Glenn Ligon*, 124.

95 "Scenes of subjection" is a reference to Saidiya Hartman's landmark critical work *Scenes of Subjection*, discussed in chapter 1.
96 Fred Moten's concept of "blur" also seems resonant here, perhaps especially in his reading of Charles Gaines's *Librettos* in *Black and Blur*. For more on Ligon's smudging, see work by Darby English and Huey Copeland in *Glenn Ligon*; as well as Whitney Museum curator Scott Rothkopf's introduction to *Glenn Ligon: America*. Also see chapter 4, "Time, Race, and Biology: Fanon, Freud, and the Labors of Race," in Musser, *Sensational Flesh*, for more on "racialization through stickiness" in Ligon's *Door Paintings*.
97 *Oxford English Dictionary Online*, s.v. "stereotype," Oxford University Press, www.oed.com.
98 Glissant, *The Poetics of Relation*, 189. Glissant writes:

Agree not merely to the right to difference but, carrying this further, agree also to the right to opacity that is not enclosure within an impenetrable autarchy but subsistence within an irreducible singularity. Opacities can coexist and converge, weaving fabrics. To understand these truly one must focus on the texture of the weave and not on the nature of its components. For the time being, perhaps give up this old obsession with discovering what lies at the bottom of natures. There would be something great and noble about initiating such a movement, referring not to Humanity but to the exultant divergence of humanities. Thought of self and thought of other here become obsolete in their duality. Every Other is a citizen and no longer a barbarian. What is here is open, as much as this there. I would be incapable of projecting from one to the other. This-here is the weave, and it weaves no boundaries. The right to opacity would not establish autism; it would be the real foundation of Relation in freedoms. (Glissant, *The Poetics of Relation*, 190)

99 Edwards, "Blackness in Abstraction."
100 Ligon, "Blue Black, Black and Blue," 13.
101 Ligon, "Blue Black, Black and Blue," 14.

4. DIFFICULT PLEASURES

Epigraph: Wang, "The Coral Tree," 99.

1 While some of Cha's biographies claim that she was murdered by a stranger, Cathy Park Hong's meticulous examination of the evidence surrounding Cha's death and the paper trail that followed suggests that Cha knew her murderer. On November 5, 1982, Cha was raped and murdered by Joseph Sanza, a security guard at the Puck Building where her husband, Richard Barnes, was documenting the building's renovation and where Sanza killed Cha. Undoubtedly Cha's race and gender were significant in Sanza's decision to target her. In her chapter on Cha in *Minor Feelings*, Hong gives a comprehensive account of the event and the experiences of the loved ones who survived Cha. Significantly, Hong also argues that critics have done Cha a disservice by avoiding the topic of how she died—including her sexual assault—in their scholarly work. However well-meaning or

protective these silences may have been, Hong argues that the scholars seeking to shield Cha's legacy from "the sordid forces of her rape and murder . . . may have been too effective," erasing the reality of the violence and contributing to a larger culture of silence around violence against Asian women, sexual and otherwise (Hong, *Minor Feelings*, 164). I am not certain what the most ethical way to address or not address the realities of Cha's death might be. Like Cha's earlier critics, I am wary of morbid spectacularization, or reading her work and life only through her death. How sickeningly unjust for such an incandescent body of work to be associated with such violence. However, Hong's point resounds with moral clarity. How can Cha be mourned without some public reckoning with her death? Mourning Cha as an individual also requires an examination of the structural violence experienced by Asian women, including sexual violence. This has become even clearer since the increase in anti-Asian violence since the COVID-19 pandemic, its most gruesome iteration being the Atlanta massacre on March 16, 2021, in which eight people were killed, six of them Asian women, at an Atlanta spa, where the shooter reportedly murdered in order to "eliminate" the "temptation" presented by the Asian women who worked there (Kindig, "The Violent Embrace"). To write around Cha's death is perhaps to participate in silences that are systemic and harmful. I encourage the reader to spend a few moments (at least) to pause in their reading to contemplate this loss. For those seeking a quite detailed account of how Cha died, the experience of her family, the process of convicting Sanza, and Cha's legacy, Hong's *Minor Feelings* is essential reading.
2 Wu and Min, "Cici Wu and Yong Soon Min."
3 Wu and Min, "Cici Wu and Yong Soon Min," 17.
4 Hong, *Death beyond Disavowal*, 78.
5 Hong, *Death beyond Disavowal*, 78.
6 Xiang, *Tonal Intelligence*, 133.
7 Hong, *Death beyond Disavowal*, 66. See Ferguson, *Aberrations in Black*; Kim, *The Ends of Empire*; Lowe; *Immigrant Acts*; Melamed; *Represent and Destroy*; and Rodríguez, *White Reconstruction*.
8 The Combahee River Collective, "Letter to HERESIES," 129.
9 The Heresies Collective was based in New York City, and its founding members included some very influential voices at the intersection of feminism and the art world, including Lucy Lippard, Harmony Hammond, Mary Beth Edelson, and Susana Torre. However well-meaning in its intention to support the work and perspectives of women, Heresies came under fire early on in its existence for its exclusion of women of color and particularly queer women of color. When the Mother Collective recruited mostly women of color for the volunteer editorial collective for their issues focused on race and racism (in response to the Combahee letter), the volunteer editors had mixed responses to the experience, suggesting that *HERESIES* continued to unevenly address the conditions of racism that shaped the organization. Cha's contribution to the 1982 "Women's Pages" issue

arrived during a time when the question of how Heresies might become an antiracist as well as feminist organization was still being actively debated.
10. See editorial statements from *HERESIES* volumes 8 and 15.
11. Browne et al., "Issue 15 Editorial Statement," 73.
12. *HERESIES* is available in a free online archive at http://heresiesfilmproject.org.
13. Hong, *Death beyond Disavowal*, 63.
14. Saltzstein, "Overlooked No More."
15. Hong qtd. in Saltzstein, "Overlooked No More."
16. Cho, "Mel-*han*-cholia," 413.
17. Hong, *Minor Feelings*, 45.
18. Hong, *Minor Feelings*, 45.
19. See Cumings, *The Korean War*; Kim *Ends of Empire*; Kim *The Intimacies of Conflict*.
20. Cho, "Mel-*han*-cholia," 413.
21. See Xiang's *Tonal Intelligence* on tone and affect in Cha in connection with the Cold War.
22. For a rare scholarly reading that showcases Cha's wit, see Joseph Jonghyun Jeon's reading of Cha's *Surplus Novel*, a piece in which Cha takes a racist joke (presumably lobbed against her) and cuttingly undermines its stupidity, in *Racial Things, Racial Forms*.
23. Lewallen, *The Dream of the Audience*, 3.
24. See Lewallen and Rinder in *The Dream of the Audience*, 2001.
25. Lewallen, introduction to *The Dream of the Audience*, 3.
26. Roh, Huang, and Niu, "Technologizing Orientalism," 2. The term *techno-Orientalism* was first coined by Kevin Morley and David Robins in *Spaces of Identity*.
27. See Anne Anlin Cheng's concept of "the yellow woman" in *Ornamentalism*, 2018.
28. Hong, *Minor Feelings*, 170.
29. Said, *Orientalism*, 138.
30. Parreñas and Tam, *The Force of Domesticity*, 113–14.
31. Lee, "Staying In," 29.
32. Halberstam, *The Queer Art of Failure*, 131.
33. See Bow *Racist Love*; Cheng. *Ornamentalism*; Shimizu, *The Hypersexuality of Race*; and Nguyen, *A View from the Bottom*.
34. Theresa Hak Kyung Cha Conceptual Art Archive, "Biography of Theresa Hak Kyung Cha (1951–1982)."
35. Kelley, *Freedom Dreams*, 159.
36. Modernist studies scholar Susan Stanford Friedman reads Cha and Aimé Césaire together through the framework of the diasporic long poem in *Planetary Modernisms*.
37. On Cha and Korean female identity, see also Kang, *Compositional Subjects*; and Cheng, *The Melancholy of Race*.
38. On the transformation of *Dictee*'s reputation and audiences, see Yu, *Race and the Avant-Garde*.

39 Mayukh Sen argues that "Cha's virtual vanishing from cultural memory feels both unfair and unsurprising. *Dictee*'s artistic rebellion may have prevented wider audiences from flocking to the work. Her unruliness, however, has been the point of entry for a number of Asian American writers she inspired who have achieved more mainstream prominence than she did in life or in death. This cruel dissonance speaks to her work's foresight. She imagined a form of expression that was situated along the uncomfortable fault lines between modes of art" ("A Kind of Blueprint").
40 See Yu, "A Vision of Asian-American Presence"; and Han, "Shortcuts to Identity."
41 Lewallen, *The Dream of the Audience*, 21–24.
42 The term *Third Cinema* is generally linked to the 1970 essay by Fernando Solanas and Octavio Getino "Toward a Third Cinema," in which they make the argument for the decolonizing, anti-capitalist, and democratizing power of cinema: "The anti-imperialist struggle of the peoples of the Third World and of their equivalents inside the imperialist countries constitutes today the axis of world revolution. *Third cinema* is, in our opinion, the cinema that *recognizes in that struggle the most gigantic cultural, scientific, and artistic manifestation of our time*, the great possibility of constructing a liberated personality with each people as the starting point—in a word, the *decolonization of culture*" (Solanas and Getino, "Toward a Third Cinema," 2). See also Espinosa, "For an Imperfect Cinema."
43 *The Dream of the Audience*, 2–3.
44 Baudry, "The Apparatus," 106.
45 Plato's allegory of the cave seeks to explain how humans without knowledge of the world of forms perceive reality. In the allegory, prisoners in a cave are chained to face the cave wall and cannot turn their heads. Behind them is a fire and between the fire and the prisoners, people walk by holding objects and making sounds, which cast shadows on the wall and create echoes in the cave. Plato argues that the prisoners would mistake the shadows and echoes for reality, unable to see the real sources behind them.
46 Baudry, "The Apparatus," 112–13.
47 Baudry, "The Apparatus," 111.
48 Baudry, "The Apparatus," 108.
49 Barthes, "Upon Leaving the Movie Theater, 1–2.
50 Trinh, "White Spring," 36.
51 For an analysis of Daoism and Korean shamanism in Cha's work, see Stalling, "Pacing the Void." This chapter will not explicitly take up the spiritual aspects of Cha's work and its explorations of being and nonbeing that depart from conventional Western notions of the liberal subject. While this chapter cannot do justice to this important aspect of Cha's work, I will note that Cha's studies of both Eastern and Western spiritual traditions are crucial to fully appreciating the complexity of her art and writing.
52 Cha, "Paths," 2.
53 The *Zhuangzi* is a fragmented, at times even self-contradictory text—a collection of anecdotes, arguments, images, and short narratives grouped loosely around

themes. It is very unlikely that these texts were all written by the same person, although they are attributed to the figure of Zhuang Zhou. Interestingly, the story that immediately precedes the butterfly dream in the section titled "Equalizing Assessment of Things" considers a dialogue between shadows: "The penumbra said to the shadow, 'First you were walking, then you were standing still. First you were sitting, then you were upright. Why can't you decide on a single course of action?' The shadow said, 'Do I depend on something to make me as I am? Does what I depend on depend on something else? Is my dependence like the case of the snake's skin or the cicada's shell? How would I know why, I am so or not so?'" (*Zhuangzi*, 21). This is a fascinating passage to read in conjunction with Cha's own preoccupation with shadows and interdependence.

54 Cha, "Paths," 2.
55 This story is told particularly well in Yu's *Race and the Avant-Garde*. See also Cathy Park Hong's chapter on Cha in *Minor Feelings* for more on Cha and her impact on Asian American readers and writers. Alarcón and Kim, *Writing Self, Writing Nation*; Hong, *Minor Feelings*; Yu, *Race and the Avant-Garde*.
56 Ingold, *Imagining for Real*, 120.
57 Ingold, *Imagining for Real*, 128.
58 Maliangkay, "The Power of Representation," 213.
59 Naficy, "Theorizing 'Third World' Film Spectatorship," 187.
60 Naficy, "Theorizing 'Third World' Film Spectatorship," 185.
61 Naficy, "Theorizing 'Third World' Film Spectatorship," 189–90.
62 Maliangkay, "The Power of Representation," 223.
63 According to research by Dong Hoon Kim, the vast majority of films shown in Korea during the colonial period were from the United States, Europe, and Japan. A very small minority of locally produced Korean films were available. For more on cinema culture in colonial Korea, see Kim, *Eclipsed Cinema*.
64 The voyeurism in this section likely makes reference to Jean-Louis Baudry's and Christian Metz's theories of cinematic voyeurism, "the idea of an unauthorized voyeurism that does not have the counterpart of the exhibitionism of the object observed and in which the voyeur, who is concealed, derives comfort from not being seen" (*Apparatus*, 359–60).
65 Cha, *Dictee*, 94.
66 Cha, *Dictee*, 96.
67 While cinema (both mainstream and avant-garde) has historically excluded women and filmmakers of color and contributed to sexist and racist cultural epistemologies, experimental cinema has also been fertile ground for women artists and artists of color throughout the twentieth century. See Diawara, *Black American Cinema*; Feng, *Screening Asian Americans*; Noriega, *Chicanos and Film*; Trinh, *Women, Native, Other*.
68 Casid, *Scenes of Projection*, 25.
69 The "Erato/Love Poetry" section also prominently features excerpts from the memoir of nineteenth-century French Catholic martyr Thérèse de Lisieux, *Story*

of a Soul (1898). In these excerpts, Lisieux compares herself to Joan of Arc in a manner that invites queer and erotic readings. The "Erato/Love Poetry" section also includes photographs of Lisieux dressed as Joan of Arc, promotional materials from a play that Lisieux wrote and starred in, as Joan, of course.

70 Marks, *The Skin of the Film*, xi.
71 Marks, *The Skin of the Film*, xi–xii.
72 Marks, *The Skin of the Film*, xiii.
73 See Carroll, "Remains to be Seen."
74 Sedgwick, *Touching Feeling*, 13.
75 For a critical meditation on what Sedgwick misses about touch and texture particularly in regard to Black subjectivity, see Rizvana Bradley's "The Vicissitudes of Touch."
76 Muñoz, *Disidentification*, 12.
77 Yu Guan Soon's name is transliterated in several different ways. I use the transliteration used by Cha in *Dictee*.
78 Lee, "Rewriting Hesiod," 87.
79 See Cho, "Anticipating Citizenship"; Phu, *Picturing Model Citizens*; Pegler-Gordon, *In Sight of America*.
80 Cheng, *The Melancholy of Race*, 248.
81 One of the signature techniques found in Cha's work is the use of reproduced images in her slideshows, artist's books, and in *Dictee*. These reproductions, like the group photograph that includes Yu Guan Soon, are not always "good" copies of the image, often creating new visual barriers to understanding the image and the "clarity" of its significance and signification through the effects of reproduction. Hito Steyerl argues in her essay "In Defense of the Poor Image" that the poor visual quality of images is a reflection of its alternative circulation: "The circulation of poor images creates a circuit, which fulfills the original ambitions of militant and (some) essayistic and experimental cinema—to create an alternative economy of images, an imperfect cinema existing inside as well as beyond and under commercial media streams." The poor image "thus constructs anonymous global networks just as it creates a shared history. It builds alliances as it travels, provokes translation or mistranslation, and creates new publics and debates" (Steyerl, "In Defense of the Poor Image," 42).
82 Sen, "The Radical Afterlives of Theresa Hak Kyung Cha."
83 Chang et al., *After La vida nueva*, 60.
84 Chang et al., *After La vida nueva*, 7.
85 Chang et al., *After La vida nueva*, 18.
86 Chang et al., *After La vida nueva*, 53. My deep thanks to Cici Wu for providing additional details regarding both *Foreign Object #1 Fluffy Light* and *Upon Leaving the White Dust*.
87 Planning documents made by Cha suggest that that she planned to edit this footage further and add more images and text. Cha's sister Bernadette's comments on the film offer insights into how *White Dust*, like *Dictee*, took an autotheoreti-

cal approach to Korean history and exile, creating imagery that traversed the personal, political, and historical. In her planning documents for *White Dust*, Cha discussed how she wanted the project to serve as a means of creating connections across ethnic difference to form a sense of Asian solidarity, writing, "I would like to bring forth in this book, all the elements that are historical to lessen the physical geographical distance as well as the psychological distance of the Asian people from other ethnic cultures. The causes for the Korean War, and the reasons for the division of Korea into North and South, and the perpetuating conditions of Cold War will contribute to the understanding of Korea and Asia as whole cultures, not merely state their economic and political status as nations" (Cha, "White Dust From Mongolia," 2).

88 Here we recall Sianne Ngai's now classic definition of cute: a commodity aesthetic marked by "smallness, compactness, softness, simplicity, and pliancy" that aestheticizes powerlessness provoking both tender and aggressive feelings in the viewer.
89 Cici Wu, *Upon Leaving the White Dust*, Canal 47, 2018, https://47canal.us.
90 Video element from *Upon Leaving the White Dust* can be seen here: https://47canal.us.
91 Wu, *Upon Leaving the White Dust*, 1.
92 Wu, *Upon Leaving the White Dust*, 1.

CONCLUSION

1 Hong and Ferguson, introduction to *Strange Affinities*, 1–2.
2 Lowe, *The Intimacies of Four Continents*. On the history of Afro-Asian relations, see Ho and Mullen, *Afro Asia*; Jung, *The Rising Tide of Color*; Kee, *The Geometries of Afro Asia*; Prashad, *Everybody Was Kung Fu Fighting*.
3 Kee, *Geometries of Afro Asia*, 14.
4 Kee, *Geometries of Afro Asia*, 14.
5 See Maynard and Simpson, *Rehearsals for Living*, as well as Gilmore's foreword to that book.
6 Ault, *Felix Gonzalez-Torres*, 160.

BIBLIOGRAPHY

"After La vida nueva: Week 1." *Artist's Space*. https://artistsspace.org. Accessed December 9, 2021.

Ahmed, Sara. *The Cultural Politics of Emotion*. Edinburgh: Edinburgh University Press, 2014.

———. *The Promise of Happiness*. Durham, NC: Duke University Press, 2010.

Alarcón, Norma, and Elaine H. Kim, eds. *Writing Self, Writing Nation: A Collection of Essays on* Dictee *by Theresa Hak Kyung Cha*. Berkeley, CA: Third Woman Press, 1994.

Albers, Josef. *Interaction of Color*. New Haven, CT: Yale University Press, 2013.

Allen, Jafari S. *There's a Disco Ball between Us: A Theory of Black Gay Life*. Durham, NC: Duke University Press, 2022.

Anker, Elizabeth. *Ugly Freedoms*. Durham, NC: Duke University Press, 2022.

Appiah, Kwame Anthony. *Lines of Descent: W. E. B. Du Bois and the Emergence of Identity*. Cambridge, MA: Harvard University Press, 2014.

Appy, Christian. *American Reckoning: The Vietnam War and Our National Identity*. New York: Penguin, 2016.

———. "What Was the Vietnam War About?" *New York Times*, March 26, 2018.

Arendt, Hannah. *Lectures on Kant's Political Philosophy*. Chicago: University of Chicago Press, 1993.

Art21. "An Artist's Life: Jack Whitten." March 21, 2018. Video, 9:19. https://art21.org.

Aubrey, Timothy. *Guilty Aesthetic Pleasures*. Cambridge, MA: Harvard University Press, 2018.

Ault, Julie, ed. *Felix Gonzalez-Torres*. Gottingen: SteidlDangin, 2006.

Avilez, GerShun. *Radical Aesthetics and Modern Black Nationalism*. Champaign: University of Illinois Press, 2016.

Baker, Houston. *Modernism and the Harlem Renaissance*. Chicago: University of Chicago Press, 2013.

Barthes, Roland. "Upon Leaving the Movie Theater." In *Apparatus: Cinematographic Apparatus: Selected Writings*, edited by Theresa Hak Kyung Cha, 1–4. New York: Tanam, 1980.

Batchelor, David. *Chromophobia*. London: Reaktion, 2000.

Baudry, Jean-Louis. "The Apparatus." *Camera Obscura* 1, no. 1 (1976): 104–26.

Berkeley Art Museum. "Biography of Theresa Hak Kyung Cha (1951–1982)." Theresa Hak Kyung Cha Conceptual Art Archive, Berkeley Art Museum, University of California, Berkeley. https://oac.cdlib.org/.

Berlant, Lauren. "Humorlessness (Three Monologues and a Hairpiece)." *Critical Inquiry* 43, no. 4, 2017: 305–40.

———, ed. *Reading Sedgwick*. Durham, NC: Duke University Press, 2019.

Berlant, Lauren, and Sianne Ngai. "Comedy Has Issues." *Critical Inquiry* 43, no. 2 (Winter, 2017): 233–49.

Bernasconi, Robert. "Kant as an Unfamiliar Source of Racism." In *Philosophers on Race: Critical Essays*, edited by Julie K. Ward and Tommy L. Lott, 145–66. Malden, MA: Blackwell, 2002.

———, ed. *Race*. Malden, MA: Blackwell, 2001.

Bernasconi, Robert, and Sybil Cook, eds. *Race and Racism in Continental Philosophy*. Bloomington: Indiana University Press, 2003.

Bhabha, Homi. *The Location of Culture*. New York: Routledge, 1994.

Bindman, David. *Ape to Apollo: Aesthetics and the Idea of Race in the 18th Century*. Ithaca, NY: Cornell University Press, 2002.

Blazwick, Iwona, and Magnus Af Petersons, eds. *Adventures of the Black Square: Abstract Art and Society 1915–2015*. Munich: Prestel, 2015.

Blocton, Lula Mae, Yvonne Flowers, Valerie Harris, Zarina Hashmi, Virginia Jaramillo, Dawn Russell, and Naeemah Shabazz, eds. "Third World Women: The Politics of Being Other." *HERESIES* 8 (1979).

Bloom, Paul. *Against Empathy: The Case for Rational Compassion*. New York: Harper Collins, 2016.

Bost, Darius. *Evidence of Being: The Black Gay Cultural Renaissance and the Politics of Violence*. Chicago: University of Chicago Press, 2018.

Bow, Leslie. *Betrayal and Other Acts of Subversion: Feminism, Sexual Politics, and Asian American Women's Literature*. Princeton, NJ: Princeton University Press, 2001.

———. *Racist Love: Asian Abstraction and the Pleasures of Fantasy*. Durham, NC: Duke University Press, 2022.

Bradley, Rizvana. "Vicissitudes of Touch: Annotations on the Haptic." *the b20 review*, November 21, 2020. www.boundary2.org.

Briante, Susan. *Defacing the Monument*. Blacksburg, VA: Noemi, 2020.

Broomer, Stu, et al. "Black." *arts/canada* 24, no. 113 (1967): 13–14.

Brown, Adrienne. "Hard Romping: Zora Neale Hurston, White Women, and the Right to Play." *Twentieth-Century Literature* 64, no. 3, (September 2018): 295–316.

Browne, Vivian E., Cynthia Carr, Michele Godwin, Hattie Gossett, Carole Gregory, Sue Heinemann, Lucy R. Lippard, May Stevens, Cecilia Vicuña, and Sylvia Witts Vitale, eds. "Racism Is the Issue." *HERESIES* 15 (1982).

Bryan-Wilson, Julia. "Remembering Yoko Ono's *Cut Piece*." *Oxford Art Journal* 26, no. 1, 2003, 99–123.

Buchloh, Benjamin. "Conceptual Art 1962–1969: From the Aesthetic of Administration to the Critique of Institutions." *October* 55 (1990): 105–43.

———. *Neo-avantgarde and the Culture Industry: Essays on European and American Art 1955–1975*. Cambridge, MA: MIT Press, 2000.

Butler, Judith. *Precarious Life: The Powers of Mourning and Violence.* New York: Verso, 2004.
Butler, Judith, Ernesto Laclau, and Slavoj Žižek. *Contingency, Hegemony, Universality: Contemporary Dialogues on the Left.* New York: Verso, 2000.
Carby, Hazel. "The Politics of Fiction, Anthropology, and the Folk: Zora Neale Hurston." In *New Essays on Their Eyes Were Watching God*, edited by Michael Awkward, 71–94. New York: Cambridge University Press, 1991.
Carpio, Glenda. *Laughing Fit to Kill: Black Humor in the Fictions of Slavery.* New York: Oxford University Press, 2008.
Carr, Brian. "Paranoid Interpretation, Desire's Nonobject, and Nella Larsen's 'Passing.'" *PMLA* 119, no. 2 (2004): 282–95.
Carroll, Rachel Jane. "Remains to Be Seen: Black Feminist Art and US Militarism in Asia." *Social Text* 41, no. 1 (2023): 47–70.
Casid, Jill. *Scenes of Projection: Recasting the Enlightenment Subject.* Minneapolis: University of Minnesota Press, 2015.
Castronovo, Russ. "Beauty along the Color Line: Lynching, Aesthetics, and the 'Crisis.'" *PMLA* 121, no. 5 (October 2006): 1443–59.
Cecire, Natalia. *Experimental: American Literature and the Aesthetics of Knowledge.* Baltimore, MD: John Hopkins University Press, 2019.
Cha, Theresa Hak Kyung. *Apparatus: Cinematic Apparatus: Selected Writings.* New York: Tanam, 1980.
———. *Dictee.* Berkley: University of California Press, 2001.
———. "Paths." Master's thesis, University of California, Berkeley, 1978.
———. "White Dust from Mongolia." Theresa Hak Kyung Cha Conceptual Art Archive. Berkeley Art Museum, University of California, Berkeley, 1980.
Chandler, Nahum Dimitri. *Toward a New History of the Centuries: On the Early Writings of W. E. B. Du Bois.* New York: Fordham University Press, 2014.
Chang, Jeff. *Who We Be: The Colorization of America.* New York: St. Martin's, 2014.
Chaouli, Michel. *Thinking with Kant's Critique of Judgment.* Cambridge, MA: Harvard University Press, 2017.
Cheng, Anne Anlin. "Ornamentalism: A Feminist Theory for the Yellow Woman." *Critical Inquiry* 44, no. 3 (Spring 2018): 415–46.
———. *The Melancholy of Race.* New York: Oxford University Press, 2000.
———. *Second Skin: Josephine Baker and the Modernist Surface.* New York: Oxford University Press, 2011.
———. "Wounded Beauty: An Exploratory Essay on Race, Gender, and the Aesthetic Question." *Tulsa Studies in Women's Literature* 19, no. 2 (2000): 191–217.
Cho, Jennifer. "Mel-*han*-cholia as Political Practice in Theresa Hak Kyung Cha's *Dictée*." *Meridians: Feminism, Race, Transnationalism* 19 (supplement 2020): 410–34.
Cho, Lily. "Anticipating Citizenship: Chinese Head Tax Photographs." In *Feeling Photography*, edited by Elspeth Brown and Thy Phu, 158–80. Durham, NC: Duke University Press, 2014.

Chong, Doryun, Michio Hayashi, Fumihiko Sumitomo, and Kenji Kajiya, eds. *From Postwar to Postmodern: Art in Japan 1945–1989*. New York: Museum of Modern Art, 2012.

Chong, Sylvia Shin Huey. *The Oriental Obscene: Violence and Racial Fantasies in the Vietnam Era*. Durham, NC: Duke University Press, 2012.

Chuh, Kandice. *The Difference Aesthetics Makes: On the Humanities 'After Man.'* Durham, NC: Duke University Press, 2019.

Combahee River Collective. "Letter to HERESIES." *HERESIES* 4 (1977): 129.

Concannon, Kevin. "Yoko Ono's *Cut Piece*: From Text to Performance and Back Again." *PAJ: A Journal of Performance and Art* 30, no. 3 (2008): 81–93.

Copeland, Huey. *Bound to Appear: Art, Slavery, and the Site of Blackness in Multicultural America*. Chicago: University of Chicago Press, 2013.

Crafton, Donald. *Emile Cohl, Caricature, and Film*. Princeton, NJ: Princeton University Press, 2014.

Crawford, Margo Natalie. *Black Post-Blackness: The Black Arts Movement and Twenty-First Century Aesthetics*. Champaign: University of Illinois Press, 2017.

Crimp, Douglas. "Introduction: AIDS: Cultural Analysis/Cultural Activism." *October* 43, (Winter 1987): 3–16.

Crone, Rainer, and David Moos. *Kazimir Malevich: The Climax of Disclosure*. Chicago: University of Chicago Press, 1991.

Cronin, Gloria, ed. *Critical Essays on Zora Neale Hurston*. New York: G. K. Hall, 1998.

Cumings, Bruce. *The Korean War: A History*. New York: Random House, 2011.

Danto, Arthur. "Black, White, Gold: Monochrome and Meaning in the Art of Louise Nevelson." In *The Sculpture of Louise Nevelson: Constructing a Legend*, edited by Brooke Kamin Rapaport, 39–48. New Haven, CT: Yale University Press, 2007.

Day, Iyko. "Afro-Feminism before Afropessimism: Meditations on Gender and Ontology." In *Anti-Blackness*, edited by Moon-Kie Jung and João H. Costa Vargas, 60–81. Durham, NC: Duke University Press, 2021.

De Duve, Thierry. *Aesthetics at Large: Art, Ethics, and Politics*. Chicago: University of Chicago Press, 2018.

Diawara, Manthia. "The Absent One: The Avant-Garde and the Black Imaginary in *Looking for Langston*." *Wide Angle* 13, no. 3–4 (1991): 96–109.

Diawara, Manthia, ed. *Black American Cinema*. New York: Routledge, 2012.

D'Souza, Aruna. *Whitewalling: Art, Race & Protest in 3 Acts*. New York: Badlands, 2018.

Du Bois, W. E .B. *The Oxford W. E. B. Du Bois Reader*. Edited by Eric Sundquist. Oxford: Oxford University Press, 1996.

———. *The Souls of Black Folk*. New York: Oxford University Press, 2007.

Dunne, Carey. "Art Historians Find Racist Joke Hidden under Malevich's *Black Square*." *Hyperallergic*, November 13, 2015. https://hyperallergic.com/.

Dyer, Richard. *White: Essays on Race and Culture*. New York: Routledge, 2013.

Edelheit, Martha, Valerie Jaudon, Joyce Kozloff, Melissa Meyer, Carrie Rickey, Elizabeth Sacre, Miriam Schapiro, Elizabeth Weatherford, and Sally Webster, eds. "Women's Traditional Arts and the Politics of Aesthetics." *HERESIES* 4 (1977).

Edwards, Adrienne. "Blackness in Abstraction." *Art in America*, January 5, 2015, www.artnews.com.

Edwards, Erica R. Foreword to *The Terms of Order: Political Science and the Myth of Leadership*. Chapel Hill: University of North Carolina Press, 2016.

Elcott, Noam M. *Artificial Darkness: An Obscure History of Modern Art and Media*. Chicago: University of Chicago Press, 2016.

English, Darby. *1971: A Year in the Life of Color*. Chicago: University of Chicago Press, 2016.

———. *How to See a Work of Art in Total Darkness*. Cambridge: MIT Press, 2010.

English, Daylanne. *Unnatural Selections: Eugenics in American Modernism and the Harlem Renaissance*. Chapel Hill: University of North Carolina Press, 2005.

Espinosa, Julio García. "For an Imperfect Cinema." Translated by Julianne Burton. *Jump Cut* 20 (1979): 24–26.

Espiritu, Yến Lê. "About Ghost Stories: The Vietnam War and 'Rememoration.'" *PMLA* 123, no. 5 (2008): 1700–2.

Feng, Peter X., ed. *Screening Asian Americans*. New Brunswick, NJ: Rutgers University Press, 2002.

Ferguson, Roderick A. *Aberrations in Black: Toward a Queer of Color Critique*. Minneapolis: University of Minnesota Press, 2003.

Flam, Jack, and Miriam Deutch. *Primitivism and Twentieth-Century Art: A Documentary History*. Berkeley: University of California Press, 2003.

Folgarait, Leonard. *Painting 1909: Pablo Picasso, Gertrude Stein, Henri Bergson, Comics, Albert Einstein, and Anarchy*. New Haven, CT: Yale University Press, 2017.

Foucault, Michel. *Discipline and Punish: The Birth of the Prison*. New York: Vintage, 1995.

Francis, Jacqueline. *Making Race: Modernism and 'Racial Art' in America*. Seattle: University of Washington Press, 2012.

Fredrickson, Laurel. "*Trap*: Kate Millett, Japan, Fluxus and Feminism." *Women & Performance* 19, no. 3 (2009): 337–67.

Freeman, Elizabeth. "Turn the Beat Around: Sadomasochism, Temporality, History." *Differences* 19, no. 1 (2008): 32–70.

Ganeri, Jonardon. *Attention Not Self*. Oxford: Oxford University Press, 2017.

Gibson, Ann Eden. "Color and Difference in Abstract Painting." In *The Feminism and Visual Culture Reader*, edited by Amelia Jones, 192–204. New York: Routledge, 2003.

Gilmore, Glenda. *Defying Dixie: The Radical Roots of Civil Rights, 1919–1950*. New York: W. W. Norton, 2009.

Gilmore, Ruth Wilson. "Race and Globalization." In *Geographies of Global Change: Remapping the World*, edited by R. J. Johnson, Peter J. Taylor, and Michael Watts, 261–74. New York: Wiley Blackwell, 2002.

Glissant, Édouard. *Poetics of Relation*. Translated by Betsy Wing. Ann Arbor: University of Michigan Press. 1997.

Gluck, Mary. *Popular Bohemia: Modernism and Urban Culture in Nineteenth-Century Paris*. Cambridge, MA: Harvard University Press, 2008.

Goings, Kenneth. *Mammy and Uncle Moses: Black Collectibles and American Stereotyping*. Bloomington: Indiana University Press, 1994.

Goldsby, Jaqueline. *A Spectacular Secret: Lynching in American Life and Literature*. Chicago: University of Chicago Press, 2006.

Graeber, David. *The Utopia of Rules: On Technology, Stupidity, and the Secret Joys of Bureaucracy*. New York: Melville House, 2016.

Greenberger, Alex. "An Old-School Painter Adapts to a New World Order: Jack Whitten's 50-Year Evolution." *Artnews*, January 19, 2016. www.artnews.com.

Gunning, Tom. "In Your Face: Physiognomy, Photography, and the Gnostic Mission of Early Film." *Modernism/Modernity* 4, no.1 (1997): 1–29.

Halberstam, Jack. *The Queer Art of Failure*. Durham, NC: Duke University Press, 2011.

Hall, Stuart. *The Hard Road to Renewal: Thatcherism and the Crisis of the Left*. New York: Verso, 1988.

Han, Simon. "Shortcuts to Identity: How We Tell Asian American Stories." *Literary Hub*, February 12, 2021. https://lithub.com.

Harney, Stefano, and Fred Moten. *The Undercommons: Fugitive Planning and Black Study*. New York: Minor Compositions, 2013.

Harper, Phillip Brian. *Abstractionist Aesthetics: Artistic Form and Social Critique in African American Culture*. New York: New York University Press, 2015.

Harris, Michael. *Colored Pictures: Race and Visual Representation*. Chapel Hill: University of North Carolina Press, 2003.

Hartman, Saidiya V. *Scenes of Subjection: Terror, Slavery, and Self-Making in Nineteenth-Century America*. New York: Oxford University Press, 1997.

———. "Venus in Two Acts." *Small Axe* 26, no. 2 (June 2008): 1–14.

———. *Wayward Lives, Beautiful Experiments: Intimate Histories of Social Upheaval*. New York: W. W. Norton, 2019.

Ho, Fred, and Bill V. Mullen. *Afro Asia: Revolutionary Political and Cultural Connections*. Durham, NC: Duke University Press, 2008.

Hong, Cathy Park. "Delusions of Whiteness in the Avant-Garde." *Lana Turner* (November 3, 2014). https://arcade.stanford.edu.

———. *Minor Feelings: As Asian American Reckoning*. New York: Penguin Random House, 2020.

Hong, Grace Kyungwon. *Death beyond Disavowal: The Impossible Politics of Difference*. Minneapolis: University of Minnesota Press, 2015.

Hong, Grace Kyungwon, and Roderick Ferguson, eds. *Strange Affinities: The Gender and Sexual Politics of Comparative Racialization*. Durham, NC: Duke University Press, 2011.

Huang, Vivian L. "Inscrutably, Actually: Hospitality, Parasitism, and the Silent Work of Yoko Ono and Laurel Nakadate." *Women & Performance* 28, no. 3 (2018): 187–203.

Hughes, Langston. *The Big Sea: An Autobiography*. New York: Hill and Wang, 1993.

———. *Fight for Freedom and Other Writings on Civil Rights*. Edited by Christopher C. De Santis. Columbia: University of Missouri Press, 2001.

Hurston, Zora Neale. "How It Feels to Be Colored Me." In *I Love Myself When I Am Laughing and Then Again When I Am Looking Mean and Impressive*, edited by Alice Walker, 152–55. New York: Feminist Press at CUNY, 1979.
Ingold, Tim. *Imagining for Real: Essays on Creation, Attention and Correspondence*. New York: Routledge, 2021.
Ishizuka, Karen L. *Serve the People: Making Asian America in the Long Sixties*. New York: Verso, 2016.
Javadizadeh, Kamran. "The Atlantic Ocean Breaking on Our Heads: Claudia Rankine, Robert Lowell, and the Whiteness of the Lyric Subject." *PMLA* 134, no. 3, 2019: 475–90.
Jenkins, Ulysses, dir. *Inconsequential Doggereal*. Video, 1981.
———. *Mass of Images*. Video, 1978.
Jeon, Joseph Jonghyun. *Racial Things, Racial Forms: Objecthood in Avant-Garde Asian American Poetry*. Iowa City: University of Iowa Press, 2012.
Johnson, Abby Arthur, and Ronald Maberry Johnson. *Propaganda and Aesthetics: The Literary Politics of African-American Magazines in the Twentieth Century*. Amherst: University of Massachusetts Press, 1991.
Johnson, Barbara. *A World of Difference*. Baltimore, MD: John Hopkins University Press, 1987.
Johnson, Gaye Theresa, and Alex Lubin, eds. *Futures of Black Radicalism*. New York: Verso, 2017.
Johnson, James Weldon. "Lynching: America's National Disgrace." *Current History* 19, no. 4 (1924): 596–601.
Julien, Isaac. "Confessions of a Snow Queen: Notes on the Making of the Attendant." *Critical Quarterly* 36, no.1 (1994): 120–26.
———, dir. *Looking for Langston*. Strand Releasing, 2007. DVD.
Julien, Isaac, et al. *RIOT*. New York: Museum of Modern Art, 2013.
Julien, Isaac, and Kobena Mercer. "De Margin and De Centre." *Screen* 29, no. 4 (Autumn 1988): 2–11.
Jung, Moon-Ho, ed. *The Rising Tide of Color: Race, State Violence, and Radical Movements across the Pacific*. Seattle: University of Washington Press, 2014.
Kang, Laura Hyun Yi. *Compositional Subjects: Enfiguring Asian/American Women*. Durham, NC: Duke University Press, 2002.
Kant, Immanuel. *The Critique of Judgment*. Translated by James Creed Meredith. Oxford: Oxford University Press, 2008.
———. *The Critique of Judgment*. Translated by Werner S. Pluhar. Indianapolis, IN: Hackett, 1987.
———. *The Critique of the Power of Judgment*. Translated by Paul Guyer and Eric Matthews. Cambridge, UK: Cambridge University Press, 2000.
———. *Observations on the Feeling of the Beautiful and Sublime and Other Writings*. Edited by Patrick Frierson and Paul Guyer. New York: Cambridge University Press, 2011.

Kee, Joan. *The Geometries of Afro Asia: Art beyond Solidarity*. Oakland: University of California Press, 2023.
Keeling, Kara. "Looking for M—Queer Temporality, Black Political Possibility, and Poetry from the Future." *GLQ* 15, no. 4 (2009): 565–82.
Kelley, Robin D. G. "Foreword." In *Black Marxism: The Making of the Black Radical Tradition*, by Cedric J. Robinson, xi–xxvi. Chapel Hill: University of North Carolina Press, 2000.
———. *Freedom Dreams: The Black Radical Imagination*. Boston: Beacon, 2002.
Kim, Byron. "Byron Kim by Adam Simon." Interviewed by Adam Simon. *Bomb Magazine* February 21, 2014. https://bombmagazine.org.
———. "Byron Kim Oral History Interview." Interviewed by Ann Shi. Houston Asian American Archives Oral History Collection, April 8, 2021. https://haaa.rice.edu.
Kim, Daniel. *The Intimacies of Conflict: Cultural Memory and the Korean War*. New York: New York University Press, 2020.
Kim, Dong Hoon. *Eclipsed Cinema: The Film Culture of Colonial Korea*. Edinburgh: Edinburgh University Press, 2017.
Kim, Jodi. *The Ends of Empire: Asian American Critique and the Cold War*. Minneapolis: University of Minnesota Press, 2010.
Kindig, Jessie. "The Violent Embrace." *Boston Review*, April 5, 2021. https://bostonreview.net.
Kirschke, Amy Helene. *Aaron Douglas: Art, Race, and the Harlem Renaissance*. Jackson: University of Mississippi Press, 1995.
Laclau, Ernesto. *Emancipation(s)*. New York: Verso, 1996.
Larsen, Nella. *Quicksand and Passing*. Edited by Deborah McDowell. Brunswick, NJ: Rutgers University Press, 1986.
Law, Ian. *Red Racisms: Racism in Communist and Post-Communist Contexts*. London: Palgrave MacMillan, 2012.
Lee, Kun Jong. "Rewriting Hesiod, Revisioning Korea: Theresa Hak Kyung Cha's *Dictee* as a Subversive Hesiodic 'Catalogue of Women.'" *College Literature* 33, no. 3 (2006): 77–99.
Lee, Summer Kim. "Staying In: Mitski, Ocean Vuong, and Asian American Asociality." *Social Text* 37, no. 1 (2019): 27–50.
Lewallen, Constance. *The Dream of the Audience: Theresa Hak Kyung Cha (1951–1982)*. Berkeley: University of California Press, 2001.
Ligon, Glenn. "Blue Black, Black and Blue." *Blue Black*. St. Louis: Pulitzer Arts Foundation, 2017.
———. *Glenn Ligon: Some Changes*. Toronto: Power Plant, 2005.
———. "Glenn Ligon Speaks about His Curatorial Project 'Encounters and Collisions.'" *Art Forum*, June 5, 2015. www.artforum.com.
Lipsitz, George. *The Possessive Investment in Whiteness: How White People Profit from Identity Politics*. Philadelphia: Temple University Press, 2006.
Locke, Alain. *The New Negro*. New York: Simon and Schuster, 1997.
Lorde, Audre. *Sister Outsider: Essays and Speeches*. Berkeley, CA: Crossing Press, 2007.

Lott, Eric. *Love and Theft: Blackface Minstrelsy and the American Working Class*. New York: Oxford University Press, 2013.
Lowe, Lisa. *Immigrant Acts: On Asian American Cultural Politics*. Durham, NC: Duke University Press, 1996.
MacDonald, Scott, and Yoko Ono. "Yoko Ono: Ideas on Film: Interview/Scripts." *Film Quarterly* 43, no. 1 (1989): 2–23.
Maeda, Daryl J. *The Chains of Babylon: The Rise of Asian America*. Minneapolis: University of Minnesota Press, 2009.
Malevich, Kazimir. "From Cubism to Futurism to Suprematism: The New Painterly Realism." In *Russian Art of the Avant-Garde: Theory and Criticism, 1902–1934*, edited and translated by John Bowlt, 116–35. New York: Viking, 1976.
Maliangkay, Roald. "The Power of Representation: Korean Movie Narrators and Authority." *Journal of Korean Studies* 16, no. 2 (2011): 213–29.
Marinetti, F. T. *The Futurist Manifesto (aka The Founding and Manifesto of Futurism)*. *UbuWeb*, February 20, 1909. https://ubu.com.
Marks, Laura. *The Skin of the Film: Intercultural Cinema, Embodiment, and the Senses*. Durham, NC: Duke University Press, 2000.
Marriott, David. *Haunted Life: Visual Culture and Black Modernity*. New Brunswick, NJ: Rutgers University Press, 2007.
Maynard, Robyn, and Leanne Betasamosake Simpson. *Rehearsals for Living*. Chicago: Haymarket, 2022.
McKittrick, Katherine. *Sylvia Wynter: On Being Human as Praxis*. Durham, NC: Duke University Press, 2015.
McMillan, Uri. *Embodied Avatars: Genealogies of Black Feminist Art and Performance*. New York: New York University Press, 2015.
Melamed, Jodi. *Represent and Destroy: Rationalizing Violence in the New Racial Capitalism*. Minneapolis: University of Minnesota Press, 2011.
Mercer, Kobena. "Dark and Lovely Too: Black Gay Men in Independent Cinema." In *Experimental Cinema: The Film Reader*, edited by Wheeler Winston and Audrey Dixon Foster, 325–38. London: Routledge, 2002.
———. "Reading Racial Fetishism." In *Fetishism as Cultural Discourse*, edited by Emily Apter and William Pietz, 307–30. Ithaca, NY: Cornell University Press, 1993.
———. *Welcome to the Jungle: New Positions in Black Cultural Studies*. New York: Routledge, 1994.
Miller, Monica. *Slaves to Fashion: Black Dandyism and the Styling of Black Diasporic Identity*. Durham, NC: Duke University Press, 2009.
Millett, Kate. *Sexual Politics*. New York: Columbia University Press, 2016.
Milner, John. *Kazimir Malevich and the Art of Geometry*. New Haven, CT: Yale University Press, 1996.
Min, Susette. *Unnamable: The Ends of Asian American Art*. New York: New York University Press, 2018.

Morgan, Jessica, ed. *Ellen Gallagher*. Boston: Institute of Contemporary Art Boston, 2001. Exhibition catalogue.

Morrison, Toni. "James Baldwin: His Voice Remembered; Life in His Language." *New York Times*, December 20, 1987.

——. *Playing in the Dark: Whiteness and the Literary Imagination*. New York: Vintage, 1993.

Moten, Fred. *Black and Blur*. Durham, NC: Duke University Press, 2017.

——. *In the Break: The Aesthetics of the Black Radical Tradition*. Minneapolis: University of Minnesota Press, 2003.

——. *Stolen Life*. Durham, NC: Duke University Press, 2018.

——. *Universal Machine*. Durham, NC: Duke University Press, 2018.

Muñoz, José Esteban. *Cruising Utopia: The Then and There of Queer Futurity*. New York: New York University Press, 2009.

——. *Disidentification: Queers of Color and the Performance of Politics*. Minneapolis: University of Minnesota Press, 1999.

Munroe, Alexandra, and Yoko Ono. *YES Yoko Ono*. New York: Abrams, 2000.

Musser, Amber Jamilla. *Sensational Flesh: Race, Power, and Masochism*. New York: New York University Press, 2014.

Naficy, Hamid. "Theorizing 'Third World' Film Spectatorship." In *Rethinking Third Cinema*, edited by Wimal Dissanayake and Anthony Guneratne, 183–201. New York: Routledge, 2003.

Nechepurenko, Ivan. "Examination Reveals a Mysterious Message on Malevich's 'Black Square' Painting." *New York Times*, November 18, 2015, https://artsbeat.blogs.nytimes.com/.

Nelson, Maggie. *On Freedom: Four Songs of Care and Constraint*. New York: Random House, 2021.

Ngai, Mae. *Impossible Subjects: Illegal Aliens and the Making of Modern America*. Princeton, NJ: Princeton University to Press, 2014.

Ngai, Sianne. *Our Aesthetic Categories: Cute, Zany, Interesting*. Cambridge, MA: Harvard University Press, 2012.

——. *Theory of the Gimmick: Aesthetic Judgment and the Capitalist Form*. Cambridge, MA: Harvard University Press, 2020.

——. *Ugly Feelings*. Cambridge, MA: Harvard University Press, 2005.

Nguyen, Mimi Thi. *The Gift of Freedom: War, Debt, and Other Refugee Passages*. Durham, NC: Duke University Press, 2012.

Nguyen, Tan Hoang. *A View from the Bottom: Asian American Masculinity and Sexual Representation*. Durham, NC: Duke University Press, 2014.

Nguyen, Viet Thanh. *Nothing Ever Really Dies: Vietnam and the Memory of War*. Cambridge, MA: Harvard University Press, 2016.

Noriega, Chon A. *Chicanos and Film: Representation and Resistance*. Minneapolis: University of Minnesota Press, 1992.

Nussbaum, Martha. *Upheavals of Thought: The Intelligence of Emotions*. Cambridge, UK: Cambridge University Press, 2003.

Odell, Jenny. *How to Do Nothing: Resisting the Attention Economy*. New York: Melville House, 2019.
Ongiri, Amy Abugo. *Spectacular Blackness: The Cultural Politics of the Black Power Movement and the Search for a Black Aesthetic*. Charlottesville: University of Virginia Press, 2010. Print.
Ono, Yoko. "Declaration of Nutopia—April 1, 1973." *Imagine Peace*, April 1, 2015, https://www.imaginepeace.com/archives/23831.
———. "The Feminization of Society." *New York Times*, February 23, 1972, 41.
———. *Grapefruit: A Book of Instructions and Drawings*. New York: Simon and Schuster, 2000.
Painter, Nell Irvin. *The History of White People*. New York: W. W. Norton, 2010.
Parreñas, Rhacel Salazar, and Winnie Tam. *The Force of Domesticity: Filipina Migrants and Globalization*. New York: New York University Press, 2008.
Pegler-Gordon, Anna. *In Sight of America: Photography and the Development of U.S. Immigration Policy*. Berkeley: University of California Press, 2009.
Perreault, John. "The Art Cops Return: Fluxus Must Die!" *Artopia*, April 26, 2011. www.artsjournal.com.
Perrée, Rob. *Cover to Cover: The Artist's Book in Perspective*. Rotterdam: Nai, 2002.
Phu, Thy. *Picturing Model Citizens: Civility in Asian American Visual Culture*. Philadelphia: Temple University Press, 2011.
Plant, Deborah. *Every Tub Must Sit on Its Own Bottom: The Philosophy and Politics of Zora Neale Hurston*. Urbana: University of Illinois Press, 1995.
Prashad, Vijay. *Everybody Was Kung Fu Fighting: Afro-Asian Connections and the Myth of Cultural Purity*. Boston, MA: Beacon Press, 2001.
Rankin, John. *Letters on American Slavery*. New York: Arno, 1969.
Reed, Anthony. *Freedom Time*. Baltimore, MD: John Hopkins University Press, 2014.
Reddy, Chandan. *Freedom with Violence: Race, Sexuality, and the U.S. State*. Durham, NC: Duke University Press, 2011.
Reed, Ishmael. "The Black Artist: Calling a Spade a Spade." *Arts Magazine* (May 1967): 48–49.
Robinson, Cedric J. *Black Marxism: The Making of the Black Radical Tradition*. Chapel Hill: University of North Carolina Press, 2000.
———. *The Terms of Order: Political Science and the Myth of Leadership*. Chapel Hill: University of North Carolina Press, 2016.
Rodríguez, Dylan. *White Reconstruction: Domestic Warfare and the Logics of Genocide*. New York: Fordham University Press, 2020.
Roelofs, Monique. "Racialization as Aesthetic Production: What Does the Aesthetic Do for Whiteness and Blackness and Vice Versa?" In *White on White/Black on Black*, edited by George Yancy, 83–124. New York: Rowman and Littlefield, 2005.
Roh, David S., Betsy Huang, and Greta A. Niu. "Technologizing Orientalism: An Introduction." In *Techno-Orientalism: Imagining Asia in Speculative Fiction, History, and Media*, edited by David S. Roh, Betsy Huang, and Greta A. Niu, 1–20. New Brunswick, NJ: Rutgers University Press, 2015.

Rose, Barbara. *Art as Art: The Selected Writings of Ad Reinhardt*. Berkeley: University of California Press, 1991.

Rosenthal, Angela. *No Laughing Matter: Visual Humor in Ideas of Race, Nationality, and Ethnicity*. Hanover, NH: Dartmouth College Press, 2016.

Ross, Stephen, and Allana C. Lindgren, eds. *The Modernist World*. New York: Routledge, 2017.

Rothkopf, Scott. *Glenn Ligon: America*. New Haven, CT: Yale University Press, 2011.

Said, Edward. *Orientalism*. New York: Knopf Doubleday, 2014.

Saltzstein, Daniel. "Overlooked No More: Theresa Hak Kyung Cha, Artist and Author Who Explored Identity." *New York Times*, January 7, 2022.

Sammond, Nicholas. *Birth of an Industry: Blackface Minstrelsy and the Rise of American Animation*. Durham, NC: Duke University Press, 2015.

Saunders, Raymond. *Black Is a Color*. Self-published, 1967.

Scarry, Elaine. *On Beauty and Being Just*. Princeton, NJ: Princeton University Press, 1999.

Sedgwick, Eve Kosofsky. *Touching Feeling: Affect, Pedagogy, Performativity*. Durham, NC: Duke University Press, 2003.

Sen, Mayukh. "A Kind of Blueprint: The Radical Vision of Theresa Hak Kyung Cha's *Dictée*." *Nation*, August 20, 2020. www.thenation.com/.

Sexton, Jared. "Basic Black." *liquid blackness* 5, no. 2 (2021): 74–83.

Shah, Nayan. *Contagious Divides: Epidemics and Race in San Francisco's Chinatown*. Berkeley: University of California Press, 2001.

Sharpe, Christina. *In the Wake: On Blackness and Being*. Durham, NC: Duke University Press, 2016.

Shatskikh, Aleksandra. *Black Square: Malevich and the Origin of Suprematism*. New Haven, CT: Yale University Press, 2012.

———. "Inscribed Vandalism: *The Black Square* at One Hundred." *e-flux* 85 (October 2017). www.e-flux.com.

Sherrard-Johnson, Cherene. *Portraits of the New Negro Woman: Visual and Literary Culture in the Harlem Renaissance*. New Brunswick, NJ: Rutgers University Press, 2007.

Shimizu, Celine Parreñas. *The Hypersexuality of Race: Performing Asian/American Women on Screen and Scene*. Durham, NC: Duke University Press, 2007.

Sillman, Amy. *Faux Pas. Selected Writings and Drawings*. Paris: After 8 Books, 2020.

Silva, Denise Ferreira da. "In the Raw." *e-flux* 93 (September 2018): 1–9. www.e-flux.com.

———. *Toward a Global Idea of Race*. Minneapolis: University of Minnesota Press, 2007.

Sjöholm, Cecilia. *Doing Aesthetics with Arendt: How to See Things*. New York: Columbia University Press, 2015.

Smethurst, James. *The African American Roots of Modernism: From Reconstruction to the Harlem Renaissance*. Chapel Hill: University of North Carolina Press, 2011.

Solanas, Fernando, and Octavio Getino. "Toward a Third Cinema." *Cinéaste* 4, no. 3 (Winter 1970–71): 1–10.
Stalling, Jonathan. *The Poetics of Emptiness: Transformations of Asian Thought in American Poetry*. New York: Fordham University Press, 2010.
Steyerl, Hito. "In Defense of the Poor Image." In *The Wretched of the Screen*, 31–45. Berlin: Sternberg, 2012.
Strings, Sabrina. *Fearing the Black Body: The Racial Origins of Fat Phobia*. New York: New York University Press, 2019.
Táíwò, Olúfẹ́mi O. *Elite Capture: How the Powerful Took Over Identity Politics (And Everything Else)*. Chicago: Haymarket, 2022.
Tate, Claudia. *Allegories of Political Desire: The Black Heroine's Text at the Turn of the Century*. New York: Oxford University Press, 1992.
———. "*Passing*: A Problem of Interpretation." *Black American Literature Forum* 14, no. 4 (1980): 142–46.
Tate, Shirley Anne. *Black Beauty: Aesthetics, Stylization, Politics*. Burlington, VT: Ashgate, 2009.
TateShots. "Jack Whitten—'The Political Is in the Work.'" Tate Modern, October 6, 2017. YouTube video, 5:59. www.youtube.com/watch?v=QzxhXbXGeTc.
Taussig, Michael. *What Color Is the Sacred?* Chicago: University of Chicago Press, 2010.
Taylor, Keeanga-Yamahtta, ed. *How We Get Free: Black Feminism and the Combahee River Collective*. Chicago: Haymarket, 2017.
Taylor, Paul C. *Black Is Beautiful: Philosophy of Black Aesthetics*. Malden, MA: Wiley Blackwell, 2016.
Terada, Rei. *Looking Away: Phenomenality and Dissatisfaction, Kant to Adorno*. Cambridge, MA: Harvard University Press, 2009.
Tibebu, Teshale. *Hegel and the Third World: The Making of Eurocentrism in World History*. Syracuse, NY: Syracuse University Press, 2011.
Trinh, T. Minh-ha, "White Spring." In *The Dream of the Audience: Theresa Hak Kyung Cha (1951–1982)*, edited by Constance Lewallen and Lawrence Rinder, 33–50. Berkeley: University of California Press, 2001.
———. *Women, Native, Other: Writing Postcoloniality and Feminism*. Bloomington: Indiana University Press, 1989.
Tucker, Irene. *The Moment of Racial Sight: A History*. Chicago: University of Chicago Press, 2012.
Ty, M. "The Riot of the Literal." *Oxford Literary Review* 42, no. 1 (2020): 76–108.
Vogel, Shane. *The Scene of Harlem Cabaret: Race, Sexuality, Performance*. Chicago: University of Chicago Press, 2009.
Voon, Claire. "Dread Scott Discusses Controversial Lynching Banner That Sparked Threats." *Hyperallergic*, July 21, 2016. https://hyperallergic.com/.
Walker, Alice. *In Search of Our Mothers Gardens*. New York: Mariner, 2003.
Walker Art Center. "Jack Whiten on Mapping the Soul." September 3, 2015. YouTube video, 2:51. Transcribed by the author. www.youtube.com/watch?v=V1mI71d2Plc.

Wall, Cheryl A. "Passing for What? Aspects of Identity in Nella Larsen's Novels." *Black American Literature Forum* 20, no. 1–2 (1986): 97–111.

———. *Women of the Harlem Renaissance*. Bloomington: Indiana University Press, 1995.

———. *Worrying the Line: Black Women Writers, Lineage, and Literary Tradition*. Chapel Hill: University of North Carolina Press, 2005.

Wang, Dorothy. *Thinking Its Presence: Form, Race, and Subjectivity in Contemporary Asian American Poetry*. Stanford, CA: Stanford University Press, 2014.

Wang, Jackie. *The Sunflower Cast a Spell to Save Us from the Void*. New York: Nightboat, 2021.

Watney, Simon. *Policing Desire: Pornography, AIDS, and the Media*. London: Cassell, 1997.

Watts, Eric King. *Hearing the Hurt: Rhetoric, Aesthetics, and Politics of the New Negro Movement*. Tuscaloosa: University of Alabama Press, 2012.

Weheliye, Alexander G. *Habeus Viscus: Racializing Assemblages, Biopolitics, and Black Feminist Theories of the Human*. Durham, NC: Duke University Press, 2014.

Westheider, James. *The African American Experience in Vietnam: Brothers in Arms*. New York: Rowman and Littlefield, 2008.

Whitten, Jack. "An Interview with Artist Jack Whitten." Interview by Linda DeBerry. *Crystal Bridges Museum of American Art*. January 23, 2018. https://crystalbridges.org.

———. "Jack Whitten." Interview by Kenneth Goldsmith. *Bomb*, no. 48 (summer 1994): 36–41.

Wiener, John. *Gimme Some Truth: John Lennon and the FBI*. Berkeley: University of California Press, 2000.

Wilderson, Frank B., III. "Afropessimism and the Ruse of Analogy: Violence, Freedom Struggles, and the Death of Black Desire." In *Anti-Blackness*, edited by Moon-Kie Jung and João H. Costa Vargas, 37–59. Durham, NC: Duke University Press, 2021.

Wispé, Lauren. "History of the Concept of Empathy." In *Empathy and Its Development*, edited by Nancy Eisenberg and Janet Strayer, 17–37. Cambridge, UK: Cambridge University Press, 1987.

Wolff, Larry. *Inventing Eastern Europe: The Map of Civilization on the Mind of the Enlightenment*. Stanford, CA: Stanford University Press, 1994.

Wu, Cici, and Yong Soon Min. "Cici Wu and Yong Soon Min." In *The Book of Gossip*, edited by Weiyi Chang, Sofia Jamal, Colleen O'Connor, and Patricio Orellana, 8–19. New York: Whitney Independent Study Program, 2020. https://artistsspace.org.

Wynter, Sylvia. "Unsettling the Coloniality of Being/Power/Truth/Freedom: Towards the Human, after Man, Its Overrepresentation—An Argument." *New Centennial Review* 3, no. 3 (Fall 2003): 257–337.

Xiang, Sunny. *Tonal Intelligence: The Aesthetics of Asian Inscrutability During the Long Cold War*. New York: Columbia University Press, 2020.

Yoshimoto, Midori. *Into Performance: Japanese Women Artists in New York*. New Brunswick, NJ: Rutgers University Press, 2005.

Yu, Brandon. "A Vision of Asian-American Cinema That Questions the Very Premise." *New York Times*, February 11, 2021.

Yu, Timothy. *Race and the Avant-Garde: Experimental and Asian American Poetry Since 1965*. Stanford, CA: Stanford University Press, 2009.

Zerilli, Linda. *Feminism and the Abyss of Freedom*. Chicago: University of Chicago Press, 2005.

———. "This Universalism Which Is Not One." *Diacritics* 28, no. 2 (1998): 2–20.

Ziporyn, Brook, trans. *Zhuangzi: The Complete Writings*. Indianapolis: Hackett, 2020.

INDEX

Page numbers in *italics* indicate Figures.

abstraction, 36; Blackness in, 148–49; of chromatic black, 147, 160, 161; geometric, 138; in "How It Feels to Be Colored Me," 149, 151, 154–56; racialization relation to, 135, 142, 146; racism relation to, 128, 235n13; realism compared to, 168; social meaning relation to, 157; stereotype as, 143–44, 150, 159–60

absurdism: of Ono, 87–88; of war, 115; whimsy compared to, 97

absurdist humor, 13

administration, aesthetic judgment relation to, 111

administrative forms, 88, 89; as poetry, 100, 103–4, 108–9, 111; whimsy in, 107–8

aesthetic. *See specific topics*

aesthetic judgment: administration relation to, 111; beauty in, 73–74, 75, 78, 80; Blackness in, 54; of cinema, 164, 175; dominance relation to, 11–12; domination relation to, 65–66, 67, 94; dreaminess relation to, 174; empathy in, 55–56; ethics relation to, 191; forms relation to, 34; identity relation to, 80–81; Kantian mode of, 42, 46–47, 48, 55, 68, 69; in *Looking for Langston*, 76–77, 82; in *Passing*, 63–64, 65–68; power relation to, 6, 35, 67, 94; reality relation to, 186, 211; social relation and, 12–13, 20, 191, 212–13; taste relation to, 48–50; whimsy relation to, 96, 122, 212

aesthetic satisfaction, passivity of, 156

aesthetic theory, 212; of Du Bois, 58–59, 60, 71, 85, 235n15; Enlightenment relation to, 6; purposiveness in, 52, 96; racial capitalism relation to, 5, 12; whiteness relation to, 31

"affectable subjects," 139–40

affective experiences, 15, 135; beauty in, 14

Afro Asia, 214

After La vida nueva (exhibition), 203–5, 210

Ahmed, Sara, 14

AIDS pandemic, 72, 73

Akinsha, Konstantin, 145

Alarcón, Norma, 182, 203

Allais, Alphonse, 143

Allen, Jafari, S., 71, 83

Allende, Salvador, 204

anti-colonial feminism, 191, 202

"The Apparatus" (Baudry), 185

Apparatus (Cha), 184, 187, 208

Appiah, Kwame Anthony, 58

Appy, Christian, 116

arbitrary, rationalism relation to, 90

Armstrong, Louis, 162

art. *See specific topics*

Artists Space, 236n28

Arts Incohérents, 142–43, 144–45

Asian American feminism, 178–79

Asian female subjectivity, 182

Asianness, 28

Asian racialization, 179

Asian women: immigration of, 104–5; racial capitalism relation to, 178; racial fetishism of, 106–7, 179; stereotypes of, 178–79, 230n17; violence against, 242n1
Atkins, Robert, 176
attention: beauty relation to, 17–18; forms relation to, 4, 22–23, 25, 54, 175, 191–92; pleasure relation to, 5; self affected by, 24–25
Aubrey, Timothy, 16–17, 19
audience, artist relation to, 190, 191
automatic writing, 180
avant-garde: anti-Blackness in, 28; dreaminess relation to, 181–82; fetishization relation to, 72; *Grapefruit* as, 91; race relation to, 26; racism relation to, 7–8, 124

Baldessari, John, 98
Baldwin, James, 74
Barthes, Roland, 186–87, 188, 192, 194, 208
Batchelor, David, 152
Baudry, Jean-Louis, 184–85, 186, 196
beauty, 13; in aesthetic judgment, 73–74, 75, 78, 80; aesthetic pleasure relation to, 34–35, 62; in affective experiences, 14; in Black aesthetics, 35, 39–41, 54; in Black experimentalism, 85; for Black liberation, 55, 60; Blackness relation to, 52–53, 59–60; in *Critique of Judgment*, 34–35, 46–47; disdain for, 16; domination relation to, 40; empathy relation to, 55, 57; feminism relation to, 223n4; freedom relation to, 48, 60, 61, 63, 69; in Harlem Renaissance, 40–41, 42; in *Looking for Langston*, 73–76, 79, 82–84, 85; oppression relation to, 17–18; in *Passing*, 69–70; pleasure relation to, 53–54; in political critique, 15, 212; politics relation to, 57; social change relation to, 45; social relation and, 59; transformation relation to, 70–71; truth relation to, 60; violence relation to, 62–63; whimsy compared to, 96–97; whiteness relation to, 57, 64, 70, 76, 78
"Bed-In for Peace" (Ono and Lennon), 230n16
Ben Hur (film), 197
Berlin International Film Festival (1989), 43
Bernasconi, Robert, 51, 52
Bhabha, Homi, 106–7, 143–44
Bilhaud, Paul, 142–43
black, chromatic, 131–32; abstraction of, 147, 160, 161; Blackness relation to, 129, 130, 133–34, 147; in color-based abstraction, 134; in *FIRE!!*, 157; racism relation to, 146, 236n28
Black aesthetics, 44, 212; beauty in, 35, 39–41, 54; universality in, 42
The Black Book (Mapplethorpe), 75–76
Black experimentalism: beauty in, 85; in *Looking for Langston*, 70
Black gay cultural renaissance, 43
Black liberation, 55, 59, 60
"black light," 235n16
Black Marxism (Robinson), 31–32, 221n2
black masculinity, 158–59
Black Monoliths (painting series), 129–31
Blackness, 28, 75, 81; in abstraction, 148–49; in aesthetic judgment, 54; beauty relation to, 52–53, 59–60; black monochrome painting relation to, 36, 144; chromatic black relation to, 129, 130, 133–34, 147; fetishization of, 72; objectification relation to, 65; in *Passing*, 68; stereotypes of, 241n77
anti-Blackness, 28, 126
Blackness in Abstraction (exhibition), 147–48, 162
Black queer politics, pleasure relation to, 84
Black radicalism, 53–54, 74, 223n13
Black Skin, White Masks (Fanon), 151
Black Square (painting). *See* Malevich, Kazimir

Black women, objectification of, 64–65
Blue Black Boy (painting), 162
Blue Black (exhibition), 162–63
Blue Black (sculpture), 162
Blue (film), 162
Bora, Renu, 198
"born: Bird Year." *See Grapefruit*
Bost, Darius, 43
Bow, Leslie, 106
Briante, Susan, 87
Brixton Riots, 226n83
bureaucracy, 101
"Butterfly Dream" (Zhou), 190–91

Cacho, Lisa Marie, 30–31
Cage, John, 24, 91, 229n7
"Can You Party (Club Mix)" (song), 84–85, 227n95
Carver, George Washington, 131
Casid, Jill, 196
Castronovo, Russ, 59
Cecire, Natalia, 26–27, 44
Centre d'Etudes Americain du Cinema, in Paris, 181, 184
Cervenak, Sarah Jane, 51
Cha, Theresa Hak Kyung, 36–37, 212–13, 242n1; Apparatus of, 184, 187, 208; *Commentaire* of, 187–88, 194, 196; dreaminess of, 164, 174–76, 177, 179–80, 188–89; experimentalism of, 173–74; in *HERESIES*, 170; Julien compared to, 166–67; *After La vida nueva* relation to, 205; Ono compared to, 177–78; at University of California, Berkeley, 180–81, 183–84; *White Dust from Magnolia* of, 205, 206, 207–8, 209–10, 247n87; in woman-of-color feminism, 170–71; Zhou effect on, 190–91; Zurita relation to, 204. *See also Dictee* (Cha)
Chambers-Letson, Joshua, 33
Chambers Street salons, 229n10
Chandler, Nahum Dimitri, 59
Chaouli, Michel, 16, 17

Cheng, Anne Anlin, 39–40, 64–65, 201; on beauty, 75
Chile, 204
Cho, Jennifer, 172
Chong, Sylvia, 116, 120
Chromophobia (Batchelor), 152
Chuh, Kandice, 11
cinema: aesthetic judgment of, 164, 175; attention in, 192; colonialism relation to, 196–97, 198; in *Dictee*, 194–96, 197; disidentification in, 199–200; dreaminess in, 183, 184; eroticism in, 186–88; experimental, 246n67; in Korea, 246n63; movietelling in, 192–94; night labor relation to, 188–89; Plato's cave compared to, 184–85; Third Cinema, 183–84, 245n42; voyeurism relation to, 246n64
cinematic close-up, 165
civilization, communicability relation to, 52
Clark, Edward, 234n6
Cohl, Emile, 143
Cold War, 169–70, 173
collage: paint-as, 124; unconscious relation to, 180; video, 1–4, 6
collectivity: aesthetic judgment relation to, 48; universalism relation to, 79
colonialism, 29, 107, 139, 204; chromatic whiteness relation to, 152; cinema relation to, 196–97, 198; of Japan, 193–94, 200–201; manila envelope relation to, 109–10; power of, 143–44; Vietnam War relation to, 233n60
color: freedom relation to, 140, 153, 212; interpretation of, 140–41; race relation to, 110, 132–33, 144, 146, 157, 163–64; subjugation relation to, 152–53; suprematism relation to, 137
color-based abstraction, 163; *Black Square* as, 124–25; chromatic black in, 134; freedom relation to, 126, 138, 141–42, 159, 161–62; in "How It Feels to Be Colored Me," 149, 151, 154–56; of Whitten, 129. *See also* abstraction

Combahee River Collective, 170
Combat de nègres dans une tunnel (Negroes fighting in a tunnel) (painting), 142
Commentaire (Cha), 187–88, 194, 196
"common sense" (*sensus communis*), 47, 55
communal experience, 200
communicability, civilization relation to, 52
comparative analytic, 30–31
conceptualism, 91–92, 231n34; of Ono, 94–95, 117, 212; social meaning relation to, 157; whimsy in, 98, 99
conch motif, in *Looking for Langston*, 77–78
context, forms relation to, 32
Contextures (Kraft), 3, 221n3
Copeland, Huey, 158–59
"The Coral Tree" (Wang, J.), 165
Crawford, Margo, 235n16
Crimp, Douglas, 73
Crisis (Du Bois), 60–61
"Criteria of Negro Art" (Du Bois), 41–42, 59, 62
critique, 10; of gaze, 17–18; of pleasure, 20; political, 15, 212; shared realities relation to, 13. See also aesthetic judgment
Critique of Judgment (Kant), 13, 16, 31, 78; beauty in, 34–35, 46–47; "Criteria of Negro Art" compared to, 41–42; purposiveness in, 51; whimsy in, 35–36, 88–89, 95–96
The Cultural Politics of Emotion (Ahmed), 14
culture: material conditions relation to, 9; suprematism relation to, 139
curation, meaning in, 162
curriculum vitae (CV), 102, 103, 104; labor relation to, 105–6; as poetry, 107
Cut Piece (Ono), 103
CV. *See* curriculum vitae

Darwinism, social, 139
Defacing the Monument (Briante), 87

"Delusions of Whiteness in the Avant-Garde" (Hong, C.), 7–8
"The Developer," 123–24
The Dialectic of Sex (Firestone), 113
Diawara, Manthia, 71–72
Dictee (Cha), 37, 168–69, 173, 174, 193, 245n39; challenging nature of, 171–72, 183; cinema in, 194–96, 197; legacy of, 203; mixed-media text as, 192; reproduction in, 210, 247n81; Soon in, 201–2; texture in, 198–99; *White Dust from Magnolia* compared to, 209; *Writing Self, Writing Nation* on, 182
difference: difficulty relation to, 174–75; politics of, 171; in racial capitalism, 169
difficulty, 37, 210; difference relation to, 174–75; of dreaminess, 180
dilmaj (movie translator), 193
Discipline and Punish (Foucault), 114–15
disdain, for beauty, 16
disidentification, 199–200
Disidentification (Muñoz), 222n2
distress, in racial capitalism, 3–4
dominance: aesthetic judgment relation to, 11–12; of Malevich, 138–39, 141; minoritarian aesthetics relation to, 32–33, 34
domination: aesthetic judgment relation to, 65–66, 67, 94; beauty relation to, 40; freedom relation to, 139, 141; stereotype relation to, 144; in suprematism, 140
Douglas, Aaron, 156–57
dreaminess: aesthetic judgment relation to, 174; avant-garde relation to, 181–82; of Cha, 164, 174–76, 177, 179–80, 188–89; in cinema, 183, 184; difficulty of, 180; ethics relation to, 200
Dreyer, Carl Theodor, 165, 197
Du Bois, W. E. B., 43–44, 157; aesthetic theory of, 58–59, 60, 71, 85, 235n15; in *Black Monoliths*, 130–31; *Crisis* of, 60–61; "Criteria of Negro Art" of, 41–42, 59, 62

de Duve, Thierry, 10, 13
Dyer, Richard, 222n1

education, 98–99
Edwards, Adrienne, 146–47, 148, 162
Einfühlung ("feeling into"), 56
ekphrastic tableaux, 63, 64
empathy: in aesthetic judgment, 55–56; beauty relation to, 55, 57; identity relation to, 225n49
English, Darby, 127, 134, 234n6
Enlightenment: aesthetic theory relation to, 6; beauty relation to, 41; global systems affected by, 5; Human relation to, 11; racism of, 50
erotic beauty, 75
eroticism, in cinema, 186–88
Espiritu, Yến Lê, 115–16
essentialism, of "pure color," 140
ethics, 36–37; aesthetic judgment relation to, 191; of aesthetic pleasure, 15, 215–16; dreaminess relation to, 200
ethnic studies, 213
evolution, of art, 138
EXCERPTS FROM: ΔIKTH DIKTE 딕테/딕티 for DICTEE (Lew), 193
exclusion, of minoritized artists, 126–28
existential terror, 3
experimentalism. *See specific topics*
expression, stereotype effect on, 154

Falconetti, Renée, 165, 166, *166*, 197, 199
Fanon, Frantz, 151
fantasy, 81, 84
feeling, 215; beauty relation to, 46; forms relation to, 14–15, 123; of reality, 211
"feeling into" (*Einfühlung*), 56
feminism: anti-colonial, 191, 202; Asian American, 178–79; beauty relation to, 223n4; woman-of-color, 169–71, 189, 191
"The Feminization of Society" (Ono), 113
Ferguson, Roderick, 213–14

fetishization, 72, 223n5. *See also* racial fetishism
Film No. 4 (Bottoms) (film), 85–86, 233n63; as conceptualism, 117; identity in, 89; whimsy in, 112, 118–19
FIRE!! (magazine), 156–57
Firestone, Shulamith, 113
Fludd, Robert, 240n59
Fluxus, 91–92, 229n10; Millett relation to, 232n51; whimsy in, 93
football, 2
Foreign Object #1 Fluffy Light (Wu), 205, 206, 206–7
forms: administrative, 88, 89, 100, 103–4, 107–9, 111; aesthetic judgment effect on, 34; attention relation to, 4, 22–23, 25, 54, 175, 191–92; context relation to, 32; experimentalism relation to, 21, 22; feeling relation to, 14–15, 123; racialization relation to, 151; violence relation to, 11, 23
Foucault, Michel, 114–15
freedom, 13, 81; aesthetic pleasure relation to, 15–16, 36, 216; beauty relation to, 48, 60, 61, 63, 69; color-based abstraction relation to, 126, 138, 141–42, 159, 161–62; color relation to, 140, 153, 212; domination relation to, 139, 141; experimentalism relation to, 22, 135; political violence relation to, 30; power relation to, 146; prohibition relation to, 19–20; supremation relation to, 137; whiteness relation to, 68, 69; white supremacy relation to, 236n28
Freud, 232n52
"From Cubism to Futurism to Suprematism" (Malevich), 137–38, 140, 141–42
Funk Lessons (Piper), 98
futurism, 239n47
The Futurist Manifesto (Marinetti), 238n38

Gallagher, Ellen, 147–49, 160
Ganeri, Jonardon, 23

Gaugin, Paul, 238n44
gay clubs, 228n107
gaze, 17–18, 40
gendered bodies, whimsy of, 114–15
genital essentialism, 112
geometric abstraction, 138
German Romanticism, 58–59, 60
Gilmore, Ruth Wilson, 216, 221n13
Gilroy, Paul, 72
Glissant, Édouard, 160–61
global ideology, neoliberalism as, 204
global systems, 3, 5
González-Torres, Félix, 216–18
Gossett, Hattie, 170
Graeber, David, 100–101
Grapefruit (Ono), 85–86, 87–88, 90–91, 99–100, 230n24; identity in, 89, 108; poetry in, 102–4; "Questionnaire" in, 108–9, 110–11; whimsy in, 92, 94
Groce, Dorothy "Cherry," 226n83
Guilty Aesthetic Pleasures (Aubrey), 16–17
Gupta, Sunil, 71

Habeas Viscus (Weheliye), 30
haiku, 229n9
Halberstam, Jack, 179
han (melancholy), 172–73
Harlem Renaissance, 35, 226n72; beauty of, 40–41, 42; *FIRE!!* in, 156–57; Julien compared to, 55; *Looking for Langston* relation to, 44–45, 70–72; primitivism in, 241n89
Harper, Phillip Brian, 127
Hartman, Saidiya, 39, 54, 62; *Scenes of Subjection* of, 56–57; on suffering, 120
Heaven (gay club), 228n107
Helms, Jesse, 75–76
Hemphill, Essex, 84–85
HERESIES (arts journal), 170, 243n9
hierarchy, 19; aesthetic judgment relation to, 11, 50; white supremacy relation to, 12
Hong, Cathy Park, 7–8, 171; *Minor Feelings* of, 172–73

Hong, Grace Kyungwon, 71–72, 169, 171; *Strange Affinities* of, 213–14
"How It Feels to Be Colored Me" (Hurston), 150; abstraction in, 149, 151, 154–56; Ligon affected by, 157–58; primitivism in, 154, 241n89; racialization in, 153–54
How to Do Nothing (Odell), 24
Huang, Vivian, 107
Hughes, Langston, 44, 71, 74, 84–85
Human, Enlightenment relation to, 11
humor, 228n2; absurdist, 13; incongruity theory of, 114; subversive power of, 96; whimsy relation to, 97
Hurrell, George, 39
Hurston, Zora Neale, 126, 152, 241n77; "How It Feels to Be Colored Me" of, 149–51, 153–56, 157–58, 241n89; Ligon affected by, 158–59, 160

Ichiyanagi, Toshi, 104
iconography, 67
identity: aesthetic judgment relation to, 80–81; disidentification of, 199; empathy relation to, 225n49; in *Grapefruit*, 89, 108; of minoritized artists, 128; racial capitalism relation to, 106; universalism relation to, 79
imagination: of Ono, 122; paperwork effect on, 102
immigration: paperwork for, 231n35; to US, 104–5
Immigration and Naturalization Act (1965), 105
immigration policy, 29; racism in, 104–5; in US, 107, 109, 206–7
imperialism, 29
incongruity theory, of humor, 114
Inconsequential Doggereal (video collage), 1–2, 3–4, 6
Indigenous peoples, 49–50
Ingold, Tim, 23; on attention, 191–92
instruction, in conceptualism, 98

interiority, 140, 155
interpretation, 106–7; of color, 140–41; experimentalism relation to, 3–4, 5, 22–23, 26–27; in movietelling, 193–94; stereotypes relation to, 179
interpretive practices, 162
intervention, aesthetic, in *Inconsequential Doggereal*, 3
In the Break (Moten), 65
Iran, 193

Japan, 109; colonialism of, 193–94, 200–201
Jarman, Derek, 162
Jarrett, Cynthia, 226n83
Javadizadeh, Kamran, 100
Jenkins, Ulysses, 1–3, 4, 6
Johnson, Barbara, 151
Johnson, Lyndon B. (LBJ), 120, 121
Johnson-Reed Act (1924), 105
Jones, Wayson, 84–85
Julien, Isaac, 42, 197, 223n5; Cha compared to, 166–67; Harlem Renaissance compared to, 55. See also *Looking for Langston*

Kant, Immanuel: *Critique of Judgment* of, 13, 16, 31, 34–36, 41–42, 46–47, 51, 78, 88–89, 95–96; Du Bois compared to, 61; racism of, 50–53; on taste, 49–50; on whimsy, 97
Kantian mode, of aesthetic judgment, 42, 46–47, 48, 55, 68, 69
Kaprow, Allan, 102
Kee, Joan, 214
Keeling, Kara, 71
Kelley, Robin D. G., 57, 181
Kellgren, Nina, 71
Kelly, Ellsworth, 162–63
Kim, Byron: Ligon relation to, 236n26; *Synecdoche* of, 110, 132–33, 144, 236n25
Kim, Elaine H., 182, 203
King, Martin Luther, Jr., 131

Kirchhoff, Gustav, 132
koan, 229n9
Korea: cinema in, 246n63; *han* in, 172–73; March First Movement in, 200; movietelling in, 192–94; South, 169
Korean War, 167, 173
Kraft, William, 3, 221n3
Kusama, Yayoi, 115, 233n57

labor, 105–6, 107
Laclau, Ernesto, 79, 227n98
Larsen, Nella, 41–42; aesthetic theory of, 85; on beauty, 62–63; experimentalism of, 43–44
Last Exhibition of Futurist Painting 0.10, 136
"La vida nueva" (poem), 204
LBJ. *See* Johnson, Lyndon B.
Lee, Kung Jong, 200
Lee, Min Jin, 171–72
Lee, Summer Kim, 179
Lennon, John, 104, 230n16, 230n17
Lévy, Jules, 142
Lew, Walter K., 192–93
Lewallen, Constance, 176
liberalism: racial capitalism relation to, 231n40; universalism of, 122
Ligon, Glenn, 157; *Blue Black* exhibition of, 162–63; B. Kim relation to, 236n26; *Untitled (I Feel Most Colored When I Am Thrown against a Sharp White Background)* of, 158–59, 160–61
Lipps, Theodor, 56, 66
de Lisieux, Thérèse, 246n69
Locke, Alain, 157
London, 233n63
looking, acts of, 166; communal experience of, 200
Looking for Langston (film), 39–40, 43, 81; beauty in, 73–76, 79, 82–84, 85; conch motif in, 77–78; Harlem Renaissance relation to, 44–45, 70–72; *Passing* compared to, 77, 79–80; texture in, 198

Lorde, Audre, 75, 169
Lowe, Lisa, 28–29, 214
lyric poetry, 100

MacDonald, Scott, 118
mainstream, experimentalism compared to, 21–22
Malevich, Kazimir, 126, 238n44; *Black Square* of, 124–25, 136, 142, 144–45, 163, 236n28, 240n66; dominance of, 138–39, 141; "From Cubism to Futurism to Suprematism" of, 137–38, 140, 141–42; in Paris, 239n47; on pure color, 150
Maliangkay, Roald, 193–94
manila envelope, 109–10
Mapplethorpe, Robert, 75–76, 119
March First Movement, 200
Marinetti, F. T., 238n38
Marks, Laura, 197–98
Marshall, Kerry James, 162
martyr narrative, 202, 246n69
masculinity, 178; black, 158–59; violence relation to, 112, 116–17
material conditions, culture relation to, 9
McMillan, Uri, 65
meaning, perception relation to, 162
melancholy (*han*), 172–73
Melville, Herman, 151
Mercer, Kobena, 72, 76, 127
military violence, 116
Millett, Kate, 113, 232n51
Min, Yong Soon, 168
minimalism, of Ono, 87
Minor Feelings (Hong, C.), 172–73
minoritarian aesthetics, 32–33, 34
minoritized artists, 43; exclusion of, 126–28; experimentalism of, 25, 215; identity of, 128; universality from, 80; in US, 213
misogyny, 168
mixed-media text, 192
modernism, psychology relation to, 180

modernist primitivism, 138
monochrome paintings, 124–25, 212, 240n59; *Black Monoliths* as, 129–31; Blackness relation to, 36, 144; *Black Square* as, 136, 142, 163; *Negroes Battling in a Cave at Night* as, 147–49; racism in, 142–43, 144–45, 161, 163
morality, beauty relation to, 53
Morrison, Toni, 74, 151
Moscow, Russia, Tretyakov Gallery in, 144–45, 240n66
Moten, Fred, 52–53, 54, 133; on Blackness, 81; *In the Break* of, 65
movietelling, 192–94
movie translator (*dilmaj*), 193
mulatta, 63, 66, 67, 226n72
Muñoz, José Esteban, 32–33, 71–72, 76, 122; on disidentification, 199; *Disidentification* of, 222n2; on radical politics, 81; on utopia, 121
Munroe, Alexandra, 99–100
Museum of Modern Art, New York, 233n57

Naficy, Hamid, 193, 196
The Narrative of Arthur Gordon Pym (Poe), 151
National Endowment for the Arts, 76
nationalist ideologies, of US, 116, 231n40
Négritude movement, 181
Negroes Battling in a Cave at Night (painting), 147–49
Negroes fighting in a tunnel (*Combat de nègres dans une tunnel*) (painting), 142
neoliberalism, 169; as global ideology, 204
Nevelson, Louise, 125
Newman, Donald, 236n28
New Queer Cinema movement, 43
New Right, 72–73, 75–76
New York City: *HERESIES* (arts journal), 243n9; Museum of Modern Art in, 233n57
New York Times (newspaper), 145, 171

Ngai, Mae, 104, 105
Ngai, Sianne, 13, 46, 119
Nguyen, Mimi Thi, 116
night labor, 188–89, 196
novelty, in experimentalism, 21
Nugent, Richard Bruce, 74–75

objectification, 64–65
Observations on the Feeling of the Beautiful and Sublime (Kant), 50–51
Odell, Jenny, 24–25
On Beauty and Being Just (Scarry), 17–18
"On Film" (Ono), 112, 113–14, 119–20
Ono, Yoko, 35–36, 230n17; absurdism of, 87–88; "Bed Peace" of, 230n16; Cage compared to, 229n7; Cha compared to, 177–78; Chambers Street salons of, 229n10; conceptualism of, 94–95, 117, 212; *Cut Piece* of, 103; *Grapefruit* of, 85–91, 99–100, 102–4, 108–9, 110–11, 230n24; imagination of, 122; Millett relation to, 232n51; "On Film" of, 112, 113–14, 119–20; text-based art of, 92; whimsy of, 88, 89
opacity, 242n98
oppression, 3; art relation to, 9–10; beauty relation to, 17–18; experimentalism relation to, 6, 22
Orientalism (Said), 178
Other Things Seen, Other Things Heard (performance), 165, 166, *166*, *167*, 177, 185–86; dreaminess in, 176, 177; viewership in, 199. *See also* Cha, Theresa Hak Kyung

Page Act (1875), 104–5, 107
pain, 33–34
paint-as-collage, 124
painting-as-process, 123
paperwork, 89, 90; bureaucracy relation to, 101; in *Grapefruit*, 102–3; for immigration, 231n35; labor for, 107; poetry in, 100, 103–4, 107, 108–9, 111

Paris, France: Centre d'Etudes Americain du Cinema in, 181, 184; Malevich in, 239n47
Park, Chung-hee, 167
Parreñas, Rhacel Salazar, 178
Passing (Larsen), 41–42; aesthetic judgment in, 63–64, 65–68; beauty in, 69–70; Blackness in, 68; *Looking for Langston* compared to, 77, 79–80; objectification in, 64, 65; *Quicksand* compared to, 62–63
The Passion of Joan of Arc (film), 165, 166, *166*, 197–98; texture in, 199
passivity, of aesthetic satisfaction, 156
passports, 217–18
Patterson, Benjamin, 98–99
Patterson, Orlando, 223n3
perception, meaning relation to, 162
Perreault, John, 93
petitions, 118, 121
Pinochet, Augusto, 204
Piper, Adrian, 98
Plato's cave, 184–85, 245n45
Playing in the Dark (Morrison), 151
pleasure. *See specific topics*
Pluhar, Werner S., 228n2
PMLA (journal), 128
Poe, Edgar Allen, *The Narrative of Arthur Gordon Pym* of, 151
poetry: administrative forms as, 100, 103–4, 108–9, 111; CV as, 107; in *Grapefruit*, 102–4
police, 101, 226n83
political critique, beauty in, 15, 212
political violence, freedom relation to, 30
politics, 81; aesthetic pleasure relation to, 15–16, 17, 19; beauty relation to, 57; Black queer, 84; of difference, 171; ethnic studies relation to, 213; experimentalism relation to, 9; freedom relation to, 19; racial formation effect on, 28–29; of representation, 56
Pond (Patterson, B.), 99

pop art, 231n34
possession, aesthetic pleasure as, 20
potential affect, 187
Pound, Ezra, 22, 44–45
power, 18; aesthetic judgment relation to, 6, 35, 67, 94; beauty relation to, 76, 79; of colonialism, 143–44; freedom relation to, 146; minoritarian relation to, 33
primitivism: in "How It Feels to Be Colored Me," 154, 241n89; modernist, 138
prohibition, freedom relation to, 19–20
propaganda, 59
psychology, modernism relation to, 180
purposiveness: in aesthetic theory, 52, 96; in Critique of Judgment, 51

queer Black universalism, 78
"Questionnaire" in Grapefruit, 108–9, 110–11
Quicksand (Larsen), Passing compared to, 62–63

race. See specific topics
racial capitalism, 29, 93, 221n2; aesthetic theory relation to, 5, 12; Asian women relation to, 178; bureaucracy relation to, 101; difference in, 169; distress in, 3–4; experimentalism in, 25; identity relation to, 106; immigration policy relation to, 105; liberalism relation to, 231n40; Vietnam War relation to, 233n60; violence relation to, 8
racial fetishism: of Asian women, 106–7, 179; in Looking for Langston, 70
racial formation, in US, 28–29, 35–36
racialization: abstraction relation to, 135, 142, 146; aesthetic form relation to, 151; aesthetic judgment relation to, 50; Asian, 179; experimentalism relation to, 214; in "How It Feels to Be Colored Me," 153–54; Ligon exploration of, 160; minoritarian aesthetics relation to, 34

racial pseudoscience, 133
racial terrorism, in US, 55
racial violence, 70
racism, 221n13; abstraction relation to, 128, 235n13; avant-garde relation to, 7–8, 124; in black monochrome painting, 142–43, 144–45, 161, 163; chromatic black relation to, 146, 236n28; in immigration policy, 104–5; of Kant, 50–53; of New Right aggression, 72–73; scientific, 138–39; systemic, 168; violence of, 134
radical politics, fantasy relation to, 81
Rankin, John, 56–57
rationalism: arbitrary relation to, 90; in US, 97; violence relation to, 212
rationality, whimsy relation to, 89–90
Reagan, Ronald, 1, 72
realism, 146; abstraction compared to, 168; experimentalism versus, 157, 182, 183; white supremacy relation to, 175
realist representation, 127
reality, 245n45; aesthetic judgment relation to, 186, 211; cinema relation to, 184–85
Reddy, Chandan, 89–90
Reinhardt, Ad, 236n28
relational pleasure, 121
representation, 137, 138; politics of, 56; realist, 127
reproduction, in Dictee, 210, 247n81
Rich, B. Ruby, 71
Robinson, Cedric J., 31–32, 45, 221n2, 223n13
Robinson Crusoe style hypothetical, 49
Rodriguez, Dylan, 11–12
Roelofs, Monique, 50
romance, of minoritarianism, 33
Rosen, Andrea, 216–17
Royal House, 84–85, 227n95

Said, Edward, 178
Salon des Indépendants, 239n47

Saltzstein, Dan, 171–72
Santayana, George, 58
Sanza, Joseph, 168, 242n1
Saunders, Raymond, 134
Scarry, Elaine, 17–18, 19; on beauty, 40
Scenes of Subjection (Hartman), 56–57
scientific racism, 138–39
Sedgwick, Eve Kosofsky, 198, 228n101
self: aesthetic judgment relation to, 54; attention effect on, 24–25; empathy relation to, 57
Seminar II: American Studies (Patterson, B.), 99
sensus communis ("common sense"), 47, 55
seriousness, violence relation to, 114
Sexton, Jared, 125–26
sexual assault, 242n1
Sexual Politics (Millett), 113
shared realities, critique relation to, 13
Shatskikh, Aleksandra, 136
Sherrard-Johnson, Cherene, 63, 67
Shklovsky, Victor, 94
da Silva, Denise Ferreira, 50, 138, 227n98; on "affectable subjects," 139–40
Sin ch'ul, 194
Slavery and Social Death (Patterson, O.), 223n3
Smile TV, 120–21
"Smoke, Lilies, and Jade" (Nugent), 74–75
social change: beauty relation to, 45; experimentalism relation to, 9
social death, 223n3
social meaning, conceptualism relation to, 157
social relation: aesthetic judgment relation to, 12–13, 20, 191, 212–13; aesthetic pleasure relation to, 4, 6, 10, 211, 215–16; beauty relation to, 59; experimentalism relation to, 8; surrealism relation to, 181
society, 48–49
Song Books (Cage), 24
Soon, Yu Guan, 200–202
Sŏ Sangp'il, 194, 197
South Korea, neoliberalism in, 169
sovereignty, interiority challenging, 155
state violence, 73, 90, 114, 120
status quo, experimentalism relation to, 122
Stein, Gertrude, 44–45
stereotypes: as abstraction, 143–44, 150, 159–60; of Asian women, 178–79, 230n17; of Blackness, 241n77; expression affected by, 154
Strange Affinities (Hong, G., and Ferguson), 213–14
The Subject is Jazz (television program), 85
subjugation, color relation to, 152–53
subordination, 8
subversive power, of humor, 96
suffering, 34, 120
suprematism, 136, 137–38, 141–42; culture relation to, 139; domination in, 140
surrealism, 3, 181
Synecdoche (painting series), 110, 132–33, 236n25; abstraction in, 144
systemic racism, 168

Táíwò, Olúfẹ́mi O., 33–34
Tam, Winnie, 178
Tanam Press, 184
taste, aesthetic judgment relation to, 48–50
Taussig, Michael, 152–53
Taylor, Cecil, 236n28
Taylor, Paul C., 50
Teaching a Plant the Alphabet (film), 98
techno-Orientalism, 178
Terada, Rei, 93–94
text-based art, 91–92
texture, 198–99, 242n98
Thatcher, Margaret, 72
Thinking with Kant's Critique of Judgment (Chaouli), 16
Third Cinema, 183–84, 245n42

Thomas, Michael Tilson, 24
Thurman, Wallace, 157
Tottenham Broadwater Farm Riots, 226n83
transformation, 94; beauty relation to, 70–71; color relation to, 133; experimentalism relation to, 22; pleasure relation to, 113
trauma, 34, 177
Tretyakov Gallery, in Moscow, 144–45, 240n66
Trinh T., Minh-Ha, 196
truth, beauty relation to, 60
Ty, M., 133

Ultriusque Cosmi (engraving), 240n59
unconscious, collage relation to, 180
United States (US), 232n52; Chile relation to, 204; Cold War of, 169–70, 173; immigration policy in, 104–5, 107, 109, 206–7; Korea relation to, 173; minoritized artists in, 213; nationalist ideologies in, 116, 231n40; racial formation in, 28–30, 35–36; racial terrorism in, 55; rationalism in, 97; state violence in, 73; Vietnam War relation to, 115–16, 233n60
universalism: of abstraction, 135; identity relation to, 79; of liberalism, 122; queer Black, 78
universality, 9–10; of administrative forms, 108; in Black aesthetics, 42; from minoritized artists, 80; whiteness relation to, 41, 100
University of California, Berkeley, 180–81, 183–84
Untitled (I Am Not Tragically Colored) (painting), 162
Untitled (I Feel Most Colored When I Am Thrown against a Sharp White Background) (painting), 158–59, 160–61
Untitled (Passport) (sculpture), 216–18
Untitled (Policeman) (painting), 162

"Upon Leaving the Movie Theater" (Barthes), 186–87, 194; *Upon Leaving the White Dust* relation to, 208
Upon Leaving the White Dust (Wu), 207–8, *208*, *209*, 209–10
uprisings, against white supremacy, 4
US. *See* United States
utopia, 81, 121
The Utopia of Rules (Graeber), 100–101

value, 21, 31
vandalism, 240n66
Van Der Zee, James, 39, 222n2
vexed topics, pleasure in, 15
Vietnam War, 114; South Korea in, 169; whiteness relation to, 233n60; white supremacy relation to, 115–17
viewership, 199
violence, 6; against Asian women, 242n1; beauty relation to, 62–63; experimentalism relation to, 122; forms relation to, 11, 23; masculinity relation to, 112, 116–17; military, 116; police relation to, 101; political, 30; racial, 70; racial capitalism relation to, 8; of racism, 134; rationalism relation to, 212; seriousness relation to, 114; state, 73, 90, 114, 120; whimsy relation to, 36, 93; whiteness relation to, 152; white supremacy relation to, 12
voyeurism, 194, 246n64

Wang, Dorothy, 26, 127–28
Wang, Jackie, 165
war, absurdism of, 115
Warhol, Andy, 162
Watney, Simon, 73
Weems, Carrie Mae, 162
Weheliye, Alexander, 30, 31
Western aesthetic model, 10
whimsy, 35–36, 85–86, 228n2; in administrative forms, 107–8; aesthetic judgment relation to, 96, 122, 212; beauty

compared to, 96–97; in conceptualism, 98, 99; in *Critique of Judgment*, 95–96; in *Film No. 4 (Bottoms)*, 112, 118–19; in Fluxus, 93; of gendered bodies, 114–15; in *Grapefruit*, 92, 94; humor relation to, 97; of Ono, 88, 89; rationality relation to, 89–90
White Dust from Magnolia (film), 205, 206, 207–8, 209–10, 247n87
White (Dyer), 222n1
white experimentalists, 26
whiteness, 53, 151; aesthetic pleasure relation to, 11–12; aesthetic theory relation to, 31; avant-garde relation to, 7–8; beauty relation to, 57, 64, 70, 76, 78; experimentalism relation to, 27–28; freedom relation to, 68, 69; immigration policy relation to, 109; universality relation to, 41, 100; Vietnam War relation to, 233n60; violence relation to, 152
whiteness, chromatic, 151; white supremacy relation to, 152
"White Spring" (Trinh), 188
white supremacy, 204; Blackness relation to, 28; chromatic whiteness relation to, 152; freedom relation to, 236n28; hierarchy relation to, 12; of Kant, 50–51, 52; realism relation to, 175; suffering relation to, 120; uprisings against, 4; Vietnam War relation to, 115–17; violence relation to, 12
Whitney Museum of American Art, 203–4
Whitten, Jack, 123–24, 126, 140, 159; *Black Monolith* of, 129–31; Ligon compared to, 160
Wispé, Lauren, 56
woman-of-color feminism, 169, 170–71, 189, 191
women. *See* Asian women; Black women
Writing Self, Writing Nation (Alarcón and Kim, E.), 182, 203
Wu, Cici, 168–69, 171, 212; *Foreign Object #1 Fluffy Light* of, 205, 206, 206–7; *Upon Leaving the White Dust* of, 207–8, *208*, 209, 209–10
Wynter, Sylvia, 139

Xiang, Sunny, 169

Yoshimoto, Midori, 99–100

Zerilli, Linda, 79
Zhou, Zhuang, 190–91, 245n53
Zhuangzi (Zhou), 190–91, 245n53
Zurita, Raúl, 204

ABOUT THE AUTHOR

RACHEL JANE CARROLL is ACLS Emerging Voices Fellow at the University of Illinois, Urbana-Champaign. Her work can be found in *Criticism, The Oxford Handbook of Twentieth-Century American Literature, Social Text*, and elsewhere.

www.ingramcontent.com/pod-product-compliance
Lightning Source LLC
Chambersburg PA
CBHW020359080526
44584CB00014B/1085